Practical Internet Server Configuration

Learn to Build a Fully Functional
and Well-Secured Enterprise Class
Internet Server

Robert La Lau

Apress®

Practical Internet Server Configuration

Robert La Lau
Blain, France

ISBN-13 (pbk): 978-1-4842-6959-6   ISBN-13 (electronic): 978-1-4842-6960-2
https://doi.org/10.1007/978-1-4842-6960-2

Managing Director, Apress media LLC: Welmoed Spahr
Acquisitions Editor: Louise Corrigan
Development Editor: James Markham
Coordinating Editor: Nancy Chen

Cover designed by eStudioCalamar

Cover image designed by Freepik (www.freepik.com)

Distributed to the book trade worldwide by Springer Science+Business Media New York, 1 New York Plaza, New York, NY 10004. Phone 1-800-SPRINGER, fax (201) 348-4505, e-mail orders-ny@springer-sbm.com, or visit www.springeronline.com. Apress Media, LLC is a California LLC and the sole member (owner) is Springer Science + Business Media Finance Inc (SSBM Finance Inc). SSBM Finance Inc is a **Delaware** corporation.

For information on translations, please e-mail booktranslations@springernature.com; for reprint, paperback, or audio rights, please e-mail bookpermissions@springernature.com.

Apress titles may be purchased in bulk for academic, corporate, or promotional use. eBook versions and licenses are also available for most titles. For more information, reference our Print and eBook Bulk Sales web page at http://www.apress.com/bulk-sales.

Any source code or other supplementary material referenced by the author in this book is available to readers on GitHub via the book's product page, located at www.apress.com/9781484269596. For more detailed information, please visit http://www.apress.com/source-code.

Printed on acid-free paper

I'll explain it one more time...

Table of Contents

About the Author

Robert La Lau has been active on the internet since the mid-1990s. What started as a hobby—playing around with Linux and developing small games and applications using Perl, HTML, and JavaScript—turned into a job when he became a full-time freelance web developer in 1999. Shortly thereafter, a web hosting server and freelance Linux and FreeBSD administration were added. In the years that followed, new programming languages were learned, and software development was added to the range of services offered. In his spare time, Rob was involved in several smaller and larger open source projects; among other things, he was the initiator and first administrator for the official online KDE forums. After 15 years of freelance IT work, Rob thought he'd had enough of IT work, finished his running affairs, and left the Netherlands to discover the world. However, the IT kept calling him, and once installed in his new home country France, he decided to return to his old métier. Only this time, it was not to get his own hands dirty in the field, executing orders for clients, but to transfer his knowledge and experience onto the next generations of system administrators and developers. He rebooted his IT career translating and narrating educational books and videos, taught some Unix classes, and seems to have found his destination publishing books now.

About the Technical Reviewer

Kenneth "Ken" Hess is a freelance writer, editor, podcaster, filmmaker, and visual artist. He writes about a variety of technologies ranging from open source software to storage to virtualization. Ken is a Linux, Windows, and Virtualization administrator with more than 20 years of experience.

CHAPTER 1

Introduction and Preparations

There are various reasons why people (business or private) would prefer to take the hosting of services such as websites and email into their own hands. There are just as many reasons why people wouldn't want to do that.

The most important reasons for in-house hosting are **confidentiality** and **control**. It might, for instance, be undesirable to store the business communication (email, online help desk) with an external party; the storage of client data may be another reason to prefer a self-managed solution. If the server must run custom software, it may even be impossible (or extremely expensive) to host it with a third party.

The most important reasons to delegate the hosting are **expertise** and **time**; both are required to keep a server up to date, to monitor it, and to create backups. Everybody will have to decide for themselves about the time available for server maintenance. This book will at least try to bring the knowledge to the required level and provide the system administrator with a good starting point by guiding them through the initial configuration of the server; it will also provide the system administrator with tools for finding additional information.

This book takes the reader from a *vanilla* server—a server with only the operating system installed, without any modifications, as it may be supplied by a hosting provider, for example—to a fully functional internet server that is ready to be deployed. The resulting server will provide all services that may be expected from an internet server (DNS, email hosting, web hosting, etc.). This server will be secured adequately, and the system administrator will dispose of the expertise necessary to keep the system up to date, to monitor it, and to create and restore backups.

© Robert La Lau 2021
R. La Lau, *Practical Internet Server Configuration*, https://doi.org/10.1007/978-1-4842-6960-2_1

Addendum

An online addendum for this book, providing configuration and script examples, as well as links to additional information, is freely accessible to anyone at `www.librobert.net/book/internet/addendum`.

Free Software

All the software discussed in this book is so-called *free software*. This means that for all software the source code is freely available and may be verified and even modified by the user prior to installation. Many, including the author of this book, are convinced that this openness benefits the efficiency, stability, and security of the software, because bugs and leaks are found sooner and are therefore also repaired more rapidly.

Even though *free software* does not per definition mean that the software is available without cost, this is the case for the software discussed in this book. Obviously, this does not mean that donations to these projects are not appreciated: the vast majority of free software developers develop the software in their free time, and donations are not only used to enable developers to spend more time on their project but also to pay for infrastructure like test computers, web hosting, and so on; a donation can help guarantee that the development of the software you use can continue at the same or even a higher level.

For that matter, free software projects are also often looking for reinforcements, not only developers but also user interface experts, designers, translators, authors of documentation and web content, system administrators, moderators for internet forums, and so on.

Required Knowledge and Experience

To be able to follow the instructions in this book, one does not need a vast amount of preliminary Unix expertise. It is desirable that the reader already had a first successful encounter with Unix and understands concepts like the command-line interface and the configuration by means of text files. The functioning of the operating system itself will only be discussed briefly, and the reader is expected to know basic commands like `cd`, `ls`, `cat`, `less`, and `tar`.

As the server described here is a *headless* server (a server without monitor, keyboard, and mouse) and not a workstation or a personal computer, no graphical user interface will be installed.

I have tried my best to make this book understandable and interesting in both language and contents and for both beginning and experienced system administrators.

Required Time and Motivation

After reading this book and following the instructions, the reader will have a working internet server. But this does not mean that the work is done. Each computer needs monitoring and maintenance, and for a server that is directly connected to the internet, this is more true than for any other computer. Attempts will be made to gain unauthorized access to the server, and it is the system administrator's responsibility to make every effort to ensure the confidentiality of the data on the server and to prevent the deployment of the server for unintended goals.

This book explains how to keep the installed software up to date and gives tips for the monitoring of the server. However, all these pointers are virtually useless without the two most important tools a system administrator has: time and motivation. The organization will have to realize that system administration is not a side project: time will have to be scheduled structurally to prevent the maintenance from falling behind and the server from becoming vulnerable. The system administrator will have to realize that they will not always be able to shut the door at 5 in the afternoon: if, for instance, there is an email problem, this problem will need to be solved at the latest the next morning before the start of the working day.

After installation and initial configuration, I advise to structurally schedule half a working day per week for the maintenance of the server. At another moment in the week, another hour could be scheduled for a quick check (e.g., the entire Friday morning for maintenance and an hour on Tuesday morning for some quick checks).

Obviously, the actual time needed is somewhat dependent on the use of the server. With the configuration discussed here, dozens of websites can be hosted without problem, and email for hundreds of users can be handled. In these cases, chances are that more time is necessary. And if the server is used for a single small website and the email for two or three users, maintenance may eventually not require more than half a day in two weeks. But half a working day per week is a solid rule of thumb for the time needed to analyze log files, fine-tune the system, update the software, increase the expertise, and maybe answer users' questions.

And of course it must be possible to liberate the system administrator immediately in case of an emergency, like a crash or a breach of security, for ad hoc work.

If it is clear beforehand that it will be problematic to schedule this time, it might be better to delegate the maintenance of the server to the provider.

External Account for Email and Disk Space

It is advisable to create an external mail account for the system administrator (or the team of system administrators). If a problem occurs that prevents the company server to be used for mail handling, this external account can be used to communicate with external parties.

In addition, mail accounts often dispose of some extra disk space that might be used to store data outside of the company infrastructure. Examples of this data would be important passwords, important contact addresses, and so on. Obviously, externally stored files must be encrypted and not with a key that is stored on the company server; *zip* and *OpenDocument* can both be encrypted using a password. This password should be saved on paper to ensure its availability even if the company infrastructure is not accessible.

It is important that parties like the provider and the data center know this address and have it on file, so that in the event of an emergency, the communication can be picked up directly via this address without the need to convince these parties first that this is indeed an authorized address.

This email address should be configured to also forward all received emails to the regular address for the system administrator(s) to prevent mails from being lost; after all, in practice, the external account will not be checked daily.

As this account will mainly be used to send and receive confidential information and privacy laws in Europe are more strict than in most other places, it might be desirable to select a European provider for this account. The online addendum for this book contains a list containing some examples of suited email providers.

When a system administrator leaves, the password for this account should **always** be changed.

Selecting a System and a Provider

Both the choice of system and the choice of hosting provider depend on many factors, of which the majority are personal demands, wishes, and preferences. It is therefore impossible to give a blueprint for the choice of these matters.

Some guidelines and pointers follow that might prove practical when making these choices.

Hardware

One of the first choices to be made for the acquisition of a server is the choice of the hardware to be used. What are the minimum specifications for the server? Should it be a physical server or a virtual machine?

Physical Server or Virtual Machine?

Before comparing the pros and cons of physical servers and virtual machines, a definition of both devices should be formulated.

A physical server is a combination of hardware (motherboard, processor, memory, etc.) and software (the operating system and the applications). The server is allocated to a single customer, and the system administrator or team of administrators responsible for the server maintains the entire server and has full control of the server.

A virtual machine consists of only software: the "hardware" for the server has been virtualized, and the physical hardware harboring the server is shared between multiple virtual machines. This physical hardware may consist of a single server of a cluster of servers; a so-called *hypervisor* distributes the capacities of the physical hardware between the virtual machines it manages, according to the specifications made by the administrator of the physical hardware. The administrator for the virtual machine only manages the virtual machines assigned to them within the limits set by the *hypervisor* administrator. The virtual machines are also called *guest* and the hypervisor *host*.

The most important advantages of a physical server over a virtual machine are the complete confidentiality and control: after the transfer of the server and the changing of the passwords, only the server administrator decides who is granted access and who is not. Due to the existence of tools like *libguestfs*, a hypervisor administrator can always gain access to the virtual machines in their care. Obviously, this does not mean that they will, but the possibility must be considered, especially if the confidentiality of the data on the server is important.

Where confidentiality plays a less prominent role or the guarantees of the provider provide sufficient confidence, this accessibility may also be an advantage: the creation and restoration of backups may then be delegated to the provider, which could save quite some work and time for the system administrator.

Another advantage of virtual machines is the ease with which they can be scaled up and repaired. If, for example, the memory of a physical server breaks down, the server will usually need to be turned off to replace the memory. If the capacities for a physical server no longer suffice, a new server will have to be assembled, installed, and configured, after which the data must be copied from the old server to the new server. Since the hardware for a virtual machine has been virtualized, the hypervisor administrator can add memory or disk space by simply changing the software settings. And in a worst-case scenario, the virtual machine can be moved to a different hypervisor, minimizing the *downtime* (unavailability).

And finally, the financial cost of a virtual machine may be more attractive than that of a physical server. On the one hand, virtual machines share their hardware, and even though the specifications for a server for multiple virtual machines will be more impressive than those for a single physical server, the specifications for hardware for ten virtual machines will most certainly not be tenfold those of a physical machine. On the other hand, because of its easy scalability, a virtual machine can be acquired more cautiously, while a physical server will usually be purchased with some overcapacity in order to accommodate growth. It must be stated, though, that prices for physical servers drop currently.

Minimum Specifications

Obviously, it is impossible to list the minimum specifications for an internet server, as these depend strongly on the purpose of the server: a server that handles enormous amounts of website visitors and/or emails has different specifications from a server that handles the email for a company of five employees and hosts a single website for some dozens of visitors per day.

In general, it could be stated, however, that the minimum specifications are not as tough as one would think. It is tempting to order the most powerful server in the provider's list, and if the budget permits this, it will most certainly not hurt, but generally, this is not necessary.

For a server as discussed in this book—DNS, email, web hosting, address books, calendars, and shared files, plus monitoring and backup—for an organization with a few dozen or a hundred employees and hosting a few websites serving several thousands of visitors per day, a quad core machine with 8GB of memory should largely suffice. Since disk space is not expensive, it is not necessary to skimp on this, but it is good to keep in mind that a website usually does not require a lot of space; obviously, the required space increases if employees share many files.

It doesn't need much argumentation that if it concerns a server for a family, on which several dozen mails a day are handled, one or two websites are hosted with at most a few dozen visitors per day, and five to ten people synchronize their mobile phones, the cheapest server from the list can be chosen.

Operating System

Most system administrators, including the author of this book, agree that Unix-like systems are the most suited operating systems for servers: more than 70% of all internet servers run a Unix variant, more than half of which are Linux; this includes Google, Facebook, Twitter, and Amazon servers. In addition to those, the International Space Station, the Large Hadron Collider, the *ground stations* of NASA and SpaceX, and the American nuclear submarine fleet also run on Linux.

Linux variants are called distributions, or simply distros.

To discuss an important portion of the spectrum and leave the reader/system administrator free in their choice, this book discusses three different Unix variants:

- **FreeBSD**

  This is a *BSD* (not Linux), which means it is related to *OpenBSD*, *NetBSD*, and *DragonFly BSD*. The version used when writing this book is *FreeBSD 12.0-RELEASE*.

- **Debian**

  With a first release in 1993, this is one of the oldest Linux distributions. Many other distributions were based on Debian, including *Knoppix, Ubuntu, Linux Mint, Kali Linux*, and *Whonix*. While writing this book, *Debian 9 (Stretch)* was used.

- **CentOS**

  This distro is based on *Red Hat Enterprise Linux*, which means it is related to *Fedora*, *CloudLinux*, and *Oracle Linux*. The version used while writing this book is *CentOS 7*.

Even though many other variants exist and they all have their pros and cons, a limit must be set to the number of variants discussed. With these three systems, a large portion of the field is covered, and the system administrator who decides to continue and grow will, without a doubt, develop their own preference, based on their personal wishes, demands, and experiences. (For those interested, the author of this book prefers *FreeBSD* on the server and *Gentoo Linux* on the desktop.)

Chances are that the system administrator reading this book already has a preference, be it from experience or from hearsay. If this is not the case, all three options discussed are equally valid, and the choice could even be made with a game of heads or tails; the study must start somewhere, and the system administrator who still has a full career before them will, without any doubt, encounter all three of these Unix-like operating system families sooner or later.

This book starts with a server as furnished by a *colocation provider*: the operating system has been installed, the network has been configured, a root password has been set, and usually one user has been created. If this book is used for an office or home server or a virtual machine for practice, these first steps have not been set yet. The installation images for the mentioned systems, as well as for most other Unix-like systems, assist the user in the configuration of the network and the creation of the first user, which ensures that after installation, the system is in the state that is expected at the start of this book.

Since providers often use modified installation images—to ensure the correct configuration of the network interfaces when the system boots, for example—it is not absolutely certain which software is already installed on the new server. This book presumes therefore a new, fresh installation from an image without modifications.

File System

Several file systems exist, which all have their pros and cons, depending on the server's function. However, generally providers do not provide a choice of file system for preinstalled servers. For the server as described in this book, this is not a problem: the default file systems (*ext4* or *XFS* for Linux and *UFS* for FreeBSD) will do fine. The system administrator who really needs a different file system probably also has other wishes that are not discussed in this book.

Provider

The selection of the appropriate provider starts with a comparison of the websites of different providers. Some things to pay attention to:

- **Guarantees for *uptime* and availability**

  An unavailable server is useless. No provider will guarantee *100%*, though, because that would not leave any space for unforeseen circumstances.

- **Backup electricity**

  Is the server eligible for electricity from a generator in case of a power outage (and for how long)?

- ***DDoS* protection**

  A *DDoS (Distributed Denial-of-Service) attack* is an attack where large numbers of requests are sent to the server from multiple locations on the internet in order to make the server unavailable to legitimate users or to make it collapse under the amount of work. A colocation provider can offer protection from this sort of attack and often does so on different levels at different rates.

- **Service level**

  Is staff available 7 days a week, 24 hours a day, within 15 minutes? Or is the system administrator expected to be more autonomous? It is not necessarily a problem if the service level is not as high, but in that case, the data center should not be too far away to enable the system administrator to visit the data center if necessary.

- **Physical access**

  If the need may arise to visit the server every once in a while, the door policy for the data center should permit the system administrator to access 24 hours per day and preferably without an appointment.

During this selection, it is recommendable to also pose questions per email and phone. This is a simple way to test the response times.

Obviously, later it should be verified that these promises are also reflected in the contract.

In the considerations regarding the selection of a provider, it may be desirable to take into account that privacy regulations in Europe are stricter than in the vast majority of the rest of the world. Companies that store data for European users and select an American provider must at least verify that the selected provider has been certified through the *Privacy Shield* program. It may also be interesting to take into account that countries like Switzerland, Germany, the Czech Republic, and Iceland have no laws that can force a system administrator to hand over passwords or keys.

Finally, it is important that the provider offers a *remote console*. A *remote console* enables the system administrator to log on to the provider's network via the internet and to log on to the server's console from within that network as if they are at the server with a monitor and keyboard. This presents the system administrator with a backdoor, for example, in case of network trouble on the server (most system administrators have locked themselves out at least once while configuring the firewall). Without this *remote console*, the system administrator would be forced to go to the data center in case of network trouble to solve the problems on the console. A remote console may also be called *KVM over IP* (*Keyboard, Video, Mouse over Internet Protocol*) or *IPMI* (*Intelligent Platform Management Interface*).

BIOS or UEFI Configuration

Because of the diversity in BIOS and UEFI settings, it is impossible to discuss them all. But with a few pointers and a bit of common sense, each system administrator should be able to correctly configure the BIOS or UEFI.

The provider should be able to document how to access the BIOS or UEFI settings remotely (or their virtual equivalent in the case of a virtual machine).

Configure the machine to automatically turn itself on after a power outage. No matter how inconvenient it is, if a power outage switches off the server, it is even more inconvenient if the server does not automatically power on after the outage. Always assume that in the case of a power outage, the provider will have more important priorities than to send an administrator to your server to flip the switch.

Do not set a boot password. If the server automatically starts after a power outage, it is not very practical if it then waits for a password before booting the operating system.

Do set a password for access to the BIOS or UEFI settings. If these settings have not been secured with a password, it would suffice to wait for a reboot, or even force one, to change all these settings. Store this password securely but locatable; it will be used so little that nobody will remember it when it is needed.

Disable devices like USB, parallel port, and CD or DVD. A server does not need these devices, but an attacker could use them to gain access to the server.

Disable all power-saving features.

Log On to the New Server

After the selection of the hardware and the provider and the configuration of the BIOS/UEFI, it is time to log on to the new server for the first time. The provider documents how this works in their specific case.

The provider has probably enabled *SSH access* to the server. If this is the case, then the provider also documents how to access the server over *SSH*; the configuration of the SSH server and accessing the server over SSH are discussed extensively in a later chapter of this book.

It is also possible that access is only permitted through the remote console that was discussed before. In this case, the provider will also document how to access the server. If the server in question is a home server or a virtual machine on the PC, there obviously is no remote console, and the keyboard and monitor can be used as usual.

To not get too much ahead of the subject matter, it is acceptable for now to log on with the username *root* (a Unix system's administrator). In a following chapter, direct access to this account will be blocked for security reasons.

On a standard FreeBSD or Debian install, direct access to the root account has been blocked already. It is possible that the provider has undone this setting when installing the server. If this is not the case, log on with the username that was created/assigned, and then use the command su - to gain administrator privileges; the system will ask for the *root* password; if the *root* password is not known, the command sudo su - should be used instead, which will ask for the user's password instead of the *root* password. Type exit to return to the "regular" user account.

Type exit to log off from the server.

Names and Addresses Used in This Book

In this book, an internet server is configured. For a server that is connected to a network, one or more IP addresses are required, and one or more domain names and hostnames are desirable.

The following information will be used for the purpose of this documentation. You will have to change it for your system.

IP Address

The IP address for a server cannot be made up; it is assigned by the provider. If the IP address assigned by the provider is not honored, the server may become unreachable.

This book assumes that the provider assigned the IP address **198.51.100.156** with *netmask 255.255.255.0*. This address is part of a range that was reserved for documentation purposes; as a result, it is impossible that it will ever collide with the address for a "real" server. The gateway that is provided by the imaginary provider is *198.51.100.1*.

For a domestic or office server, the IP address may be made up. In that case, it is important to select an IP address from one of the IP ranges reserved for private use, to prevent that it could ever collide with an IP address used on the internet. More information about this is found in Chapter 4, "Network Basics and Firewall".

Apart from the IP address for the network interface, each computer—be it a server or a PC—also has the IP address *127.0.0.1*. This IP address is used for network traffic between the computer and itself. The virtual network interface for this IP address is called the *loopback device*.

Since the implementation of *IPv6* (*Internet Protocol version 6*) has not yet advanced to a level where it is imperative for the functioning of an internet server and there are no parts of the public internet that are unreachable over *IPv4*, *IPv6* is not discussed in this book.

Domain Names

Even though a domain name is not strictly necessary for the operation of a server—only the IP address is essential—one will generally want to link one or more domain names to the IP address, as this permits the use of identifiable addresses for email and websites. Contrary to an IP address, a domain name can be chosen freely and is registered with a *registrar*; usually it is the provider who takes on this function. Obviously, each domain name can only be registered by a single owner, so the possibility to register a certain domain name depends on the availability of that name.

Normally, the registration of a domain name requires at least two DNS servers. These servers register the link between the IP address and the domain name. As the *primary DNS server*, the IP address for the current server can be given—the IP address that was assigned by the provider in the previous section. The provider will usually offer to function as the *secondary DNS*, but the system administrator is free to select a different server; several companies offer this as a free or paid service, or a second private server could be used. The secondary DNS server periodically copies its data from the primary DNS server. DNS will be discussed in more detail later in this book.

The server in this book will handle traffic for the domain names **example.com**, **example.edu**, and **example.org**, with *example.com* as its primary domain. Like the IP address that was chosen for this book, these domain names have been reserved for documentation purposes; nobody can register them, and they cannot collide with domain names on the internet.

The imaginary provider, *ExampleNET*, uses the domain name *example.net*.

A domain name registration is always valid for a certain period, often 1 or 2 years. Remember to renew your registration before it expires, to prevent someone else from registering the domain name—either to use it or to sell it back to you at a high charge. Normally, you will be alerted by your provider when a registered domain name is about to expire.

However, once you have registered one or more domain names, you will receive emails with some regularity about the renewal of your registrations. Do not respond to these emails unless you are absolutely sure that they originate from your provider. If you sign with another provider, this new provider can transfer your domain name and charge you more for the same registration.

Hostname

A *host* is a computer in a network. Since names are easier to retain than IP addresses, computers in a network are normally assigned names as well: this is the *hostname*. The system administrator can freely assign these hostnames; most administrators select names from a certain theme, like musical instruments, or names from television series or films.

The theme used in this book is colors. The name for the server is **green**. This makes the full hostname (or *Fully Qualified Domain Name [FQDN]*) **green.example.com**. A next server could then be called *red.example.com*.

Obviously, later in this book, *aliases* like *www.example.com* will be created.

Usernames

When examples require usernames, the names *diane* and *dimitri* will be used; clearly, the proper names that go with those usernames are *Diane* and *Dimitri*.

Conventionally, usernames are written in lowercase Latin characters, but uppercase letters are permitted. Digits, the dot, the underscore, and the dash are permitted as well, but usernames cannot start with a dash. Diacritics like *é* and *à* are not permitted.

Summary

This chapter discussed the preliminary knowledge and the available time that the (future) system administrator is expected to have. Furthermore, some pointers were given for the acquisition of a server, be it a physical or a virtual one, and the configuration of its BIOS or UEFI. Lastly, some conventions used in this book were explained.

The next chapter will kick off the "real" system administration with some basic information about Unix and POSIX and about the discussed systems FreeBSD, Debian, and CentOS in particular. Pointers to additional documentation, both installed locally and on the internet, will also be given.

CHAPTER 2

Unix and POSIX in a Few Words

BSD and Linux are both Unix-like systems (or Unices), systems that descend from or are inspired by Unix, the operating system that was first developed in the 1960s by Bell Labs, part of AT&T, the American phone company.

POSIX (*Portable Operating System Interface*) is a standard that defines the minimal set of functionalities, commands, and interfaces, as well as the directory structure, that a system must implement to be considered a Unix system.

About Unix and POSIX alone, entire books can be written. Since others have done so, this chapter will only highlight a few subjects that are important for this book. The interested reader will find more detailed information in the book store, in the library, and on the internet.

User Accounts

As with any modern operating system, each user on a Unix system has their own account. This account is used for the storage of personal settings and files, and it enables the system administrator to configure access to files, directories, applications, and devices on user level. Apart from that, some installed applications—the so-called daemons—also have their own account; this enables the system administrator, for instance, to limit the web server's access rights to the directories containing the websites.

The administrator account on a Unix system is called *root*; this account is comparable to the account called *admin* or *administrator* on other systems, and it is the only account with sufficient permissions to modify every part of the system. Generally, there is no physical user behind the root account; instead, it is an account that is used by selected system administrators to execute certain administration tasks.

R. La Lau, *Practical Internet Server Configuration*, https://doi.org/10.1007/978-1-4842-6960-2_2

15

User accounts and permissions will be discussed in more detail later in this book.

Each user account is normally accompanied by a *home directory*. This is the directory that has been assigned to the user for the storage of personal files; the user's personal settings are also stored in this directory.

Shell

When the user logs on to the system, they land in an environment where commands can be entered; this is called the *shell*. The shell waits for commands from the user and executes those with the help of the installed applications. Apart from the applications installed on the system, the shell also brings its own set of commands. The exact set of commands and their respective syntaxes depend on the shell being used. Different shells exist, and even though their functionality is largely the same, regular Unix users generally develop a preference for a certain shell, for example, based on the available keyboard shortcuts, or the syntax of built-in commands. The most commonly used shell is *Bash*; this is the default shell for many Linux systems, and most users don't bother trying other shells.

The POSIX standard dictates that a shell named sh must be installed in any case and that this shell's commands use the syntax of the *Shell Command Language*, which is also defined in POSIX. Often, sh (which is installed as /bin/sh on FreeBSD and Linux) is a redirection to Bash. If Bash is executed as /bin/sh, it assumes sh behavior as much as possible; if Bash is executed as itself, it deviates from sh in certain respects, and it has more extended possibilities. On FreeBSD, sh is the default shell; Chapter 3, "Software Management", explains how to install Bash on FreeBSD.

The interface that waits for the user to insert commands to be executed is called the *command-line interface* (*cli*).

By means of a *prompt*, an identifiable string of characters, the shell indicates that a command may be entered. Many shells follow the convention of making the prompt end in a dollar sign ($) if the user is logged on as a regular user and in a hash sign (#) if the user is logged on as root. This book follows that same convention; the command

```
$ ls /usr/bin
```

is to be executed as a regular user, and the command

```
# ls /usr/sbin
```

must be executed as root. Clearly, the dollar and hash signs themselves are not entered. If a distinction must be made between the different systems described, this book may sometimes represent the prompt as follows:

```
bsd$ command bsd user
bsd# command bsd root

linux$ command linux user
linux# command linux root
```

or even

```
freebsd$ command freebsd user
freebsd# command freebsd root

debian$ command debian user
debian# command debian root

centos$ command centos user
centos# command centos root
```

In those cases, the prefix linux does not mean that the command in question is present on all Linux distributions, but only concerns the Linux variants Debian and CentOS that are described in this book.

Many commands accept short and long variants for their parameters; the following commands, for instance, are equal:

```
$ ls -l
```

```
$ ls --long
```

This book will describe the long variants, if available. The short variants can be found in the documentation for the commands. The installed documentation will be discussed at the end of this chapter.

To enter a command definitively, the *Enter* key is pressed; as long as the *Enter* key has not been pressed, the command may still be modified. To jump to the next line without immediately entering the command, for example, for readability, *Enter* should be immediately prepended with a backslash (\); the shell will then show an alternative prompt on the next line and wait for more input.

```
$ ls \
> /usr/bin
```

This technique will also be used in this book for lines of sample code that are too long for the page. In those cases, the backslash will be shown in the example, but not the alternative prompt, for example:

```
$ command --parameter1 value1 \
    --parameter2 value2 \
    --parameter3 value3
```

Commands like the preceding ones can be entered on a single line without the backslashes.

A command may be aborted without entering it by holding the *Ctrl* key and then pressing the *C*; this key combination is usually represented as ^C.

Many shells allow the use of the *Arrow up* and *Arrow down* keys to scroll through the commands that were entered before. In this fashion, instead of retyping a command, it can be reentered by looking it up in the command history and pressing *Enter*.

Shells use *output redirection* to direct the output of a command to another command or to a file, instead of sending it to the screen. The greater-than sign (>) is used to direct the output of a command to a file. The following command sends a directory listing (list of files and sub-directories) of the /etc directory to the file /root/listing, instead of sending it to the screen; if the file exists, its content will be overwritten; if the file doesn't exist yet, an empty file is created first.

```
# ls /etc > /root/listing
```

If the file exists and two greater-than signs are used, the redirected output is appended to the end of the file; if the file doesn't exist yet, an empty file is created first.

```
# ls /dev >> /root/listing
```

The *pipe* (|) allows the use of the output of one command as the input for another. The following command uses the application awk to make a list of all usernames; it then sends that list to the application grep to find all the usernames starting with di; and that output is sorted alphabetically using the application sort.

```
$ awk -F ':' '{print $1}' /etc/passwd | grep '^di' | sort
diane
dimitri
```

A common use of the pipe is the redirection of the output of a command to a pager program like `more` or `less`, if the output is more than a single screen.

```
$ find /etc -type f -print | less
```

(The less command may be terminated by pressing the *q* key.)

And vice versa, the less-than sign allows for *input redirection*. In the following example, the content of the file `list.txt` is sent by email to *diane@example.com*:

```
$ mail -s "This is the list" diane@example.com < ./list.txt
```

Two constructions that look a bit like redirection, but are not, are the control operators `&&` (two ampersands) and `||` (two pipes).

When two commands are separated by two ampersands, the second command is only executed if the first command terminates successfully.

```
$ mkdir ./testdir && cd ./testdir
```

When two commands are separated by two pipes, the second command is only executed if the first command terminates unsuccessfully.

```
$ ls ./testdir || mkdir ./testdir
```

Shell Configuration

Like virtually all Unix applications, shells are usually configured using text files. For Bash, these are `/etc/profile`, `~/.bash_profile`, and `~/.bashrc`.

The file `/etc/profile` contains the system-wide configuration. This is the first file Bash reads when the user logs on, and it contains default settings for all users. Subsequently, the file `~/.bash_profile` is read. This file is stored in the user's home directory and contains settings specifically for this user; these settings may overwrite settings from `/etc/profile`. The file `~/.bashrc` is significant mainly to shells in a graphical user interface; it is read by shells that do not require a login.

The content of these files can be diverse:

- **Environment variables**

  These are variables that influence the behavior of commands or applications. Some common environment variables, for example, are *EDITOR* and *PAGER*; these variables, respectively, define the applications used to edit and display text files. Defining these applications in variables enables other applications to execute the user's preferred applications for the modification or display of text files.

Environment variables can also be defined at a later time (using the export command), and some variables are defined by the system, like *HOME* for the home directory and *USER* for the username.

```
$ export EDITOR=nano
```

The following command displays a list of all defined environment variables:

```
$ env
```

To use an environment variable, it must be captured between curly brackets and prepended by a dollar sign:

```
# echo ${HOME}
/root
```

- **Aliases**

  Alternative names may be defined for commonly used commands to facilitate their use. The command ls -lF, for example, could be replaced with ll and the command ls -a --color=auto with la; subsequently, when these shorter alternatives are entered, the shell replaces them with the real commands and executes those.

  ```
  alias ll='ls --format=long --classify'
  alias la='ls --all --color=auto'
  ```

- **Function definitions**

  Functions are somewhat comparable to aliases, but for more than a single command: the user defines a command (the function), which in turn executes a series of other commands. The following code creates a function named sys_short that displays the current date and time and then the used and free disk space:

```
sys_short() {
  date
  df --human-readable --output=target,pcent,avail
}
```

```
# sys_short
Wed Sep  9 11:17:58 CEST 2020
Mounted on      Use% Avail
/dev             0%  2.0G
/run            11%  356M
/                1%  866G
/dev/shm         0%  2.0G
/run/lock        0%  5.0M
/sys/fs/cgroup   0%  2.0G
/boot           34%  116M
/run/user/1000   0%  396M
```

- **Commands to be executed**

    If certain commands should be executed each time the user logs on,
    they could be put in these files.

To avoid clashes, it is important to avoid aliases, functions, and the *shell scripts*
described in the following section to have the same names as existing commands.

Defined environment variables, aliases, and functions remain in memory for the
length of the session and cease to exist when the user logs off.

Just like the files listed earlier are loaded when the user logs on, the file
~/.bash_logout is loaded when the user logs off. Obviously, it is of little use defining
environment variables when logging off, but this could be used, for instance, to
empty a certain directory when logging off.

Examples of .bash_profile and .bashrc can be found in the online addendum for
this book.

Shell Script

For the execution of repetitive tasks, *shell scripts* can be created. A *shell script* is a sequence of commands in an executable text file. By creating a shell script, the commands only need to be typed once; the next time the commands must be executed, the user executes the script instead, and the shell executes all commands in the correct order. Scripts can also process user input from command-line parameters and output from another command that was redirected using a pipe, as well as interactive input.

Shell scripts can greatly simplify a system administrator's job, and when beginning a more elaborate task, it is advisable to always ask oneself whether it would be worth it to automate the task using a script; often, the answer will be affirmative.

The following is an example of a shell script:

```
#!/usr/bin/env bash
cd /data/images/all
for img in *.{jpg,png}; do
    if [ `uname` = "Linux" ]; then
        time=`stat -c "%y" "${img}" | \
            awk -F. '{print \$1}' | \
            tr ' :' '_-'`
    else
        time=`stat -f %Sm -t %Y-%m-%d_%H-%M-%S`
    fi
    sfx=${img##*.}
    cp "${img}" "/data/images/${sfx}/${time}.${img}"
done
```

It would go a bit far to dissect this example by the letter, but it is a script for the Bash shell, which copies all *JPG* and *PNG* files from the directory /data/images/all to the respective directories /data/images/jpg and /data/images/png, prepending the date and time of last modification of each file to the filename.

If this were to be executed only once, for one or just a few files, it might not be a problem to manually enter these commands. But if the source directory contains many images and/or these commands must be executed each week, for instance, it is more practical to turn it into a script; the user would then execute the name of the script, and all commands would automatically be executed in the correct order.

```
$ /usr/local/bin/copy_images.sh
```

It is advisable to provide comments in the script—explanatory text which is ignored by the interpreter—so that it is possible later to analyze what exactly the script does and why. In most shells, if not all, a comment starts with a hash sign (#) and continues to the end of the line.

Directory Structure

The directory structure of a Unix system may be dispersed over several logical and physical disks (hard disks, partitions, network nodes, etc.). Locations that are situated outside the main disk or partition can be linked to an existing directory. These links are called *mounts*, and the verb for creating these links is *to mount*; the destruction of these links is *to unmount* (even though the command for this task is umount, without the "n").

Since the system has already been installed, and hence all disks and partitions have been mounted, and this server will not make use of removable media like CDs and flash disks, mounting physical stations will not be discussed further in this book. The system administrator who wishes to learn more about this subject should investigate the documentation for the commands mount and umount and the file fstab.

An address in the directory structure is usually called a *path*. Such an address or path consists of the names of directories, separated by slashes (/). Those slashes indicate that the directory to the right of the slash is a sub-directory (or file) in the directory to the left of the slash; the path /etc/ssh/sshd_config indicates a file named sshd_config in a directory named ssh, which in turn is a sub-directory of the directory named etc.

Since additional stations are linked to directories in the file system and hence have a place within the directory structure instead of next to it, paths do not begin with a letter, as they do in Windows.

Apart from files and directories, some other important elements exist in the Unix file system:

- **Devices**

  Each device on a Unix system, physical or virtual, is linked to a special file in the file system; this file allows the communication between the system and the device. A device can be the network card, but also the random number generator that is part of the kernel.

- **Links**

  An address in the file system can refer to a device, file, or directory, but it can also refer to another address. A distinction can be made between *symbolic links*, also called *symlinks* or *soft links*, and *hard links*. A *hard link* is a second name for the same file (or actually for the same *inode*); if one of the two (or more) addresses is deleted, the file or directory will continue to exist under the other name. A *symlink* is a reference to the address of the file; if the symlink is deleted, the file will continue to exist under its original name, and if the file is deleted, the symlink is "dead": it continues to exist, but no longer refers to anything.

- **Sockets**

  Unix domain sockets are interfaces that can be used for communication between applications installed on the same machine. If an application needs to communicate with other applications, it can create a *socket*. Other applications can then send information to be processed to this socket or use it to retrieve information that was made available by the application. For processes running on the same machine, sockets are a good alternative for network traffic, because they do not require all the protocols required by network traffic and hence require less memory and processor capacity. Since *Unix domain sockets* are represented by (special) files in the file system, they cannot be used for communication between different machines. For this same reason, the access to sockets can easily be managed on the level of users and user groups.

These are the most important directories on a Unix system:

- ~

  The tilde is used to indicate the home directory. If the tilde is used without any additional information, it indicates the home directory of the current user: if the user is logged on with the username *dimitri* and executes the command `ls ~/Downloads`,

the content of the directory /home/dimitri/Downloads (Linux) or
/usr/home/dimitri/Downloads (BSD) is displayed. If the tilde is
directly followed by an existing username, it indicates the home
directory for the user in question; the path ~diane/Downloads
indicates /home/diane/Downloads and /usr/home/diane/Downloads,
respectively.

It is possible to assign different home directories to users,
individually or collectively; in this case, the reference ~ still refers to
the correct directory.

- .

  The dot indicates the current directory (or working directory), the
  directory where the user currently "resides". When the user just
  logged on, this is usually the user's home directory; otherwise,
  it is the directory where the user has brought the shell using the
  command cd (*change directory*). The command pwd (*print working
  directory*) may be used to display the path for the current directory.

- ..

  The current directory's *parent directory* (the directory above the
  current directory) is indicated with two dots. If the current directory
  is /usr/local/etc, the path ../bin refers to /usr/local/bin; the
  path ../bin is called a *relative path*, and /usr/local/bin is
  called an *absolute path*. Even though it is rarely used, this reference
  may be used in the middle of a path as well: the path
  /usr/local/etc/../share/doc references /usr/local/share/doc.

  The reference .. may be used multiple times in a single path and
  indicates the parent directory of the parent directory, then. So,
  from the directory /usr/local/etc, the path ../../bin indicates
  /usr/bin.

- `lost+found`

  One of the default file systems for Linux is *ext4*. The first directory for each *ext4* file system, just like for its predecessors *ext3* and *ext2*, is called `lost+found`. This directory is therefore not only found in the root file system on the primary disk or partition but also on all mounts of type *extended*. This directory is used by the disk checking utility `fsck` to store files and file fragments that were found during a file system check.

- `/`

  The topmost directory in the Unix directory structure is represented by a single slash and pronounced as *root directory*, or simply *root*, not to be confused with user *root*'s home directory.

- `/home`

  The directory `/home` contains the home directories for the users. On BSD systems, `/home` is a symlink to `/usr/home`, where the actual home directories are kept. On many standard installs, users' home directories are accessible (but not writable) for all users; clearly, the owner of the home directory and the system administrator can change this.

- `/root`

  The home directory for the root user is not located in `/home`, but in `/root`. There is a simple reason for this: the users' home directories are often located on a different partition or disk or even on a network station. If root's home directory was on a different partition or disk and root needs to log on to solve problems with the mounting of partitions or network stations, root would not have access to their home directory, where scripts or other tools may be stored that might be necessary to repair the problems.

- `/bin`, `/usr/bin`, and `/usr/local/bin`

  The term *bin* stems from *binaries*, even though these directories can also contain scripts; these directories contain executable files.

  The division between `/bin` and `/usr/bin` originated in the days that hard drives weren't as large, and the system grew too large for a single disk; a second disk was mounted on /usr, where the / structure was copied. The sub-directory local is meant for files that are not part of the actual operating system; home-made applications and scripts that are used on the system should be installed in /usr/local/bin.

- /sbin, /usr/sbin, and /usr/local/sbin

  Comparable to /bin, /usr/bin, and /usr/local/bin, but for *system binaries*.

- /etc and /usr/local/etc

  These directories contain the system's configuration files. These are probably the most important directories to back up regularly; more information on this later in this book. Unix-like systems are largely configured through plain text files that can be edited using the most basic text editors. The advantage of this is obvious: there is no dependence of services that need to be started, like database managers or graphical interfaces.

- /srv

  This directory is used to store data for services running on this server. As the content of this directory depends heavily on the server's function(s), the system administrator is completely free in the arrangement of files and directories within this directory. System and software updates are not allowed to touch the content of this directory. In this book, this directory is used, among other things, to store the websites and the email.

- /tmp

  This is a directory for temporary files. All system users can read and write in this directory, but files can only be deleted by their owners.

- /dev

  This is the directory where the devices are stored, which were discussed before.

One device is important enough to explain, because it is a very practical device on the one hand, but a bit counterintuitive on the other: /dev/null. If data is sent to this device, it returns a *success* signal, but does nothing with the data it received; this can be used to ignore the output of a command (by redirecting its output to /dev/null). If data is read from this device, it only returns an *end-of-file* (*EOF*), which equals the content of an empty file; this can be used to create an empty file (by sending the content of /dev/null to the file).

```
$ ls / > /dev/null
$
```

```
$ cat /dev/null > /tmp/test
```

(These may not be the most practical or logical examples, but they do demonstrate the usage of /dev/null in a single line.)

These are only a few of the directories on a Unix system. An explanation for the other directories can be found in the *Filesystem Hierarchy Standard*, which is available online.

A path may contain the wildcards * and ?, where the asterisk signifies zero or more characters and the question mark exactly one character.

```
$ ls t?st
test tost tust
```

Obviously, this is not useful for every command:

```
$ cd t?st
bash: cd: too many arguments
```

The wildcards never match the slash that is used to separate directories and files.

Files and directories of which the name begins with a dot are "hidden files". For example, these files are not displayed by default in the output of ls. To display these files, the -a parameter for ls can be used.

```
$ ls ~
$ ls -a ~
.     .bash_history    .bash_profile    .mailrc    .shrc
..    .bash_logout     .bashrc                      .profile    .vimrc
```

Hidden files and directories are often used to store personal settings. Even though the files are hidden, they are accessible like non-hidden files.

Filename Extensions

Filename extensions (.zip, .txt, .html) do not, by definition, determine the file type. Even though the extension often reasonably indicates the file type, Unix systems do not, as some other systems do, determine how to handle a file based on the extension of its filename; instead, Unix handles files based on their content. In case of doubt, the file command may be used to determine the actual file type.

A zip file:

```
$ file zipfile.zip
zipfile.zip: Zip archive data, at least v2.0 to extract
```

A shell script posing as a zip file:

```
$ file shellscript.zip
shellscript.zip: POSIX shell script, ASCII text executable
```

The extension is often omitted altogether for executable and text files.

Network Ports

Network ports, or simply *ports*, are not a specific Unix functionality. But since they are more visible both on Unix systems and on servers than they are on some other operating systems and on workstations, they are briefly discussed here.

Network ports are virtual addresses that are assigned to the various services and protocols handled by the server. The web server, for instance, gets assigned ports 80 (HTTP) and 443 (HTTPS) by default; when a web browser requests *www.example.com/index.html*, this request is sent to port 80 on the server, and a request for the *https* variant is sent to port 443. On the server side of this communication, the web server (e.g., Apache or Nginx) "listens" on those ports and responds to those requests.

It is important for a system administrator to know, or at least to know where to find, which services use which ports. This information is specifically important when resolving network problems and when configuring the firewall. The file /etc/services contains a large list of port/protocol associations.

One of the commands that allow to display a list of the ports where applications currently listen (wait for client requests) is netstat:

```
# netstat -f inet -an
```

On many Linux systems, the command ss is also available, which gives more detailed information:

```
linux# ss --listening --processes --tcp --udp
```

If this command is executed as a regular user instead of root, the output is somewhat less overwhelming (but also less detailed).

The FreeBSD administrator also has the following command at their disposal:

```
bsd# sockstat -P tcp,udp
```

Processes

Applications that are loaded into memory—which have been started and have not been terminated yet—are called *processes*. Processes can be active for a long time, like a web server that is started and then waits for client requests; processes can also be active very briefly, like the cd command, to change the working directory.

The processes could be displayed in a tree structure: every process, except for the first, is started by another process. Of course, a process can also be started by a user typing a command into the shell, but the shell is also a process; the shell, in turn, is started by the login process and so on. The very first process in this tree structure is called init, after the original *SysV init*, even though this application may be named differently nowadays; init is the first process that is started and the last process that is terminated.

Each process has a unique numeric identifier that can be used, for example, to forcefully terminate the process. This identifier is called *PID* (*process identifier*), and init has PID 1.

Furthermore, each process is started with a certain username; the process then has the same privileges as that user. When a process is started by a user, for example, by entering the command in a shell, the process usually receives the username and privileges of this user. In some cases, processes receive a different username; this is discussed later in this chapter.

Displaying Processes

Two applications to display running processes and their PIDs are ps and top.

The ps command displays a list of processes, PIDs, and some additional information. By default, only processes belonging to the current user are displayed; to display all active processes, the ax parameter is added.

```
$ ps ax
  PID     TTY      STAT     TIME     COMMAND
    1      ?       Ss       0:01     /sbin/init
  ...     ...      ...      ...      ...
 1038    tty1      R+       0:00     ps ax
```

The top command also displays information about running processes, but instead of giving a list like ps does, it periodically refreshes the screen; the consequence of this is that top does not display all processes, but only as many as fit on the screen, sorted by CPU and memory usage. Moreover, top displays information on the total usage of memory and processor capacity of the system. Pressing *q* on the keyboard terminates top.

Terminating Processes

Active processes can be forcefully terminated with the help of the kill command.

The kill command sends a *signal* to a running process. Many different signals have been defined, and the vast majority of them (except SIGKILL and SIGSTOP) can be captured and interpreted by the process; if no code has been integrated into the program to handle the signal, a standard action is executed. The list of available signals can be found on Wikipedia and is linked from this book's online addendum.

One of the available signals is SIGTERM (for *terminate*); this is the default signal sent by the kill command. This signal is sent to a process to indicate that it should terminate. The process can capture this signal and then free up memory, delete temporary files, and execute other tasks that allow it to "cleanly" terminate.

This command sends a SIGTERM to the process with PID 1035:

```
# kill 1035
```

Sometimes it happens that a process "hangs" and does not respond to a signal that was sent to it. In that case, a SIGKILL may be sent; this signal is not captured by the process, but instead instructs the kernel to terminate the process.

```
# kill -s KILL 1035
```

The -s signal parameter may be shortened to -signal, and in addition to that, each signal has a numerical value; the numerical value for SIGKILL is 9. A system administrator who wishes to unconditionally terminate a process will therefore usually execute the following command:

```
# kill -9 1035
```

Despite its name, the kill command can not only be used to terminate processes but also to send other signals to processes. The system administrator who wishes to learn how to capture and interpret signals in shell scripts searches the Bash manual for the trap command (more information about the available documentation will follow later in this chapter).

Processes that were started from the command line can usually be terminated by pressing *Ctrl-C* (*^C*); this will send a SIGINT (for *interrupt*) to the process.

```
$ while true; do date; sleep 3; done
Thu Sep 10 11:16:57 CEST 2020
Thu Sep 10 11:17:00 CEST 2020
Thu Sep 10 11:17:03 CEST 2020
^C
$
```

The easiest way to find the mapping between the names and numbers of the signals is to execute the Bash command `trap -l`. The meaning of the signals can be found online.

Switching Off/Restarting the System

Not many valid reasons exist for rebooting a server. A Unix system does not need to be rebooted when new software has been installed; this is only necessary when a new kernel has been installed. When software has been installed or updated, it suffices to restart running instances of the software, if any exist.

The only reasons for shutting down a server are hardware trouble and the decommissioning of the server.

If there is a suspicion that the server's security has been compromised, it is often best to keep the server on, but disconnect the network cables, so that the server is only accessible through the (serial) console. This allows to analyze problems and to back up any data on the server. A hacked system may not come back up after it has been switched off.

Having said that, it may be practical, especially during the installation and initial configuration, to reboot the server every now and then; this is the only way to verify that everything will come back up as it should when the server is rebooted.

To shut down the system in a "clean" and secure way, the command `shutdown` is used. This command can be configured to shut down the system at a specific time and can send a message to logged on users.

```
# shutdown -h 16:15 "Server down 4:15 pm; replacement disk."
```

The `-h` parameter ensures that the server is switched off after the system has been brought down. Instead of a specific time (`16:15`), the format `+5` may be used to shut down the server in a certain number (5 in this case) of minutes; the keyword `now` shuts down the system immediately.

The `shutdown` command is also used to reboot the system. In that case, the `-h` parameter is replaced with `-r`:

```
# shutdown -r 06:15 "Server reboot at quarter past six."
```

It may be a good idea, when the installation is finished, but the server has not yet been taken into production, to do a *hard reboot*, for example, by pulling the plug. This allows to verify that the server correctly comes back up after a power outage. Some providers allow to cut and reset the power through their web interface.

Daemons

Daemons are processes that run in the background, which means that they are not connected to a terminal, and users cannot communicate with them directly. This type of process is called *service* on some other systems. Examples of daemons are the web server and the DNS server, but also the previously discussed init, the "ancestor" of all processes. In principle, one could say that (when functioning normally) all servers are daemons, but not all daemons are servers.

Daemons often save their PID to a text file, which simplifies the recovery. Such a text file is called a *PID file* and is usually stored in /run or /var/run.

Daemons are normally, directly or indirectly, started by *root*. Clearly, it could be dangerous to also execute these processes under the *root* username; after all, this would give these processes the same privileges as *root*, which would allow them to do great damage to the server, deliberately or by accident. This is why in the past daemons were often executed with the username *nobody* and the group name *nogroup*, a user and group without special privileges. However, if different daemons are executed with the same username, they can send each other signals and sometimes also modify each other's configurations. This is why today, when a daemon is installed, a user is created specifically for this daemon, allowing a precise limitation of the privileges of each daemon.

The names of daemons often end in "d" to indicate a daemon (sshd, named, httpd, crond). However, not every process of which the name ends in a "d" is a daemon, and not every daemon has a name that ends in "d" (dovecot, freshclam).

Starting and Stopping Daemons

Daemons are normally started by init, when the system boots, but they can also be started and stopped manually.

Different variants of init exist; each Unix system has its philosophy about what is best for the system and for the users.

BSD-Style init

The init system used by BSD systems is /etc/rc.

Startup scripts for daemons are installed in the directories /etc/rc.d and /usr/local/etc/rc.d. These scripts contain functionalities for starting and stopping the daemon in question and also often for restarting, status information, and so on. These scripts also define a number of variables.

The system administrator defines in the configuration file /etc/rc.conf which daemons should be started. This works as follows:

- The startup script in /etc/rc.d or /usr/local/etc/rc.d defines the variable *rcvar*.

- The value of this variable is used as a variable in the configuration file /etc/rc.conf.

- This variable is given the value YES.

An example: the startup script /etc/rc.d/ntpd contains the following line:

```
rcvar="ntpd_enable"
```

To enable this daemon, the system administrator adds the following line to /etc/rc.conf:

```
ntpd_enable="YES"
```

When the system boots, the script /etc/rc is executed by init. This script reads its configuration from the file /etc/rc.conf and then executes various tasks, among which the execution of the startup scripts of which the *_enable* variable has been defined as YES. By means of keywords defined in the comments of the startup scripts (PROVIDE, REQUIRE, BEFORE, and KEYWORD), rc determines the order of execution of the startup scripts. When the server is shut down, `rc` uses the variables in `/etc/rc.conf` to determine which services have been started and should hence be terminated.

To manually start a daemon, for instance, right after its installation, the system administrator defines, in `/etc/rc.conf`, the variable that indicates that the service should be started and then executes the `service` command to start the daemon.

```
bsd# service ntpd start
```

The `service` command is also used to stop a daemon.

```
bsd# service ntpd stop
```

If a service is stopped and should not be started automatically when the server reboots, the variable can be removed from `/etc/rc.conf` or be given the value NO.

```
ntpd_enable="NO"
```

If the value of this variable is NO while the daemon is running, the daemon cannot be stopped using the command `service [...] stop`; the value should then be changed to YES first, or the daemon should be terminated using a command like `kill`.

To define the variable in `/etc/rc.conf`, the file can be edited using a text editor, but the `service` command can also be used:

```
bsd# service ntpd enable
bsd# service ntpd disable
```

The first command sets the value to YES, and the second sets the value to NO.

SysV-Style init

System V (pronounced *System Five*) is a Unix variant that exists since the 1980s. *System V*'s `init` system has long been the default system for starting and stopping daemons, and it still is on a large number of Linux distributions.

Like *BSD-style* `init`, the system is based on scripts that start and stop services. However, instead of a single configuration, *SysV-style* systems have *runlevels*. A *runlevel* is a collection of active and inactive daemons and network settings. By switching runlevels, a computer can quickly and easily be brought into a certain state; *runlevel 3*, for example, is traditionally the runlevel where network services have been started and the computer functions mostly as a server, while *runlevel 5* is the runlevel where the graphical interface has also been started, and therefore the computer serves as a desktop computer.

A noteworthy variant of *SysV init* is *OpenRC*, which is the default *init system* for Gentoo Linux, TrueOS, Alpine Linux, and others, and is available as an option for other Linux distributions and BSD systems.

Since the systems FreeBSD, Debian, and CentOS, which are discussed in this book, do not use *SysV init* by default, this *init system* is not discussed any further in this book.

systemd

In the past few years, a number of Linux distributions have adopted *systemd* as their default *init system*. Among these distributions are Debian and its derivatives like Ubuntu (but with Devuan and Knoppix as notable exceptions) and Red Hat Enterprise Linux with its derivatives like Fedora and CentOS.

In *systemd*, daemons are called *services*. Configuration files in /lib/systemd/system (Debian) or /usr/lib/systemd/system (CentOS) determine how services must be started and stopped and in which order. The systemctl command is used to start and stop services:

```
linux# systemctl start apache2

linux# systemctl stop apache2
```

A target is a collection of active and inactive services. These targets allow the computer to quickly and easily be brought into a certain state; for example, there are the *multi-user.target*—the default target for a server—and the *graphical.target*—the default target for a desktop computer with a graphical interface. When these targets are activated, they start and stop all services that need to be started and stopped for the target in question. The active target is displayed with the following command:

```
linux# systemctl get-default
```

More information about setting the default target is to be found in Chapter 3, "Software Management."

The `systemctl` command is also used to add services to or delete services from the current target.

```
linux# systemctl enable apache2
```

```
linux# systemctl disable apache2
```

The first command adds a service to the current target, and the second command removes a service from the target. Adding a service does not automatically start the service, and deleting a service does not automatically stop it.

When a service is added to a target, a *symlink* is created in the related sub-directory of `/etc/systemd/system` to the configuration file for the service located in `/lib/systemd/system` or `/usr/lib/systemd/system`.

The `systemctl` command without any command-line parameters displays a list of loaded targets and services.

```
linux# systemctl
```

To display the status of a single service, the following command is used:

```
linux# systemctl status apache2
```

Other Background Processes

Not all background processes are daemons. Daemons are created to run in the background; they often have built-in functionality that allows them to send themselves to the background after having been started. But other processes may be sent to the background as well.

A good example would be the previously discussed script for copying images from one directory to another. If hundreds of images are to be copied, this script could take a long time to finish, and the user will probably not want to wait until the script finishes. In that case, the user may append an ampersand (&) to the command that starts the script; the script is then sent to the background, and the user regains the command line immediately to continue their work.

```
$ /usr/local/bin/copy_images.sh &
[1] 13824
$
```

The displayed output is the *job id* (a sequence number) between square brackets, followed by the process's PID.

A list of all the processes that have been sent to the background in this fashion may be obtained using the jobs command:

```
$ jobs
[1]  +   Running   /usr/local/bin/copy_images.sh
[2]  -   Running   find / -type f -name "*x*" > ~/x-files
[3]      Running   sleep 180
```

A process that was sent to the background can be brought back to the foreground with the help of the fg command, followed by the *job id*:

```
$ fg 2
```

If the fg command is not followed by a *job id*, the process that will be brought back to the foreground is the process that is indicated with a "+" in the jobs output.

Logs

The directory /var/log contains many log files. Most of these are plain text files that can be opened using pagers like more and less.

On systems that use *systemd* as their init system, many logs have been replaced with binary files. These files cannot be opened using pagers or text editors, but only with the help of an application called journalctl.

Log files will be discussed in more detail later in this book in Chapter 15, "Backup and Monitoring".

Documentation

Documentation about concepts, configurations, and installations can be found in abundance on the internet and in books like this one. But sometimes it is practical to be able to search for small pointers in daily use, such as the allowed *command-line parameters* for a certain command.

Even though this information is obviously available online, it is good to know that virtually all applications install their own documentation on the system and that most internet forums do not appreciate questions for which the answer could just as easily be found in the documentation that is installed locally.

Man and Info Pages

The most common form of locally installed documentation are the *man pages*, where *man* is short for *manual*. Very few applications are installed without a *man page*. Some of these man pages are very elaborate, and others only give some basic information and refer the user to a website for additional information.

The command for opening a man page is simply

```
$ man ls
```

The preceding command opens the man page for the ls command.

The man page can be scrolled up and down line by line with the help of the arrow keys and page by page using the *PageUp* and *PageDown* keys; the *g* is pressed to return to the top of the page, and the *G* sends the user to the end of the page. To search a certain word or term in the man page, a slash is typed, followed by the searched word, followed by *Enter*. The man page is closed with *q* (for *quit*).

More information about the usage of man is available in man's own man page:

```
$ man man
```

The man pages are divided into nine categories or sections:

1. Commands and applications

2. System calls

3. Library calls

4. *FreeBSD*: Kernel interfaces

   Linux: Special files

5. File formats; mostly configuration files

6. Games and screensavers

7. Miscellaneous

8. Commands for system administration

9. *FreeBSD*: Kernel developers

   Linux: Kernel routines

Some commands or terms appear in multiple sections; for example, the *man page* for man in section 1 explains the use of the man command, and the *man page* for man in section 7 explains how to create a *man page*. If no section number is given, man will search the sections in the following order: 1 8 2 3 4 5 6 7 9; the first matching page will be displayed. The desired section number may be given as the first parameter:

```
$ man 7 man
```

A common convention to refer to man pages is to write the name of the man page, directly followed by the number of the section in parentheses. This convention is also applied in this book. If, later in this book, a text says "*More information about this is available in nanorc(5)*," the reader is supposed to understand without additional explanation that this means "*More information about this is available in the man page nanorc in section 5 of the man pages.*" and that this man page can be displayed with the help of the command

```
$ man 5 nanorc
```

Apart from man pages, sometimes *info pages* are referred, although this format seems to be declining in popularity; often, these info pages are just copies of the man page for the same command. However, if projects do publish real *info pages*, they are often much more elaborate than the *man pages*. Another advantage of *info pages* is that they can link between pages, both pages from the same project and pages about other commands.

Obviously, the *info* documentation is available as an *info page*:

```
$ info info
```

Press *H* for a list of key bindings for the navigation.

HTML and Text

Many packages also install HTML or plain text documentation in the directories /usr/share/doc and /usr/local/share/doc. Clearly, these files can be displayed using commands like more and less. In Chapter 3, "Software Management", a so-called *text-based web browser* will be installed, which will enable the display of HTML documents on the console.

Installed text documents are sometimes compressed using gzip or bzip2; in those cases, the respective commands zless and bzless can be used to open the documents.

On FreeBSD, many examples of scripts and configurations are installed in the directories /usr/share/examples and /usr/local/share/examples. On Linux,

these examples are often installed in sub-directories of /usr/share/doc and
/usr/local/share/doc. The following command can be used to search the directory
/usr for all directories named examples:

```
# find /usr -type d -name examples -print
```

Request for Comments (RFC)

And finally, the *RFC*s should be mentioned, even though these are not installed locally.

These documents were originally written by technicians and researchers, addressed
to their colleagues, to propose new standards for protocols. During the past decennia,
however, it has become a system to document protocols and procedures, of which a part
has eventually become an official standard and another part a de facto standard. The
RFCs describe the internet and related technologies, so they are not limited to Unix only.

Beginning or even very advanced system administrators are in no way expected
to know the RFCs by heart. But it is good to know of their existence, and the system
administrator or software developer who needs to learn the ins and outs of a certain
protocol, for example, cannot ignore the RFCs.

The online addendum for this book includes a link to the *RFC editor*, the online
database containing all the RFCs.

Summary

This chapter served as a quick primer for the less experienced BSD or Linux
administrator and as a quick refresher for the more experienced *sysadmin*. It described
some of the basic building blocks of Unix and POSIX, like the shell, the directory
structure, and file types, and it gave some quick information about network ports (that
are not Unix specific, but still quite important on a server). This chapter also explained
how processes are started, stopped, and monitored on different Unix-like systems. Lastly,
the reader got some pointers for finding additional documentation outside this book.

The next chapter will explain how to personalize the server by installing and
removing software and will guide the reader through different software management
systems.

CHAPTER 3

Software Management

Unix systems exist in many variants, and they all have their own philosophies and evolutions. One of the areas where these differences are very visible is software management.

Even though most Unix systems know how to compile the source code for applications (provided that the application developer has integrated support for the system in question), most operating systems have chosen to develop a system for software installation. Some advantages of such a system are

- The system decides where executable files, configuration files, and documentation are installed, enabling users, but also other applications, to find files in predictable locations.

- The system can resolve dependencies. An application can depend on the presence of another application or of a certain library; a software installation system can detect these dependencies and install required additional software.

- The communication with a single software repository facilitates the search for new versions of installed software.

Many of these systems publish the software in a pre-compiled form, but the systems in the BSD family, as well as some Linux distros like Gentoo, have opted for a system that downloads the source code for the software to adapt and compile it locally.

In practice, the preference for a certain software installation system is an important factor in the choice of an operating system.

In the rest of this chapter, some examples of installation and removal of applications will be given for each operating system (FreeBSD, Debian, and CentOS). First, a complete system update is done; it is advised to always assume that the system is not

43

© Robert La Lau 2021
R. La Lau, *Practical Internet Server Configuration*, https://doi.org/10.1007/978-1-4842-6960-2_3

fully up to date after an installation and that updates have been published between the compilation of the installation medium and the actual installation. Subsequently, the following applications will be installed:

- **A text editor**

    With this application, text files can be edited in the console. Since Unix systems are configured using text files, this is an essential tool. Many text editors exist for the console. For a system administrator who does not yet have enough experience to have a favorite text editor, *nano* is advised; this is an easy-to-use and intuitive editor.

- **Lynx**

    This is a so-called *text-based browser*, a web browser that is executed in the console and navigated using the keyboard. This browser is very suited for browsing the HTML documentation that many applications install into `/usr/share/doc` (and also `/usr/local/share/doc` on FreeBSD). This browser can also be a practical tool to test the website(s) installed on the server; visiting the website from the console of the machine where the website is installed eliminates network problems.

A consequence of the use of software installation systems is that the software must be adapted after being published by their respective development teams, so that it can be installed by the chosen installation system and onto the chosen operating system. As these adaptions, as well as testing them, are done by people and thus depend on the available staff and on the priorities, the available software and available software versions may differ between operating systems and distributions.

It is important to keep in mind that, besides installation and updates, the removal of software is equally important for the maintenance of the system. It is not exceptional that in time software reveals problems of stability or security, and even though this may be justifiable for software that is actually used and can usually be resolved by applying updates, there is no excuse for accepting this risk for unused software. It is therefore essential, after having experimented or having replaced a certain application with another, to remove software that is not or no longer used from the system.

FreeBSD

FreeBSD software can be divided into two categories: the base system and additional software. The base system consists of the kernel and a number of base commands and applications; this is what makes the system a FreeBSD system. The additional software consists of all the applications that are added to allow the system to perform the tasks that it was built for.

Base System

The `freebsd-update` command serves to update the base system. The configuration file for this application is `/etc/freebsd-update.conf`, and for privacy reasons, it is advised to verify that the hosting provider did not change the server to be solicited. The value for the parameter *ServerName* should be `update.freebsd.org`; if this is not the case, it can be corrected after the text editor *nano* has been installed in the next section.

The `freebsd-update` command is executed in two steps. First, the updates are downloaded, permitting the system administrator to inspect the modifications to be made:

```
freebsd# freebsd-update fetch
```

The output of this command is displayed in the *less* application; the output can be inspected with the help of the arrow keys, the *PageUp* and *PageDown* keys, and the space bar, and the application is terminated by pressing *q*.

Subsequently, the updates are installed by executing

```
freebsd# freebsd-update install
```

If during the installation something goes wrong unexpectedly, the system can be reset to the previous state with the help of the command

```
freebsd# freebsd-update rollback
```

Active applications that have been updated must be restarted for the changes to take effect. If the kernel has been updated, the system must be rebooted.

Since chances are good that the installation media do not contain the very last versions of all applications, it is advisable to execute the preceding commands directly after having completed a new installation. After that, regular checks for updates—at least once a week—will have to be performed. Later in this book, when task planning is discussed, the automation of this process will be explained.

Additional Software

FreeBSD knows two systems for the installation of additional software: *packages* and *ports*. The installation of a *package* consists of the download and installation of a pre-compiled binary file; when a *port* is installed, an application's source code is downloaded and compiled locally before it is installed.

These are some considerations that can be made when choosing between packages and ports:

- Packages have already been compiled, so their installation takes less time.

- Ports are compiled on the target system, so they are optimized for that system; packages have been compiled with options that make them run acceptably on as many systems as possible.

- The source code for ports can be verified and modified before being compiled.

- The compilation of ports allows the system administrator to enable or disable optional functionalities; for packages, this choice has already been made by someone else.

Packages and ports can be mixed on a system, so these considerations can be made for each installation.

For both packages and ports, dependencies (additional software that is required for the functioning of the initially installed software) will be found and installed automatically.

This chapter discusses both systems. Since this book also serves the beginning system administrator, the rest of this book will only use packages; this may prevent some research and debugging that may occur sometimes when installing ports because of incomplete dependencies or incompatible compilers. The more experienced user is encouraged to always use ports to optimize the installed software for the system it is used on.

On FreeBSD systems, software is often referred to in the format *category/package* (e.g., *editors/nano*). This category corresponds to the package's sub-directory in the *Ports Collection*; more information about the *Ports Collection* follows later in this chapter, in the sections about *ports*.

Package Installation

The application that is used to manipulate packages is called *pkg*. If this package is not installed, the command will propose to install it:

```
freebsd# pkg help
The package management tool is not yet installed on your system.
Do you want to fetch and install it now? [y/N]:
```

Press *y* and then *Enter*; the package will be installed and the command executed.

The pkg command accepts several sub-commands, like the preceding help. The command pkg help displays the list of all sub-commands.

The pkg search command is used to search in the list of available packages.

```
freebsd# pkg search nano
```

The result of this search is a list of all packages that have nano in their name. The second column of the output contains a short description of the found packages. It is important to always execute pkg search, even if the name of the package to be installed is known, because multiple versions of the same package may be available.

The pkg install command then starts the installation; this command asks for confirmation before any packages are actually installed.

```
freebsd# pkg install nano
Updating FreeBSD repository catalogue...
FreeBSD repository is up to date.
All repositories are up to date.
Updating database digests format: 100%
The following 3 package(s) will be affected (of 0 checked):
New packages to be INSTALLED:
        nano: 4.4
        indexinfo: 0.3.1
        gettext-runtime: 0.20.1
Number of packages to be installed: 3
The process will require 3 MiB more space.
677 KiB to be downloaded.
Proceed with this action? [y/N]: y
[1/3] Fetching nano-4.4.txz: 100% 511 KiB 523.4kB/s 00:01
```

```
[2/3] Fetching indexinfo-0.3.1.txz: 100% 6 KiB 6.2kB/s     00:01
[3/3] Fetching gettext-runtime-0.20.1.txz: 100% 160 KiB 163.6kB/s 00:01
Checking integrity... done (0 conflicting)
[1/3] Installing indexinfo-0.3.1...
[1/3] Extracting indexinfo-0.3.1: 100%
[2/3] Installing gettext-runtime-0.20.1...
[2/3] Extracting gettext-runtime-0.20.1: 100%
[3/3] Installing nano-4.4...
[3/3] Extracting nano-4.4: 100%
```

Once installed, the *nano* editor can be started with a filename as a command parameter:

```
freebsd$ nano ~/test.txt
```

or

```
freebsd# nano /usr/local/etc/nanorc
```

Within the application, help is available by pressing *Ctrl-G* or *F1*; *Ctrl-X* closes the editor. *Nano* can be configured using command-line parameters and configuration files; more information about this is available in nano(1), nanorc(5), and /usr/local/share/doc/nano.

The Lynx browser is installed in the same manner.

```
freebsd# pkg search lynx
freebsd# pkg install lynx
```

Once installed, the browser can be used to display the HTML documentation that was installed on the system or to visit websites (both local and remote):

```
freebsd$ lynx /usr/local/share/doc/nano/nano.html
```

```
freebsd$ lynx https://lynx.invisible-island.net/
```

Lynx can be configured through command-line options and configuration files; more information in lynx(1) and /usr/local/share/doc/lynx.

And then, Chapter 2, "Unix and POSIX in a Few Words", spoke of the Bash shell, which may be somewhat more user-friendly for the beginning system administrator than *sh*, FreeBSD's default shell. With the information given previously, the reader may now be expected to be able to install this shell without additional help; the package is called *bash*, and the most recent version can be installed. Chapter 5, "User Management and Permissions", will explain how to set this new shell as a user's default shell. The online addendum for this book contains the personal Bash configuration files ~/.bash_profile and ~/.bashrc that are not installed automatically on FreeBSD.

The pkg install command also allows the installation of multiple packages at the same time:

```
freebsd# pkg install nano lynx
```

More about the possibilities of *pkg* can be found in pkg(8) and the man pages that that man page refers to.

Package Updates

If no software has been installed from the *Ports Collection*, installed packages can be simply updated to the most recent available version with the help of the following command:

```
freebsd# pkg upgrade
```

This should be executed at least once a week.

If active services like daemons have been updated, they must be restarted to use the newly installed version. In the following chapters, this will be discussed individually for each service.

If software was installed from the Ports Collection, the update method for ports should be used when updating all packages.

Since FreeBSD does not record whether software was installed from a package or from a port, once installed, it is impossible to determine from which source software has been installed. Updating the software using pkg upgrade would then result in installed ports being replaced with packages, which would forfeit any optimizations and explicitly enabled functionalities. Updating packages from the Ports Collection will not harm the software. However, it is important to keep in mind that the gain in time from installing packages will be lost if packages are updated from the Ports Collection: the updates will be installed as ports, so they will be compiled locally.

Installation of the Ports Collection

To enable the installation of ports, the *Ports Collection* must be installed first. This is a directory structure that contains FreeBSD-specific compilation and installation instructions for each available port. To find out whether the Ports Collection has been installed, a simple directory listing suffices:

```
freebsd# ls /usr/ports
ls: /usr/ports: No such file or directory
```

If the directory does not exist, the Ports Collection is not installed.

The tool that is used to retrieve and update the Ports Collection is called *portsnap*; this application is part of the base system, so it is installed already. The configuration file for *portsnap* is /etc/portsnap.conf. For privacy reasons, it is recommended to verify that this file refers to the default FreeBSD server. The value for the *SERVERNAME* parameter should be portsnap.freebsd.org; if this is not the case, it can be corrected after the text editor *nano* has been installed in the next section.

The following command will take care of the initial installation of the collection:

```
freebsd# portsnap fetch extract
```

This command will take some time to execute. See portsnap(8) for more information about *portsnap*.

The files in /usr/ports are text files, and the cd, ls, more, and less commands can be used to discover their contents.

Once the Ports Collection has been installed, it can be updated to its most recent version with the help of the following command:

```
freebsd# portsnap fetch update
```

It is advised to always do this before installing new applications and before updating installed applications to a newer version.

The command that is used to compile applications (turn source code into executable files) is called make; make's sub-commands are called *targets*.

The configuration file /etc/make.conf helps optimize the compilation of applications. To avoid the chicken-and-egg situation where no application has been installed to edit text files, but the file must be created before such an application can be installed, the echo command can be used with *output redirection* to the file:

```
freebsd# echo "OPTIONS_UNSET=" >> /etc/make.conf
freebsd# echo "OPTIONS_UNSET+= CUPS" >> /etc/make.conf
freebsd# echo "OPTIONS_UNSET+= FONTCONFIG" >> /etc/make.conf
freebsd# echo "OPTIONS_UNSET+= GUI" >> /etc/make.conf
freebsd# echo "OPTIONS_UNSET+= HAL" >> /etc/make.conf
freebsd# echo "OPTIONS_UNSET+= LPT" >> /etc/make.conf
freebsd# echo "OPTIONS_UNSET+= X11" >> /etc/make.conf
freebsd# echo "DEFAULT_VERSIONS+= ssl=libressl" >> /etc/make.conf
```

The first seven lines prevent components being installed for a graphical user interface and for printing; these functionalities are not needed for an internet server and would only "pollute" the system (add complexity and risks, without giving usable functionality in return). These options may be specified on a single line, but for readability, they have been split up.

The last line assures that *LibreSSL* is used as the default SSL/TLS implementation. This encryption protocol for web and mail traffic will be discussed elaborately in Chapter 10, "Traffic Encryption: SSL/TLS".

The make command will load these settings each time it is executed to install a port.

Installation of Ports

The base directory for the Ports Collection is /usr/ports. In this directory, the command make search can be used to find applications to be installed:

```
freebsd# cd /usr/ports
freebsd# make search name=nano
```

(In the preceding command, search is the *target*.)

The result of this search is a list of all ports that have nano in their name. This list shows /usr/ports/editors/nano as the directory for the *nano* port.

```
freebsd# cd /usr/ports/editors/nano
```

When in doubt, the file pkg-descr usually contains more details about the port in question:

```
freebsd# cat ./pkg-descr
```

The following command (to be executed in the port directory) shows a complete list of all dependencies for the application to be installed:

```
freebsd# make all-depends-list
```

For many ports, the installation is configurable: certain components can be enabled or disabled, added or removed. The first time a port is installed, the system will ask which options must be enabled or disabled if any configurable options exist. These settings are then stored and reused for updates. The make config command can be used, in the port's directory, to modify stored options.

```
freebsd# make config
```

This command displays a dialog window where options can be enabled and disabled. In this dialog window, the arrow keys are used to navigate between the options, the space bar is used to enable and disable options, and the *Tab* key is used to navigate between the list with the options and the buttons; the buttons are pressed using the *Enter* key. When in doubt, the wiser option would be to not change an option; if needed, the configuration can be modified later and the application reinstalled.

To prevent the installation from being paused to configure the options for dependencies, forcing the system administrator to stay present and alert, make's config-recursive target can be used to configure all dependencies before the installation:

```
freebsd# make config-recursive
```

Repeat this command until no options are left; it could happen that in a next execution of this command options for dependencies of dependencies need to be configured.

Once the port is configured, it can be installed.

```
freebsd# make install clean
```

The source code will now be downloaded and compiled, and the resulting application will be installed. Depending on the application and on the dependencies that must be installed, this may take somewhere between some and a lot of time. However, since all options have been configured, for the application itself as well as for its dependencies, there is no need to remain present during the installation.

The make target named clean (make [...] clean) assures that all supporting and temporary files are deleted after the installation, leaving the port directory as clean as it was before the installation.

The *nano* editor has now been installed and can be started with a filename as command-line parameter:

```
freebsd$ nano ~/test.txt
```

or

```
freebsd# nano /usr/local/etc/nanorc
```

Within the application, help is available by pressing *Ctrl-G* or *F1*; *Ctrl-X* closes the editor. *Nano* can be configured using command-line parameters and configuration files; more information about this is available in nano(1), nanorc(5), and /usr/local/share/doc/nano.

The Lynx browser can be installed in the same manner:

```
freebsd# cd /usr/ports
freebsd# make search name=lynx
freebsd# cd www/lynx
freebsd# make config-recursive
freebsd# # ^^^ repeat ^^^
freebsd# make install clean
```

Once installed, the browser can be used to display the HTML documentation that was installed on the system or to visit websites (both local and remote):

```
freebsd$ lynx /usr/local/share/doc/nano/nano.html
```

```
freebsd$ lynx https://lynx.invisible-island.net/
```

Lynx can be configured through command-line options and configuration files; more information in lynx(1) and /usr/local/share/doc/lynx.

And then, Chapter 2, "Unix and POSIX in a Few Words", spoke of the Bash shell, which may be somewhat more user-friendly for the beginning system administrator than *sh*, FreeBSD's default shell. With the information given previously, the reader may now be expected to be able to install this shell without additional help; the port directory is /usr/ports/shells/bash. Chapter 5, "User Management and Permissions", will explain how to set this new shell as a user's default shell. The online addendum for this book contains the personal Bash configuration files ~/.bash_profile and ~/.bashrc that are not installed automatically on FreeBSD.

The make reinstall command can be used to reinstall installed packages, for example, when installation parameters have been changed. This command removes the installed package without removing its configuration to reinstall it immediately.

```
freebsd# cd /usr/ports/editors/nano
freebsd# make config
freebsd# make reinstall clean
```

Port Updates

Various applications exist for updating ports. The simplest of these is *portmaster*.

```
freebsd# cd /usr/ports/ports-mgmt/portmaster
freebsd# make install clean
```

The following commands are executed to update all installed packages to their most recent available versions:

```
freebsd# portsnap fetch update
freebsd# portmaster -ya
```

It is recommended to do this at least once a week.

If new configuration options have been added to the ports, the configuration dialog will be presented. Also, portmaster will ask for confirmation before removing old versions. The system administrator will therefore have to be present during the update.

The portmaster command can also be used to update a single port:

```
freebsd# portmaster editors/nano
```

Even though the preceding command contains the relative path to the port directory in /usr/ports, it is not necessary to change the working directory to /usr/ports before executing this command.

More information can be found in portmaster(8).

If active services like daemons have been updated, they must be restarted to make use of the newly installed version. This is discussed individually for each service in the following chapters.

Alternatives for *portmaster* can be found in the Ports Collection under /usr/ports/ports-mgmt.

Package and Port Information

Once installed, there is no difference between packages and ports; they are installed into the same directories and contain the same machine code, and their installation is registered in the same database. This means that once installed, packages and ports can be manipulated by the same tool. This tool is *pkg*, the same tool that was used for the installation of packages.

To obtain a list of installed packages, the following command is executed:

```
freebsd# pkg info
```

The same command, with the name of a package appended, is used to obtain more detailed information about an installed package:

```
freebsd# pkg info nano
```

The pkg command is also used to obtain information about packages that are not installed. The following command displays the description, but the %e pattern can be replaced by other patterns to display different information; more information in pkg-rquery(8).

```
freebsd# pkg rquery "%e" nano
```

The following command will display a list of all files installed by a certain package:

```
freebsd# pkg query "%Fp" nano
```

To find out which package installed a certain file, the following command is used:

```
freebsd# pkg which /usr/local/bin/nano
```

The *pkg* application can also be used to scan installed packages for known security vulnerabilities. For this to work, a database containing known vulnerabilities must be downloaded; the following command downloads this database and then executes the scan:

```
freebsd# pkg audit --fetch
```

The automation of this scan will be discussed later when task scheduling is discussed.

To check whether installed applications have been modified after being installed, the following command is used:

```
freebsd# pkg check --checksums
```

If an application has been modified after its installation, there is a possibility that it has been tampered with illegally. This would be a valid reason to disconnect the server from the network, analyze it completely, and possibly reinstall it.

It is important to keep in mind that the preceding tests are only performed on installed packages and ports and not on the base system.

Removal of Packages and Ports

And finally, pkg can also be used to remove an installed application from the system:

```
freebsd# pkg delete editors/nano
```

As in the preceding text, even though the path relative to /usr/ports is specified, it is not necessary to change the working directory to /usr/ports.

The preceding command will only remove the specified application and not the applications that were installed as dependencies for this package. It is therefore advised to always execute the following command after the removal of an application; this command will remove all unused dependencies from the system:

```
freebsd# pkg autoremove
```

More about all of the preceding information and many more possibilities of *pkg* can be found in pkg(8) and all the man pages that this man page refers to.

Restarting the Interrupted Installation of a Port

An advantage of the Ports Collection is that packages can often be fine-tuned to the demands of the server and the system administrator in a very detailed manner, thanks to the installation options. A disadvantage may be that the chosen collection of options is not always compatible, which will make the installation terminate prematurely with an error message. While this may not be a problem when this happens with a small package, it can be quite inconvenient if this happens with a large package with dozens of dependencies. Finding all these dependencies, to reset all their installation options, can be very time-consuming.

If this happens, it is more practical to restart from zero, to reset the system to the state of before the failed installation, so to say, and restart the installation with new options.

In the following example, the installation of *database/mariadb104-server* failed; this is a port with dozens of dependencies, and dependencies of dependencies. The installation failed before the requested application was installed, but many dependencies have already been installed, and all dependencies have already been configured using make config-recursive.

First, all unused dependencies can be removed. All packages that were installed as dependencies for *mariadb104-server* are marked as unused, now that *mariadb104-server* is not installed.

```
freebsd# pkg autoremove
```

And then, all temporary files (that were used during the installation) can be removed from the port directories of the requested port and all its dependencies, and all stored installation options can be removed.

```
freebsd# cd /usr/ports/databases/mariadb104-server
freebsd# make clean-depends
freebsd# make clean
freebsd# make rmconfig-recursive
```

The installation can now be restarted from make config-recursive without any traces from the failed installation.

Debian

Debian and its derivatives use so-called *Debian packages* for software installation; these packages' filenames end in .deb. The application that is used to install, update, and remove software is called apt.

The apt command will always show a list of packages to be installed, updated, or removed and will ask for confirmation before changes are made to the system.

Just like BSD systems and contrary to systems based on Red Hat Linux, the list of available software is installed locally. It is therefore recommended to always update this list before installing or updating software:

```
debian# apt update
```

Since Debian packages are not compiled locally, but instead are downloaded in pre-compiled form, it is impossible to remove certain functionalities from applications, as was done, for instance, with support for X11 (graphical user interface) for FreeBSD earlier; after all, the same packages are installed on workstations that usually do need X11 support. The consequence of this is that some installed packages are larger than their BSD counterparts and that the chance exists that more dependencies will be installed (e.g., applications and libraries necessary for the functioning of X11).

To save resources, to dam maintenance, and to limit the risks of software that runs but is not used, it is recommended to at least prevent the X Windows System from starting. To do this, the default *graphical.target* must be replaced with the *multi-user. target*:

```
debian# systemctl isolate multi-user.target
debian# systemctl set-default multi-user.target
```

The first of those two commands makes the switch to the *multi-user.target* immediately; the second command assures that the computer will start up in the *multi-user.target* after a reboot. The section "systemd" of Chapter 2, "Unix and POSIX in a Few Words", gives some background information about these targets.

The list of sources from where software may be installed is /etc/apt/sources.list. One line needs to be added to this file:

```
deb http://deb.debian.org/debian stretch-backports main
```

This source contains packages that are not available in Debian Stretch by default, but have been adapted to Stretch from later Debian (test) versions. If another Debian version is installed on the server, Stretch should obviously be replaced with that version in the preceding line.

Some providers modify the file sources.list in the installation image to point at their own mirrors for the installation of packages. From a privacy point of view, it may be desirable to correct this to refer to the default Debian mirrors. The list of official mirrors can be found on the Debian website.

When the configuration file was modified, the list of packages must be updated:

```
debian# apt update
```

Updates

Once the package database has been updated, the installed packages can be updated to the most recent available versions. It is recommended to do this directly following a new installation of a system and then repeat this regularly, for example, each week.

```
debian# apt update
debian# apt dist-upgrade
```

Installation

On Debian, *nano* is part of the default installation and does not need to be installed separately.

The *nano* text editor can be started with a filename as command-line parameter:

```
debian$ nano ~/test.txt
```

or

```
debian# nano /etc/nanorc
```

Within the application, help is available by pressing *Ctrl-G* or *F1*; *Ctrl-X* closes the editor. *Nano* can be configured using command-line parameters and configuration files; more information about this is available in nano(1), nanorc(5), and /usr/share/doc/nano.

The Lynx browser is installed with the help of the following command:

```
debian# apt install lynx
```

Once installed, the browser can be used to display the HTML documentation that was installed on the system or to visit websites (both local and remote):

```
debian$ lynx /usr/share/doc/nano/nano.html
```

```
debian$ lynx https://lynx.invisible-island.net/
```

Lynx can be configured through command-line options and configuration files; more information in lynx(1) and /usr/share/doc/lynx.

If multiple package names are given as command-line parameters, all those packages will be installed, including their dependencies.

```
debian# apt install nano lynx
```

If the apt install command is used for a package that has already been installed, the package is updated to its most recent available version.

Information

Several applications exist to obtain information about installed software, and one of those applications is apt.

This command displays a list of all installed packages:

```
debian# apt list --installed
```

Unfortunately, the output for that command is not very readable; the list looks as follows:

```
lynx-common/stable,now 2.8.9rel.1-3 all [installed,automatic]
lynx/stable,now 2.8.9rel.1-3 amd64 [installed]
nano/stable,now 3.2-3 amd64 [installed]
```

which means this:

*package/archive,*now *version architecture [install options]*

where package is the name of the package, archive is the name of the software archive from which the package was downloaded, and the word now indicates that the package is installed. The word automatic in the install options indicates that the package was installed as a dependency for another package.

Another, older command to query the database of installed packages is dpkg-query:

```
debian# dpkg-query --list
```

This command's output may be a bit clearer than that of apt list. This output can be scrolled up and down using the arrow keys and *PageUp* and *PageDown*. Press *q* to quit.

The apt command can also be used to obtain detailed information about a specific package

```
debian# apt show nano
```

or to get a list of all packages that have a certain term in their name or description:

```
debian# apt search nano
```

This last command also includes, for instance, the package *openmx* in the list of results, because the description of this package says "*package for nano-scale material simulations*".

To obtain a list of all files installed by a certain package, the dpkg-query command can be used again:

```
debian# dpkg-query --listfiles nano
```

And the other way around, to find out which package installed a certain file:

```
debian# dpkg-query --search /etc/issue
```

More information about the virtually endless list of possibilities for soliciting and manipulating the package databases is available in the respective man pages for these commands.

Removal

To uninstall packages, the commands apt-get remove and apt-get purge can be used. The first command uninstalls the package, but leaves configuration files untouched; this facilitates a possible reinstallation. The second command removes the package entirely.

```
debian# apt-get remove nano
debian# apt-get purge lynx
```

To immediately remove all packages that were installed as dependencies for the package to be uninstalled and are no longer needed now, the --autoremove parameter can be added:

```
debian# apt-get remove --autoremove nano
debian# apt-get purge --autoremove lynx
```

To remove unneeded dependencies afterward, the following command can be executed:

```
debian# apt-get autoremove
```

It is recommended to execute this command periodically to remove packages that have become superfluous after an update.

CentOS

CentOS is based on Red Hat Enterprise Linux. The name of software packages ends in .rpm, which is short for *Red Hat Package Manager*; the packages are often simply called *RPMs*. The application used to install, update, and uninstall the packages is called *yum*.

The *yum* application has a lot of configuration files: /etc/yum.conf, /etc/yum/*, and /etc/yum.repos.d/*. From a privacy point of view, it may be desirable to verify that the provider did not modify the URLs for the software repositories; in all files in the directory /etc/yum.repos.d, the parameters *mirrorlist*, *baseurl*, and *metalink* should refer to trusted URLs, preferably within the centos.org domain or potentially within the fedoraproject.org domain.

The yum command always displays a list of files to be installed, updated, or removed and asks for confirmation before any changes are made to the system.

Like Debian packages, RPMs are pre-compiled, so for systems based on Red Hat, it is also impossible to remove services like X11 from the packages. However, contrary to Debian, CentOS is booted into the *multi-user.target* (fully functional system without graphical user interface), so it is not necessary to change the target to disable X11. This can be verified in the following manner:

```
centos# systemctl get-default
multi-user.target
```

If the output of that command is not multi-user.target, the previous section, about software management on Debian, explains how to switch targets. The section "systemd" of Chapter 2, "Unix and POSIX in a Few Words", gives more background information about these targets.

Updates

As stated, yum is the command that is used to manipulate the packages.

Contrary to FreeBSD and Debian, CentOS does not have a local database of available packages. The database is available online, so CentOS always has the list with all the most recent versions at its disposal, without having to update it first.

The following command is used to update all installed packages to their most recent available versions:

```
centos# yum update
```

It is recommended to execute this command immediately after a new installation (or after delivery of the server) and regularly after that, for example, each week.

To update a single package, the name of the package is appended as a command-line parameter:

```
centos# yum update binutils
```

Installation

To fully take advantage of the functionalities of *yum*, it is recommended to install the package *yum-utils*. This package contains some additions to *yum* that can be used, for instance, to query the installed packages database.

```
centos# yum install yum-utils
```

This immediately shows that yum, like pkg on FreeBSD and apt on Debian, has a simple and somewhat predictable syntax.

The *nano* text editor is installed in the same simple manner:

```
centos# yum install nano
```

The editor itself is installed in /usr/bin, with the other binaries (on CentOS, /bin is a symlink to /usr/bin). The system-wide configuration is installed as /etc/nanorc; users can modify the settings in that file by creating a file named ~/.nanorc.

The nano text editor can be started with a filename as command-line parameter

```
centos$ nano ~/test.txt
```

or

```
centos# nano /etc/nanorc
```

Within the application, help is available by pressing *Ctrl-G* or *F1*; *Ctrl-X* closes the editor. *Nano* can be configured using command-line parameters and configuration files; more information about this is available in nano(1), nanorc(5), and /usr/share/doc/nano-*version*.

Now that the *nano* text editor is installed, it can be used immediately to disable *SELinux*. *SELinux* (*Security-Enhanced Linux*) is a system to manage access to directories and files for applications. In itself, this is a good idea, but since this system can prevent applications from functioning and *SELinux*'s log files and documentation leave some things to be desired, it is recommended to disable this system until *SELinux* has matured more.

Open the file /etc/selinux/config in nano, and change the value of the variable *SELINUX* from enforcing to permissive.

```
centos# nano /etc/selinux/config
```

```
# Old value.
 SELINUX=enforcing

# New value.
 SELINUX=permissive
```

This setting assures that *SELinux* will no longer block anything after a reboot. If this is not the right moment for a reboot, *SELinux* can be disabled until the next reboot by executing the following command:

```
centos# setenforce 0
```

The other application to be installed is the Lynx browser. The command to do so speaks for itself now:

```
centos# yum install lynx
```

Once installed, the browser can be used to display the HTML documentation that was installed on the system or to visit websites (both local and remote):

```
centos$ lynx /usr/share/doc/nano/nano.html
```

```
centos$ lynx https://lynx.invisible-island.net/
```

Lynx can be configured through command-line options and configuration files; more information in lynx(1) and /usr/share/doc/lynx-*version*.

If yum is given the names of multiple packages on the command line, all of those packages will be installed, including all their dependencies.

```
centos# yum install nano lynx
```

Information

A list of all installed packages is obtained using the command

```
centos# yum list installed
```

And a very similar command displays a list of available updates:

```
centos# yum list updates
```

The yum command is also used to obtain detailed information about a specific package:

```
centos# yum info nano
```

To obtain a list of all files installed by a certain package, the repoquery command from the *yum-utils* package can be used:

```
centos# repoquery --list nano
```

And the other way around, this command is used to find out which package installed a certain file:

```
centos# yum provides /etc/favicon.png
```

More information about *yum* and *yum-utils* can be found in yum(8), yum-utils(1), and the pages that those man pages refer to.

Removal

The yum command is also used for the removal of software:

```
centos# yum remove nano
```

The preceding command will remove the named package and any packages that depend on it.

It is recommended to also execute the command

```
centos# yum autoremove
```

every now and then to remove packages that have been installed as dependencies for other packages, but are no longer necessary.

Perl and Python

Many Perl and Python applications and libraries are available in the default software repositories for the miscellaneous operating systems. But many other applications and libraries are not, and those packages that are available are not always fully up to date.

However, Perl and Python both have their own software repositories from where packages can be installed. These repositories and the tools that come with them will not be discussed extensively, but it is good to know that they exist.

Two warnings are in place when using these repositories:

- **Consistency of the internal software database**

    The software management systems (*pkg*, *apt*, and *yum*) all maintain their own databases containing information about installed software. If a second system is used for the installation of additional software, these databases no longer reflect the exact state of the system. This may pose problems if a certain package has already been installed using the alternative application and is then installed again using the operating system's default software management system, as a dependency for some other package, for example. It is therefore important to always try and install a package from the "official" repositories first. However, sometimes a package is not available from the operating system's software repositories, or its version is too far behind on the version in the alternative repository. If this is the case, there is no choice, and the alternative package will have to be installed. Possible problems will then have to be dealt with if and when they occur, and it is the responsibility of the developers of the different systems to integrate communications between the systems.

    If at all possible, installations from the alternative repositories should be executed as regular user instead of root. The packages are then installed in the home directory and are only available to the user in question; this prevents the packages from clashing with packages that are installed system wide.

- **Reliability installed packages**

    It is important to keep in mind that these software repositories
    accept submissions from non-verified sources. Only packages
    with a good reputation, from developers with a good reputation,
    should be installed. The spelling for packages to be installed
    should be thoroughly verified (to prevent *typosquatting*). The
    source code for unknown packages should be analyzed and
    verified before installation.

    It is also important to be aware of the fact that these packages have
    not necessarily been tested explicitly for the operating system or
    distribution on which they are to be installed.

Perl: CPAN/cpan

The Perl repository is called *CPAN* (*Comprehensive Perl Archive Network*), and the
application that is used to manipulate the Perl modules is called cpan.

On FreeBSD and Debian, cpan is installed together with Perl; on CentOS, it is a
separate package.

```
centos# yum install perl-CPAN
```

The cpan command can be used directly for the installation of Perl modules, but
a more user-friendly interface to that command is cpanm, which will not only execute
cpan but will also resolve dependencies and take other work off the hands of the system
administrator. This script is installed with the help of cpan:

```
$ cpan App::cpanminus
```

The first time cpan is executed, it asks for some information. Normally, the details
proposed per default can be accepted here by pressing *Enter*. This information will be
stored to be reused on a next execution of cpan.

The application cpanm is installed in /usr/local/bin. On CentOS, this directory is
not part of the *PATH* environment variable, preventing the system from finding
the command. Therefore, on CentOS, the following small file should be saved as
/etc/profile.d/path.sh:

```
PATH="$PATH:/usr/local/bin"
export PATH
```

If users exist on the server who use *C shell* or one of its variants, the following should be saved as /etc/profile.d/path.csh:

```
setenv PATH $PATH\:/usr/local/bin
```

Log out and log back in again to have this take effect.

The cpanm command can then be used to install other Perl modules:

```
$ cpanm App::cpanoutdated
```

If cpanm is executed with an already installed module as a command-line parameter, the module will be updated to its most recent available version.

The application *cpan-outdated* (installed earlier) can be used to find out-of-date modules and to feed these to cpanm to have them updated:

```
$ cpan-outdated -p | cpanm
```

A good starting point for finding Perl modules is **www.cpan.org**, with over 192,000 modules.

The cpanm command can also be used to install Perl modules from other websites, from Git repositories, and from the local hard disk.

See cpan(1) and cpanm(1) for more information.

Python: PyPI/pip

The Python repository is called *PyPI* (*Python Package Index*), and the application that is used for the manipulation of Python packages is called *pip*.

Since Python is often available in multiple versions, it is important to install the most recent version of *pip*.

```
freebsd# pkg search pip
freebsd# pkg install py37-pip

debian# apt search pip
debian# apt install python3-pip

centos# yum search pip
centos# yum install python3-pip
```

Packages can now simply be installed using these commands:

```
freebsd$ pip install <package name>
```

```
linux$ pip3 install <package name>
```

To update installed packages to their most recent versions, the --upgrade parameter is added. This also updates packages this package depends on, if any.

```
freebsd$ pip install --upgrade <package name>
```

```
linux$ pip3 install --upgrade <package name>
```

Packages can be uninstalled with the sub-command uninstall:

```
freebsd$ pip uninstall <package name>
```

```
linux$ pip3 uninstall <package name>
```

A good starting point for finding Python packages is **pypi.org**, with over 220,000 projects.

The pip command can also be used to install Python packages from other websites, from Git repositories, and from the local hard disk.

See pip(1) for more information.

Summary

This chapter explained and demonstrated differences and similarities between the FreeBSD, Debian, and CentOS software management systems. A few tips were given for the protection of privacy and confidentiality, and a user-friendly text editor and a text-based web browser were installed. The availability and risks of the OS-independent Perl and Python software repositories CPAN and PyPI were explained, together with the tools that are used to manage the software from those repositories.

In the next chapter, the network and the firewall will be configured.

CHAPTER 4

Network Basics and Firewall

These days, it is almost unthinkable that a computer would not be connected to a network, and a server is useless without a network connection.

In this chapter, the network interface will be located, an IP address and hostname will be assigned to that network interface, and the gateway that connects this server to the internet, as well as the external DNS servers that translate between hostnames and IP addresses, will be configured.

Lastly, the firewall will be configured. A firewall is software that can block or permit network traffic to certain IP addresses and/or ports, which makes it an important component in the security of the server.

Network Configuration

The minimum network settings that need to be made for the server to be fully part of the network it is on are the following:

- **Network card**

  The system must "know" which network card must be used to communicate to the network.

- **IP address**

  The address for the server in the network.

- **Default gateway**

  The address of the server through which (the rest of) the internet can be reached.

© Robert La Lau 2021
R. La Lau, *Practical Internet Server Configuration*, https://doi.org/10.1007/978-1-4842-6960-2_4

- **DNS server(s)**

   The servers that must be consulted for the translation between hostnames and IP addresses.

The network has probably been configured already with the help of *DHCP* (*Dynamic Host Configuration Protocol*), but even if this is the case, it is recommended to make all the settings manually and disable DHCP.

The IP address, together with the netmask or the routing prefix, should be provided by the hosting provider. If it wasn't, they must be contacted.

If the server is a home or office server, the system administrator can freely choose from the following ranges of IP addresses:

- **10.0.0.0/8** (10.0.0.0–10.255.255.255)

- **172.16.0.0/12** (172.16.0.0–172.31.255.255)

- **192.168.0.0/16** (192.168.0.0–192.168.255.255)

These ranges have been reserved for private networks, so they can never clash with IP addresses used on the internet. Do not use an address that ends in .0 (network address) or .255 (broadcast address). Use a netmask of 255.255.255.0, which is the same as a routing prefix of 24; this creates a network with 254 addresses (e.g., 172.17.2.1–172.17.2.254).

The address of the gateway should also be provided by the hosting provider. For a home or office network, this is the IP address of the modem.

As discussed in the first chapter, the server in this book uses the IP address **198.51.100.156**, with a netmask of **255.255.255.0**, routing prefix **24**, and gateway **198.51.100.1**. For DNS resolving, the free and public Cloudflare/APNIC DNS servers are used; their IP addresses are **1.1.1.1** and **1.0.0.1**.

A domain name can be registered with a registrar of choice. An officially registered domain name can also be used for a home or office network, for example, the subdomain *office.example.com*; if no officially registered domain name is available, a domain name should be chosen that ends in *.lan* (*Local Area Network*) to prevent the name from ever clashing with a domain name used on the internet.

About the Netmask and the Routing Prefix

An IP address is part of a subnet; the IP address 198.51.100.156 *may*, for example, be part of the subnet with the addresses 198.51.100.0 to 198.51.100.255. It may, but it is not per definition: the netmask or routing prefix determines the size of the subnet. The netmask is a "mask" that indicates which bits of the IP address are static and thus determines the subnetwork the IP address is part of. To make this clearer, the addresses must be translated to their binary values, as shown in Table 4-1.

Table 4-1. *Translation of network addresses from decimal to binary*

	decimal	binary
IP address	198.51.100.156	11000110.00110011.01100100.10011100
Netmask	255.255.255.0	11111111.11111111.11111111.00000000
Network address	198.51.100.0	11000110.00110011.01100100.00000000
Broadcast address	198.51.100.255	11000110.00110011.01100100.11111111

Every block of an IP address consists of 8 bits (1 byte or octet). The bits in the IP address that have a value of 1 in the accompanying netmask form the network prefix, and the bits in the IP address that have a value of 0 in the accompanying netmask contain the host address; the network prefix is identical for the entire subnet. In the preceding example, 198.51.100 is the network prefix, and the last octet of the IP address is used to indicate the host.

The lowest address in the calculated subnet is the network address, which should not be used as an ordinary IP address. The highest address in the calculated subnet is the broadcast address (an address to send messages to all hosts in the subnet) and should not be used as an ordinary IP address either. The addresses between the network address and the broadcast address are the available IP addresses in the subnet in question; in the preceding example, there are 254 of those.

If the netmask in Table 4-1 were 255.255.240.0, which is 11111111.11111111.11110000.00000000 in binary notation, the network address would have been 198.51.96.0, and the broadcast address would be 198.51.111.255. This subnet would contain 4094 IP addresses.

In the example in Table 4-1, 8 bits (1 byte) are available for host addresses. The other way around, one could say that 24 bits (3 bytes) are *not* available. This is what the routing prefix indicates; a netmask of 255.255.255.0 is the same as a routing prefix of 24, and a netmask of 255.255.240.0 is equal to a routing prefix of 20 (count the values 1 in the binary representation of the netmask).

For indicating an IP address and its place within its subnet or for indicating a subnet and its size, the respective representations IP address/routing prefix and network address/routing prefix are often used, for example, 198.51.100.156/24 or 198.51.100.0/24. This is called *CIDR notation* (*Classless Inter-Domain Routing*; pronounced as a single word: cider).

Mastering the calculation of subnets, netmasks, and routing prefixes requires some practice and time. It is therefore practical to remember that a netmask of 255.255.255.0

- Is equal to a routing prefix of 24 (which is often simply pronounced as slash 24)

- Makes available 254 IP addresses

- Assures that these 254 hosts all have an address in the last block (byte) of the IP address

- Largely suffices for most home and office networks

- Is sometimes also called a class C network (class B is /16, and class A is /8)

FreeBSD

On FreeBSD, the name of the network interface is discovered using the ifconfig command. Most likely, this command will show only two interfaces, but some servers have more.

```
freebsd# ifconfig -l
em0 lo0
```

The lo0 interface is the loopback device, the virtual network interface that enables network traffic between the local machine and itself. The other interface, which is not necessarily called em0, is the network interface that must be configured.

If the preceding command shows more than two devices, `ifconfig` without the `-l` option gives more information. Among other things, this will include a line starting with `status:` in the output; if this status is `no carrier`, this means that no network cable is connected, and if the status is `active`, the cable is connected. The active network interface must be configured. If more active interfaces are available than IP addresses, the provider must be contacted, and likewise if there are no active interfaces.

This book assumes that the name of the interface to be configured is em0.

The hostname, the IP address, the netmask, and the gateway are all defined in the file /etc/rc.conf:

```
freebsd# nano /etc/rc.conf
```

```
# This server's hostname.
hostname="green.example.com"

# The IP address and the netmask for interface em0.
ifconfig_em0="inet 198.51.100.156 netmask 255.255.255.0"

# The gateway.
defaultrouter="198.51.100.1"
```

If these variables are already defined in this file, those lines should be deleted. If a variable named *ifconfig_DEFAULT* is defined, it should also be deleted.

For the hostname, the complete hostname is used, the domain name included; this is called the Fully Qualified Domain Name, or simply FQDN.

The DNS servers to be used are configured in /etc/resolv.conf. By default, however, this file is managed by the `resolvconf` daemon; this daemon is disabled first to prevent it from undoing the new settings.

```
freebsd# service resolv stop
freebsd# service resolv disable
```

The contents of /etc/resolv.conf can now be entirely replaced by these two lines:

```
nameserver 1.1.1.1
nameserver 1.0.0.1
```

Now, when the `netif` (network interface), `routing`, and `hostname` services are restarted, the new configuration will be active.

```
freebsd# service netif restart && service routing restart
freebsd# service hostname restart
```

The routing service must be restarted in the same command line as the netif service, because the restarting of the network interface automatically empties the routing table. If the routing service is not restarted immediately afterward, the server becomes unreachable and must be rebooted (clearly, this is only true if the service is managed remotely, like over SSH).

Debian

On Debian, the ip command is used to discover the name of the network interface to use.

```
debian# ip link
```

```
1: lo: <LOOPBACK,UP,LOWER_UP> mtu 65536 qdisc noqueue state UNKNOWN mode
DEFAULT group default qlen 1000
    link/loopback 00:00:00:00:00:00 brd 00:00:00:00:00:00
2: enp1s0: <BROADCAST,MULTICAST,UP,LOWER_UP> mtu 1500 qdisc mq state UP
mode DEFAULT group default qlen 1000
    link/ether 52:54:00:12:34:56 brd ff:ff:ff:ff:ff:ff
```

These lines are a bit long for the page, but it is clear that there are two interfaces: lo and enp1s0. A list a bit less cluttered can be obtained with

```
debian$ ls /sys/class/net
```

The lo interface is the loopback device, the virtual network interface that enables network traffic between the local machine and itself. The other interface, which is not necessarily called enp1s0, is the network interface that must be configured.

The network interfaces are configured in the file /etc/network/interfaces. This file probably contains a line like

```
iface enp1s0 inet dhcp
```

This means that the interface enp1s0 is configured through DHCP, so it receives its IP address from the provider's DHCP server. However, the provider assigned a static IP address, so it is a good idea to configure this manually. The preceding line (iface …) can be replaced with these lines:

```
iface enp1s0 inet static
  address 198.51.100.156/24
  gateway 198.51.100.1
```

The new configuration is loaded by restarting the *ifup@enp1s0.service*.

```
debian# systemctl restart ifup@enp1s0
```

For setting the hostname, the `hostnamectl` command is used.

```
debian# hostnamectl set-hostname green
```

The specified hostname cannot contain any dots, so the domain name is not included.

Next, the following line is added to the file `/etc/hosts`:

```
198.51.100.156     green.example.com green
```

This links the complete hostname, the domain name included, to the IP address. The complete hostname is also called the FQDN (*Fully Qualified Domain Name*) sometimes.

And finally, the name servers to be consulted are specified using two lines in the file `/etc/resolv.conf`:

```
nameserver 1.1.1.1
nameserver 1.0.0.1
```

All other lines in that file may be deleted.

CentOS

Possibly, the package NetworkManager is installed for the management of the network settings. But since this daemon is not very practical for a server with a static IP address, it needs to be disabled.

```
centos# systemctl stop NetworkManager
centos# systemctl disable NetworkManager
```

If the preceding commands show error messages, this means that the NetworkManager was not active (which was exactly why the commands were executed in the first place).

The name of the network interface can be discovered with the help of the `ip` command:

```
centos# ip link
1: lo: <LOOPBACK,UP,LOWER_UP> mtu 65536 qdisc noqueue state UNKNOWN mode
DEFAULT group default qlen 1000
    link/loopback 00:00:00:00:00:00 brd 00:00:00:00:00:00
2: ens3: <BROADCAST,MULTICAST,UP,LOWER_UP> mtu 1500 qdisc pfifo_fast state
UP mode DEFAULT group default qlen 1000
    link/ether 52:54:00:12:34:56 brd ff:ff:ff:ff:ff:ff
```

The preceding output, which is a bit cluttered because of the long lines on the narrow page, shows two interfaces: lo and ens3. The lo interface is the loopback device, the virtual network interface that enables network traffic between the local machine and itself. The other interface, which is not necessarily called ens3, is the network interface that must be configured.

The file that contains the settings for this network interface is /etc/sysconfig/network-scripts/ifcfg-ens3 (where ens3 must be replaced with the name of the network interface). This file must be replaced with a file containing the new settings.

```
centos# cd /etc/sysconfig/network-scripts
centos# mv ifcfg-ens3 ifcfg-ens3.orig
centos# nano ifcfg-ens3
```

```
# The device's name.
NAME=ens3
DEVICE=ens3

# The type of connection.
TYPE=Ethernet

# Static IP address.
BOOTPROTO=static

# Do not stop on error.
IPV4_FAILURE_FATAL=no

# Connect when the server boots.
ONBOOT=yes
```

```
# IP address, routing prefix, gateway.
IPADDR=198.51.100.156
PREFIX=24
GATEWAY=198.51.100.1

# Do not use NetworkManager to manage this interface.
NM_CONTROLLED=no

# Domain + DNS (/etc/resolv.conf).
DOMAIN=example.com
DNS1=1.1.1.1
DNS2=1.0.0.1
```

A brief explanation of the parameters that can be used in this file can be found in the file /usr/share/doc/initscripts-*version*/sysconfig.txt.

The hostname is set with the help of the hostnamectl command; this has the same effect as manually editing the file /etc/hostname.

```
centos# hostnamectl set-hostname green
```

The given hostname cannot contain any dots and thus no domain name.

Next, the following line is added to the file /etc/hosts:

```
198.51.100.156    green.example.com green
```

This links the complete hostname, the domain name included, to the IP address. The complete hostname is sometimes also called the FQDN (*Fully Qualified Domain Name*).

Now, when the network service is restarted, the new network settings take effect.

```
centos# systemctl network restart
```

Firewall

A firewall is software that blocks unwanted network traffic and permits wanted network traffic. Firewalls exist with two different scopes:

- **Network-based firewall**

    This type of firewall is placed between a network and its internet gateway or between two or more network segments and protects an entire network or network segment. A network-based firewall is usually a dedicated device, be it an appliance that was constructed specifically for this purpose or an ordinary server that was configured to function as a firewall.

- **Host-based firewall**

  This type of firewall is a piece of software that is installed on a host and protects only that specific host. The host can be a server, a workstation, or any other network node.

The firewall analyzes each IP packet that tries to enter or leave the server or the network and determines whether the packet should be blocked or permitted based on rules defined by the system administrator. This is called packet filtering.

Other functionalities exist for firewalls, like changing the destination of packets, but this book will only discuss packet filtering.

The implementation and configuration of a firewall can be complex. However, this may never be an excuse to omit or postpone it: every computer that is connected to the internet will be under attack sooner or later, and it is the system administrator's job to counter these attacks; the firewall is one of the most important tools they have to do this.

This section and the next try to create a foundation for a firewall that is effective on the one hand and easy to understand and maintain on the other. The firewall described here should be seen as the absolute minimum; the system administrator is encouraged to reevaluate and readjust the firewall constantly, with the help of the system's log files and technical literature that can be found in the bookshop and on the internet.

Firewalls exist in many shapes and forms. It is therefore important to understand that the firewall as described in this book

- Only protects the server itself and no other computers (it is a host-based firewall)

- Makes its decisions based on sources and destinations of packets and not based on the contents of sent messages (it is a packet filtering firewall)

- Sees the difference between inbound packets that try to initiate a connection and inbound packets that were sent in reply to previously sent outbound packets (it is a stateful firewall)

The firewall itself is part of the kernel (also called kernel space), and the tool to manage the kernel is part of the operating system (user space).

The firewall configuration described in this book is kept as simple as possible; these are its principles:

- All outbound traffic is permitted.

- All inbound traffic is blocked, unless an exception has been configured.

- Inbound SSH traffic is permitted, because this is the protocol that is used for system administration.

- If and when a brute-force attack is detected on the SSH port (22), traffic originating from the IP address in question will be entirely blocked for an hour.

- Known fixed IP addresses for system administrators (office, home) are never blocked.

- Inbound traffic is allowed on the ports needed to provide the services for which the server is installed (DNS, HTTP(S), SMTP, IMAP, etc.).

- Since the server is not configured to make use of IPv6, the firewall will not include any rules specifically for IPv6.

Firewall rules are specified with one or more parameters; these are the most important ones:

- The action to take for the rule: block or permit

- The direction of the analyzed packet: inbound or outbound

- The used network interface (network card, Wi-Fi adapter, loopback device, etc.)

- The address family: IPv4 or IPv6

- The internet protocol (TCP, UDP, ICMP, etc.; see /etc/protocols for a complete list)

- The source and/or destination IP address

- The source and/or destination port (see /etc/services for an extensive list)

- The TCP flags; nine control bits that can be activated or deactivated in the TCP header

A firewall always has at least one rule. This is the default rule that is applied if no other rule applies to the analyzed packet. This rule only specifies an action: block or permit.

The default rule for the firewall that is configured in this book will block all inbound traffic. In general, this is the most secure option: no traffic is permitted, unless an exception was defined explicitly for the analyzed packet. In the chapters that follow, for each service that is configured, it will be indicated how the firewall configuration must be modified to allow communication with that service.

On the contrary, the default rule for outgoing traffic is very permissive: basically, all outbound traffic is permitted. Since only system administrators have access to this server and no users who could abuse the given freedoms, a concession can be made for user convenience at the cost of rigidity of security.

The firewall configuration described in the following, both for FreeBSD and for Linux, only treats a fraction of the available possibilities.

Martians

Several ranges of IP addresses exist that are not meant for use on the internet; the IP ranges for private networks, documentation, and loopback devices have already been touched upon briefly. The collection of all these reserved addresses is sometimes called Martian addresses, or simply Martians. This originated in the days that there was no network on Mars; now that multiple man-made spacecrafts exist on and around Mars, this term may be a bit obsolete.

Since these IP addresses are not meant to be used on the internet, the firewall will unconditionally block all requests originating from these addresses to the external network interface.

FreeBSD

The FreeBSD base installation includes three different firewalls: PF, IPFW, and IPFILTER. For this book, PF was chosen on the one hand because this is also the firewall for OpenBSD (where this package originated) and DragonFly BSD and on the other hand because in the FreeBSD handbook PF is discussed before IPFW, which was developed for FreeBSD, which suggests that PF will eventually replace IPFW on FreeBSD.

The rules for PF are defined in the file /etc/pf.conf, which is loaded into the firewall with the help of the pfctl application.

The rules are applied in the order in which they are defined in `pf.conf`, and **each packet is evaluated by each rule**. So, the specified action, which can be either `pass` or `block`, is not taken as soon as a rule matches: all rules are evaluated, and the action to be taken can change multiple times; the action that will be taken is the action that remains after all rules have been evaluated.

The keyword `quick` changes this functionality: if a rule contains the word `quick`, the action is taken immediately (if the rule matches), and the packet is not evaluated by any following rules.

For ease of maintenance, several variable types can be used in `pf.conf`:

- macro

  A macro is a variable that can contain a single value. An example would be the name of a network interface. A macro is defined as follows:

  ```
  interface = "em0"
  ```

  In the rest of the script, it can then be referred as follows:

  ```
  block in on $interface from any to self
  ```

- list

  A list contains a collection of similar values, represented in curly brackets. This type of variable can be used to treat a collection of ports as a group, for example.

  ```
  pass in proto tcp to self port { http https }
  ```

  A list can also be put into a macro:

  ```
  www = "{ http https }"
  pass in proto tcp to self port $www
  ```

- table

  A table contains IP addresses (IPv4 and IPv6). The name of a table is represented in angle brackets.

  ```
  table <trusted> { 192.0.2.4 198.51.100.19 203.0.113.0/24 }
  pass in from <trusted> to self
  ```

A table allows for more efficient searching than a list. Another advantage of a table is that its contents can be modified without the need to reload the rules or restart the firewall:

```
freebsd# pfctl -t trusted -T add 192.0.2.35
```

Sample Configuration

The following is a simple but effective foundation for a firewall configuration for a FreeBSD server using the PF firewall. However, this does not complete the firewall configuration: in the following chapters, services will be added to the firewall when they are added to the server. The following configuration is but a framework that blocks inbound traffic by default and can be easily modified to permit traffic to certain ports. Without modification, this configuration is not fit for a home or office server.

This file should be saved as /etc/pf.conf.

```
# Name of the network interface.
interface = "em0"

# Allowed inbound TCP ports.
# Both names and numbers can be used.
# List may not be empty.
# Example:
#   tcp_ok = "{ 22 53 http https }"
tcp_ok = "{ 22 }"

# Allowed inbound UDP ports.
# Both names and numbers can be used.
# List may not be empty.
# Example:
#   udp_ok = "{ domain 123 }"
udp_ok = "{ 53 }"

# Trusted IP addresses (office, home, ...).
# Example:
#   table <trusted> persist { 203.0.113.26 198.51.100.43 }
table <trusted> persist { }
```

```
# Reserved IP ranges.
table <martians> const { 0.0.0.0/8 10.0.0.0/8 \
  127.0.0.0/8 172.16.0.0/12 192.0.0.0/24 192.0.2.0/24 \
  192.168.0.0/16 198.18.0.0/15 198.51.100.0/24 \
  203.0.113.0/24 }

# Allow all traffic over the loopback device.
set skip on lo0

# Block non-valid packets.
scrub in all

# Block packets with a spoofed source address.
antispoof for $interface

# Fail2ban will use this anchor to automatically
# create the necessary tables and rules.
anchor "f2b/*"

# The default policy.
block in all
pass out all keep state

# Block Martians.
block drop in quick on $interface from <martians> to any
block drop out quick on $interface from any to <martians>

# Allow trusted addresses.
pass in quick on $interface from <trusted> to any

# Explicitly allow SSH.
pass in proto tcp to $interface port 22

# Allow ping.
pass inet proto icmp icmp-type echoreq

# Allow accepted TCP traffic.
pass proto tcp from any to $interface port $tcp_ok

# Allow accepted UDP traffic.
pass proto udp from any to $interface port $udp_ok
```

Obviously, at least the name of the network interface must be verified and possibly corrected. For use in a home or office network, the rules that block Martians must be removed.

The lists *tcp_ok* and *udp_ok* cannot be empty and must always contain at least one element. To open ports in the firewall, they can simply be added to these lists.

The firewall can now be enabled and started. Attention: this will disconnect all connections (except for direct connections to the console).

```
freebsd# service pf enable
freebsd# service pf start
```

After the file /etc/pf.conf has been modified, for instance, to add or remove allowed ports, the rules must be reloaded into the firewall. Attention: this will remove all rules and table entries that were added dynamically (see in the following) without also being added to pf.conf.

```
freebsd# service pf reload
```

Firewall Manipulation

The current rules are displayed with the help of the following command:

```
freebsd# pfctl -s rules
```

To add an IP address to the table of trusted addresses, the configuration file does not need to be modified, and the rules do not need to be reloaded. The following command adds an address to the table:

```
freebsd# pfctl -t trusted -T add 203.0.113.26
```

The contents of this table are displayed with the help of the following command:

```
freebsd# pfctl -t trusted -T show
```

And when a system administrator leaves, it is a good idea to remove their personal IP address from the table:

```
freebsd# pfctl -t trusted -T delete 203.0.113.26
```

The const attribute in the definition of the <martians> table prevents the contents of this table from being modified. The persist attribute in the definition of the <trusted> table assures that this table is not deleted when empty.

Unfortunately, there is no command to export the entire firewall configuration to a file, to be recharged elsewhere, or at another moment.

The `pfctl` command manages the entire firewall and not just the tables. More information can be found in `pfctl(8)`. Example configurations are available in `/usr/share/examples/pf`.

Linux

The Linux firewall is called nftables. Many Linux servers still use iptables, but since nftables is the replacement for iptables—developed by the same team—and is part of the Linux kernel since 2014, iptables will not be discussed here. The system administrator who wishes to switch from iptables to nftables will find tips and scripts on the nftables wiki.

On CentOS, firewalld is active by default. This daemon adds a few layers on top of the firewall configuration, distancing the system administrator from their system. This daemon should therefore be disabled.

```
centos# systemctl mask --now firewalld
```

On both Debian and CentOS, the necessary kernel modules have been installed, but the user space utilities have not.

```
debian# apt install nftables
```

```
centos# yum install nftables
```

The configuration for nftables actually consists of one or more scripts that are executed to load the configuration into the firewall. The configuration file on Debian is `/etc/nftables.conf`. On CentOS, it is `/etc/sysconfig/nftables.conf`, which in turn loads one or more files from the directory `/etc/nftables`. The installed executable file is `nft`.

To facilitate going back to the original configuration, it is advised to rename the original files and start from scratch.

```
debian# cd /etc
debian# mv nftables.conf nftables.conf.orig
debian# nano nftables.conf

centos# cd /etc/nftables
centos# for f in *; do mv ${f} ${f}.orig; done
centos# nano inet-filter
```

The configuration files support two different script formats. The format described here is the format that is also produced by nft when it exports the firewall configuration to a file.

In nftables, the firewall rules are placed in so-called chains (series). There is a chain for inbound traffic, a chain for outbound traffic, and so on. In turn, these chains are placed in tables. A table is linked to an address family. The address family ip is for IPv4 traffic, and the family ip6 is for IPv6 traffic; the inet family is for both IPv4 and IPv6.

The two most important actions, called verdict statements in nftables, that can be configured in this firewall are accept and drop. The other possible verdict statements are not discussed here.

For ease of maintenance, several variable types can be used in nftables.conf:

- **Variable**

  A simple variable is defined using the keyword define. This variable can then be used throughout the script by placing a dollar sign in front of its name.

  ```
  define interface = "ens3"
  iifname $interface tcp dport 22 accept
  ```

- **Set**

  A set is a collection of similar values. A set is linked to a table. The type of the values is specified in the definition of the set. The set can then be used throughout the script by placing an at sign in front of its name. Multiple elements are separated by commas.

  ```
  table inet filter {
    set trusted {
      type ipv4_addr
      elements = { 203.0.113.26, 198.51.100.43 }
    }

    chain input {
      ip saddr @trusted accept
    }
  }
  ```

  Elements can be added to and removed from sets without the need to restart nftables.

Sample Configuration

The following is a simple but effective foundation for a firewall configuration for a Linux server that uses nftables. However, this does not complete the firewall configuration: in the following chapters, services will be added to the firewall when they are added to the server. The following configuration is but a framework that blocks inbound traffic by default and can be easily modified to permit traffic to certain ports. Without modification, this configuration is not fit for a home or office server.

```
#!/usr/bin/env nft -f
# Remove existing tables and their content.
flush ruleset

# Name of the external network interface.
define interface = "enp1s0"

# Table definition.
# Address family: inet (ipv4/ipv6)
# Name: filter
table inet filter {

  # Allowed inbound TCP ports.
  # For now an empty set.
  set tcp_ok {
    type inet_service
  }

  # Allowed inbound UDP ports.
  # For now an empty set.
  set udp_ok {
    type inet_service
  }

  # Trusted IP addresses (office, home, ...).
  # For now an empty set.
  set trusted {
    type ipv4_addr
  }
```

```
# Automatically blocked IP addresses.
# For now an empty set.
set filter {
  type ipv4_addr
}

# Reserved IP ranges.
set martians {

  # This set contains IP addresses.
  type ipv4_addr

  # The set cannot be modified, and it contains ranges.
  flags constant, interval

  # These are the reserved IP ranges.
  elements = {
    0.0.0.0/8,
    127.0.0.0/8,
    172.16.0.0/12,
    192.0.0.0/24,
    192.0.2.0/24,
    192.168.0.0/16,
    198.18.0.0/15,
    198.51.100.0/24,
    203.0.113.0/24
  }
}

# Chain definition.
# Name: input
chain input {

  # It's a filter chain for incoming traffic.
  type filter hook input priority 0

  # The default policy is to block traffic.
  policy drop
```

```
# Inbound traffic that was initiated by the server
# is allowed.
ct state established,related accept

# Traffic over the loopback device is allowed.
# Keyword iif means input interface.
iif lo accept

# Inbound traffic from trusted addresses.
# Keyword iifname means input interface name.
# Keyword ip means IPv4.
# Keyword saddr means source address.
iifname $interface ip saddr @trusted accept

# Automatically blocked IP addresses.
ip saddr @filter drop

# Reserved IP ranges.
# Keyword daddr means destination address.
ip saddr @martians drop
ip daddr @martians drop

# Explicitly allow SSH.
# Keyword dport means destination port.
iifname $interface tcp dport 22 accept

# Allowed ports.
iifname $interface tcp dport @tcp_ok accept
iifname $interface udp dport @udp_ok accept
  }
}
```

Obviously, at least the name of the network interface must be verified in the preceding script. If any fixed trusted IP addresses are available already, they can be added to the set named trusted; the set named martians can be used as an example (but the set named trusted can only contain single IP addresses and no ranges). For use in a home or office network, the rules that block Martians must be deleted.

On CentOS, before the firewall can be started, the hash sign at the beginning of the following line must be removed in the file /etc/sysconfig/nftables.conf:

```
include "/etc/nftables/inet-filter"
```

The firewall can now be enabled and started. Attention: this will disconnect existing connections (except for direct connections to the console).

```
linux# systemctl enable nftables
linux# systemctl start nftables
```

Firewall Manipulation

To open or close ports in the firewall, the following commands are employed:

```
linux# nft add element inet filter tcp_ok { http, https }
```

```
linux# nft delete element inet filter udp_ok { 123 }
```

It is probably a good idea to break down these commands:

- nft

  The command-line application.

- add element or delete element

  The action to be taken.

- inet filter

  The address family and the name of the table the set belongs to.

- tcp_ok or udp_ok

  The name of the set.

- { http, https } or { 123 }

  A comma-separated list of elements to be added or deleted. These may be names or numbers.

In this same manner, the set containing the trusted IP addresses can be manipulated.

The complete firewall configuration can be exported with the following command:

```
linux# nft list ruleset
```

If that command's output is redirected to a file to be reused, the following line must be added as the first line of that file, and the file must be made executable.

```
#!/usr/bin/env nft -f
```

If the configuration file is modified, the `nftables` daemon must be reloaded. Attention: this will also undo all modifications that were made dynamically and have not been added to the configuration file.

Brute-Force Attacks

With a brute-force attack, the attacker keeps hitting a service (often SSH) with username/password combinations, in the hopes of finding a combination that permits access to the server. Lists of commonly used usernames and passwords circulate on the internet, and so do scripts that can be used to carry out these attacks, so every server that is connected to the internet will regularly be the subject of this type of attack.

Several packages exist that can help face these attacks. Most of these packages function on the same principle: they detect failed login attempts, usually by following the log files, and take a certain action for IP addresses that are at the origin of too many failed login attempts in a certain time frame. This action is usually the blocking of the IP address, for example, by adding it to the firewall, but often these applications can also take other actions, like sending an email to the system administrator.

It is important to realize that these tools do not (or hardly) help battle distributed attacks—brute-force attacks executed from multiple computers, allowing the number of attempts *per IP address* to stay under the configured minimum.

The application that is discussed in this book is fail2ban, an application that is available for both BSD and Linux, that supports both PF and nftables, and that can follow both log files and systemd's journalctl.

```
freebsd# pkg install py37-fail2ban
```

```
debian# apt install fail2ban
```

```
centos# yum install fail2ban-server
```

Fail2ban Configuration

On FreeBSD, the configuration is installed in /usr/local/etc/fail2ban, and on Debian and CentOS, it is /etc/fail2ban. On Debian, the service is started automatically after the installation. The fail2ban configuration consists of a large number of files; however, it is not necessary to edit them all.

The files in the action.d sub-directory determine the actions that can be taken by fail2ban and how to perform these actions. Actions for the most common firewalls, as well as for sending email, are available, and normally, it is not necessary to edit the files in this directory. If a new action must be added, like sending an SMS, a new file must be created in this directory. This is not discussed in this book. Since it is possible for attackers to spoof (fake) their IP address or to launch their attack from other hacked computers, it is not advisable to create actions that launch automated counterattacks; these counterattacks could very well end up attacking computers that have little or nothing to do with the original attack.

On CentOS, additional actions can be installed; the names of these packages start with fail2ban-. On FreeBSD and Debian, all available actions have been installed already.

The files in the filter.d sub-directory define how the different log files must be analyzed to recognize possible attacks. Filters for the log files of many applications have been defined already, and normally, it is not necessary to edit the files in this directory.

The files paths-*.conf define the paths to the log files on different operating systems and do not need to be modified.

The file fail2ban.conf defines the settings for fail2ban itself. If changes need to be made to the fail2ban configuration, these must be stored in the fail2ban.d sub-directory; the file fail2ban.conf may be overwritten by software updates.

The combination of a filter and one or more actions is called a jail in fail2ban. This means that a jail determines which actions follow a match in a log file (e.g., a brute-force attack on the SSH port). Default settings for jails are defined in the file jail.conf; this file also contains some (disabled) configurations for jails for common services. Configurations for individual jails are stored in the jail.d sub-directory, and for each jail, only the settings that differ from the settings in jail.conf need to be defined. Changes to default settings in jail.conf must also be stored in the jail.d sub-directory, because jail.conf may be overwritten by software updates. To clearly differentiate between files that were installed by fail2ban (*.conf) and files created by the system administrator, the fail2ban documentation advises to use the extension .local for new files.

To begin, the default settings for jails are modified.

```
bsd# cd /usr/local/etc/fail2ban

linux# cd /etc/fail2ban

# nano jail.local
```

```
[DEFAULT]

# These hosts must never be blocked.
ignoreip = 127.0.0.1/8

# Consider 5 failed login attempts in 10 minutes
# to be a brute-force attack.
maxretry = 5
findtime = 10m

# Block IP addresses for one hour.
bantime = 1h

# Source for log lines.
#   FreeBSD : auto
#   Debian  : systemd
#   CentOS  : systemd
backend = auto

# Destination for sent emails.
# Note this address down,
# so that an alias can be created later.
destemail = fail2ban@example.com

# Sender for sent emails.
# Note this address down,
# so that an alias can be created later.
sender = fail2ban@example.com
```

```
# The default block action.
# See directory action.d/ if needed.
#   FreeBSD:
#      pf[actiontype=<allports>]
#   Debian:
#      nftables-allports
#   CentOS:
#      nftables-allports
banaction = pf[actiontype=<allports>]
```

Obviously, other settings in this file may be modified as well, but this is not necessary.

The file action.d/pf.conf defines that for the pf firewall on FreeBSD, the IP addresses to be blocked must be added to the table named f2b. This table has already been defined in the previously created pf configuration.

The file action.d/nftables-common.conf defines that for the nftables firewall on Linux, the IP addresses to be blocked must be added to the set named filter. This set has already been defined in the previously created nftables configuration.

As an example, a jail is now configured for SSH (port 22). Since the filter for sshd already exists (filter.d/sshd.conf), the base for the sshd jail has already been defined (jail.conf), and the default action has been set to the correct firewall (jail.local), enabling the jail is very simple:

```
# nano jail.d/sshd.conf
```

```
[sshd]
enabled = true
```

Then, fail2ban can be started or restarted.

```
freebsd# service fail2ban enable
freebsd# service fail2ban start

debian# systemctl restart fail2ban

centos# systemctl enable fail2ban
centos# systemctl start fail2ban
```

The configuration can now be tested by repeatedly connecting with the server through SSH and using the wrong password. The firewall will then block all attempts after the set number for the configured period of time. After that period, fail2ban removes the IP address from the firewall, and new attempts can be made.

To not overcomplicate things, fail2ban will not be mentioned in the rest of this book. However, fail2ban can also detect brute-force attacks on other services (mail server, web server, etc.). The security-conscious system administrator should make a note to return to this chapter after having completed this book, to configure fail2ban for the other services hosted on this server.

Brute-Force Attacks Against Websites

A brute-force attack can also be carried out against websites and other services that are password protected, but are not directly linked to a port. Out of the box, fail2ban cannot help battle these attacks, but most CMSs and website frameworks can be extended with plugins or modules that help fight these attacks. And of course, if these web applications log failed login attempts to a file, a fail2ban filter can be created using the existing filters as examples.

Summary

After reading this chapter, the reader should have a clear grasp of where to find the network settings for their system and how to manipulate them. Furthermore, the reader has learned to configure a firewall to keep unwanted traffic out. Lastly, a tool was discussed that can help in the automation of some defensive tasks.

The next chapter will introduce the reader to the management of users and user groups, as well as the manipulation of privileges and permissions.

CHAPTER 5

User Management and Permissions

In order to be able to define the rights of persons on the server, everyone who has access to the server gets their own username; on top of that, each user is a member of one or more groups. All files, directories, and applications on the system belong to one user and one group. The system administrator can use this system to define which individual users and which user groups have access (or not) to which directories, files, and applications.

Users and Groups

Not every employee needs an account on the server. Local accounts are only created for people who need to edit files on the server. It may be necessary sometimes to explain to a manager or director that a server password is not a status symbol and can do more bad than good in the hands of a nonexpert.

Obviously, the employees need to identify themselves to read and send mail, but this does not require a local account. The password database used for email authentication is discussed in the section "Lightweight Directory Access Protocol (LDAP)" of Chapter 11, "Databases".

Apart from an account and the username that goes with it, users are also a member of one or more groups. The first of these groups is called the *primary group* or *login group*. This is the group that is assigned to a new file or directory if the user does not explicitly specify a group upon creation, and it is also the group that is assigned to each process that is started by the user. On most modern Unix systems, the primary group is a personal group for the user that has the same name as the username; this helps to protect the confidentiality of the files in the home directory, for example. The other groups that a user is a member of are called their *secondary* or *supplementary* groups.

© Robert La Lau 2021
R. La Lau, *Practical Internet Server Configuration*, https://doi.org/10.1007/978-1-4842-6960-2_5

The system administrator is completely free in the creation and distribution of these groups, depending on the specifics of the system in question; a web server, for example, could have groups for web developers and graphic designers, while an intranet server might require groups for users who have access to certain printers and scanners, and the administrator for a desktop system could limit access to external media by creating groups for users who have access to USB ports and the DVD player.

Some Unices, including the BSD family and Red Hat Linux–based systems like CentOS, have a group named *wheel*. This is a group with elevated privileges, and all system administrators are a member of this group; the name *wheel* comes from the slang *big wheel*, which means *powerful person*. On Debian-based systems, a group called *sudo* exists, which serves the same purpose.

Apart from a name, user accounts and groups also have a numeric identifier (*id*). Or actually, the numeric identifier is more important to the system than the name: a user or group name may be changed, but the *user id* (*UID*) and *group id* (*GID*) never change. This prevents all files belonging to a person from having to be modified if their username changes; internally, the system links the files to the numerical *id*.

These numerical ids may be specified when creating a user account, but normally they are generated by the system. Systems generally reserve UIDs under 1000 for system accounts, like the accounts for daemons, and UIDs for regular users start at 1000 or 1001. Sometimes daemons are given UIDs that correspond with the port on which they operate—UID 22 for the SSH server, UID 53 for the DNS server, UID 80 for the web server, and so on; however, this is not required.

Files

User account information is stored in plain text files, as is group information.

User Accounts

The username, user id, and some other information are stored in the text file /etc/passwd. The name of this file originated in times that the encrypted password was also stored in this file. Modern Unices, however, store the passwords in a file that is only accessible to root, unlike /etc/passwd; on BSD systems, this file is called /etc/master.passwd, and on Linux systems, it is /etc/shadow.

The file /etc/passwd contains one line for each account, and each line (record) consists of seven fields, separated by colons; some examples:

```
root:x:0:0:root:/root:/bin/bash
daemon:x:1:1:daemon:/usr/sbin:/usr/sbin/nologin
bin:x:2:2:bin:/bin:/usr/sbin/nologin
nobody:x:65534:65534:nobody:/nonexistent:/usr/sbin/nologin
diane:x:1002:1003:Diane:/home/diane:/bin/bash
dimitri:x:1003:1004:Dimitri:/home/dimitri:/bin/bash
```

The meaning of the fields of each record is as follows:

- **Username**

  The name with which the user logs on to the system. The maximum length for the name is 32 characters, and it may contain only lowercase Latin letters (without accents), digits, and dash and underscore (- _); the first character can only be a letter or underscore, and the username may end in a dollar sign, but the latter is not recommended.

- **Encrypted password**

  If this field only contains an asterisk (*, BSD) or a lowercase x (Linux), this means that the system uses the shadow passwords that are stored in, respectively, /etc/master.passwd and /etc/shadow.

- **User id**

  The account's numerical id.

- **Group id**

  The numerical id for this user's primary group.

- **Free text**

  This field, historically called the *GECOS* field, often contains the user's real name nowadays. There are also systems that store multiple data here, separated by commas; in addition to the full name of the user, this can include telephone numbers, email addresses, and office numbers. The system administrator is free to use this field however they see fit, but it is important to keep in mind that the contents of this field can be read by other users. Obviously, a colon cannot be used in this field, since this is the field separator in this file.

- **Home directory**

  By default, the home directories are created in /home, but this can be modified on a user-by-user basis; for instance, on many systems, the home directory for the web server daemon is the base directory for the websites.

- **Login shell**

  The shell that is started when the user logs in. This must be an absolute path to an executable.

  If a non-existing shell is specified, the user cannot log in at the console; it is important to realize, however, that this does not automatically block logging in through other means, like FTP. If the user is not supposed to log in on the console, /sbin/nologin or /usr/sbin/nologin is often specified instead of a non-existing shell; this application displays a message to the user before disconnecting.

  Alternative shells can be tried out by installing them and starting them from the command line like any other executable; typing exit will bring the user back to the login shell. Later in this chapter, it is explained how to change the login shell.

On FreeBSD, the /etc/master.passwd file also contains one colon-separated line or record for each user, and each record consists of ten fields; some examples:

```
root:$SomeString:0:0::0:0:Charlie &:/root:/bin/csh
daemon:*:1:1::0:0:Owner of many system processes:/root:/usr/sbin/nologin
bin:*:3:7::0:0:Binaries Commands and Source:/:/usr/sbin/nologin
diane:$SomeString:1002:1003::0:0:Diane:/home/diane:/usr/local/bin/bash
```

In these records, the first field is the username; the second field contains a long string of seemingly random characters that represents the encrypted password; the third and fourth fields contain the UID and the GID, respectively; the fifth field contains the user's login class, which is not discussed in this book, and defaults to "default" if not defined; the sixth and seventh fields define when the password must be changed and when the account expires; the eighth field is the GECOS field; the ninth field specifies the home directory; and the tenth field specifies the login shell.

On Linux, the /etc/shadow file also contains one colon-separated line or record for each user, and each record consists of nine fields; some examples:

```
root:$SomeString::0:99999:7:::
daemon:*:18587:0:99999:7:::
bin:*:18587:0:99999:7:::
diane:$SomeString:18587:0:99999:7:::
```

The first of these fields is the username; the second field contains a long string of seemingly random characters that represents the encrypted password; the third field indicates when the password was last changed (in days since January 1, 1970); the fourth and fifth fields indicate the minimum age that the password must have before it can be changed and the maximum age that the password can have before it must be changed, both in days; the sixth field specifies how many days before the password expires the user will be asked to change the password; the seventh field specifies how many days after the password expiration the account will be blocked; the eighth field indicates when the account will expire (in days since January 1, 1970); the ninth field is currently unused.

Groups

The groups are stored in the file /etc/group; this file also contains the group memberships for all users. Like the passwd file, this file contains one colon-separated line for each group; some examples:

```
root:x:0:
daemon:x:1:
bin:x:2:
wheel:x:10:diane,dimitri
diane:x:1003:
dimitri:x:1004:
```

The meaning of the fields for each group is as follows:

- **Group name**

  This name may be up to 16 characters long and may only consist of lowercase Latin letters (without accents), digits, and the dash and underscore (- _); the first character can only be a letter or an underscore, and the group name may end in a dollar sign, but the latter is not recommended.

- **Encrypted keyword**

  This field is usually empty or contains an asterisk (*) to indicate that there is no password. If this field only contains an x, this means that shadow passwords are used, as described before; in this case, the group passwords are stored in /etc/gshadow. The latter only applies to Linux, though.

- **Group ID**

  The numerical identifier for this group.

- **Members**

  A comma-separated list of usernames of the members of this group.

  Only the memberships to secondary groups are recorded in /etc/group; users' primary groups are registered in /etc/passwd.

Manipulation

Even though these files are all plain text files that can be edited with the help of any basic text editor, it is strongly discouraged to do so.

The next sections describe commands that prevent the system administrator from having to directly edit these files. The system administrator who still wants to try and edit these files directly uses the commands vipw and vigr; these commands verify the syntax of the files before saving them and make sure that the user and group databases stay synchronized with the shadow password files. If vipw and vigr display messages about corrupted user or group databases, the commands chkgrp (FreeBSD) or pwck and grpck (Linux) may be able to help repair this.

However, it is strongly recommended to use the tools described in the next sections.

Account Creation

FreeBSD, Debian, and CentOS all have a command named `adduser` for creating new users. However, this is not the same application, and it works differently on all three systems.

All three systems also have a so-called *skeleton directory*. Files and directories in this directory are copied to new users' home directories. If a system administrator wishes to make certain files or directories available to all new users, they place them in the skeleton directory; this can include personal configuration files or directories like `Documents` and `Downloads` that are also found on desktop systems, and so on. The online addendum for this book contains example configuration files for Bash (`.bash_profile` and `.bashrc`) that could be copied to the skeleton directory after analysis and possible modification.

FreeBSD

On FreeBSD, `adduser` is an interactive command: if no command-line parameters are specified, the command asks for the information it needs.

An example follows. The responses follow the colons. The default responses, which are used if *Enter* is pressed without specifying an answer, are displayed in square brackets. For security reasons, the password is not echoed to the screen while it is entered.

The account is not created until the information has been verified and confirmed; as long as the information is not confirmed, the process can be aborted with ^C.

```
freebsd# adduser
Username: diane
Full name: Diane
Uid (Leave empty for default):
Login group [diane]:
Login group is diane. Invite diane into other groups? []: wheel
Login class [default]:
Shell (sh csh tcsh bash rbash nologin) [sh]: bash
Home directory [/home/diane]:
Home directory permissions (Leave empty for default): 750
Use password-based authentication? [yes]:
Use an empty password? (yes/no) [no]:
Use a random password? (yes/no) [no]:
```

```
Enter password:
Enter password again:
Lock out the account after creation? [no]:
Username  : diane
Password  : *****
Full Name : Diane
Uid       : 1002
Class     :
Groups    : diane wheel
Home      : /home/diane
Home Mode : 750
Shell     : /usr/local/bin/bash
Locked    : no
OK (yes/no): yes
adduser: INFO: Successfully added (diane) to the user database.
Add another user? (yes/no): no
Goodbye!
freebsd#
```

A configuration file can be created to modify the default answers displayed in the preceding code. See adduser(8) and adduser.conf(5) for more information.

The list of available shells is taken from /etc/shells; it is not allowed to select a shell that is not in this file.

The skeleton directory on FreeBSD is /usr/share/skel. Files in this directory for which the name starts with dot. are renamed when they are copied: dot.profile becomes .profile, dot.shrc becomes .shrc, and so on.

Another command for user management is pw. This command is not interactive and accepts many command-line parameters. See pw(8) for more info.

Debian

On Debian, adduser is a shell script that tries to be a more user-friendly interface to the useradd command that does the actual work. Since default settings, like the login shell, can be defined in the configuration file /etc/adduser.conf, creating a new account can be as simple as executing the command with a single command-line parameter:

```
debian# adduser diane
```

The default settings can be overwritten with command-line parameters:

```
debian# adduser --shell /usr/sbin/nologin diane

debian# adduser --add_extra_groups diane

debian# adduser --home /users/diane --gecos "Diane" diane
```

After the account has been created by adduser, the system administrator is asked to specify the password for the new user. For security reasons, this password is not echoed to the screen.

Once the password is set, the administrator is asked to enter additional user information. This information is stored in the GECOS field in the user database; on Debian, this field consists of five comma-separated fields. Obviously, the system administrator is still free in the interpretation of these five fields.

```
debian# adduser diane
Adding user `diane' ...
Adding new group `diane' (1002) ...
Adding new user `diane' (1002) with group `diane' ...
Creating home directory `/home/diane' ...
Copying files from `/etc/skel' ...
Enter new UNIX password:
Retype new UNIX password:
passwd: password updated successfully
Changing the user information for diane
Enter the new value, or press ENTER for the default
        Full Name []: Diane
        Room Number []: 1
        Work Phone []: 2
        Home Phone []: 3
        Other []: abc
Is the information correct? [Y/n]
debian#
```

The default responses are displayed in square brackets; they are empty in the preceding example. If two values, separated by a slash, are displayed in square brackets ([Y/n]), these are the only allowed responses with the capitalized reply being the default one.

If the new user must be made a member of additional groups, this must be done separately; this is explained later in this chapter. It is also possible to modify the *EXTRA_GROUPS* variable in /etc/adduser.conf for this purpose and then use the --add_extra_groups parameter when creating a new user.

More information can be found in adduser(8) and adduser.conf(5).

The skeleton directory is called /etc/skel on Debian.

Since adduser is a script that executes useradd, it is also possible to execute useradd directly. See the section "CentOS" for more information about useradd.

CentOS

On CentOS, adduser is a symlink to the useradd command.

Default settings for useradd can be defined in /etc/default/useradd. The file /etc/login.defs also contains some variables that influence the behavior of useradd.

All default settings can be overwritten using command-line parameters:

```
centos# useradd --comment "Diane" \
        --shell /bin/bash \
        --create-home \
        --user-group \
        --groups "wheel" \
        diane
```

More information can be found in useradd(8) and login.defs(5).

After the account has been created, the password must be set before the user can log in. For security reasons, the password is not echoed to the screen.

```
centos# passwd diane
Changing password for user diane.
New password:
Retype new password:
passwd: all authentication tokens updated successfully.
centos#
```

On CentOS, like on Debian, the skeleton directory is /etc/skel.

Password Modification

A user can change their password using the `passwd` command.

```
$ passwd
```

This command will first ask for the current password and then twice for the new password.

The root user can change the passwords for all users by giving the username as a command-line parameter. In this case, the current password is not asked.

```
# passwd diane
```

Account Modification

Just like the user can change their password, they can also change the contents of the GECOS field, as well as the login shell.

chfn

The `chfn` (*change full name*) command can be used to change the contents of the GECOS field. This command asks for five items (full name, room number, office and private phone numbers, and other information) and stores these in the GECOS field, separated by commas. On FreeBSD, this command also allows the modification of the login shell.

```
$ chfn
```

```
# chfn dimitri
```

On Linux, this is an interactive command; on FreeBSD, a text file is opened to edit the information.

On some Linux systems, the variable *CHFN_AUTH* can be defined in `/etc/login.defs` to require a password before the information can be modified. The variable *CHFN_RESTRICT* can also be defined to limit the components of the GECOS field that can be modified.

Users can only modify their own information; the root user can modify the information for all users by appending the username in question. The root user on FreeBSD can also edit other information, like the username and the password.

For more information, see `chfn(1)` and `login.defs(5)`.

chsh

The chsh command allows the modification of the login shell. On BSD, this command has the same functionality as chfn (both commands are symlinks to the actual command chpass).

```
$ chsh
```

```
# chsh dimitri
```

On some Linux systems, the *CHFN_AUTH* variable can be defined in /etc/login.defs to require a password before the login shell can be changed.

Users can only change their own login shell; root can change the login shell for all users by appending the username in question.

Only shells that are listed in the file /etc/shells can be set as the new shell. The root user does not have this limitation.

For more information, see chsh(1), login.defs(5), and on FreeBSD and Debian also shells(5).

Locking an Account

There are several reasons why a system administrator might want to block a user's access without deleting the associated account: temporary or permanent termination of activities, vandalism or misconduct, and so on; the most positive of these reasons may require the transfer of the user's documents and activities to another user, and the most negative may require the analysis of the user's documents and actions or even their transfer to authorities.

Often, changing the password is not enough for completely blocking a user's access; the use of SSH keys (discussed extensively in Chapter 7, "Secure Shell (SSH)"), for instance, circumvents effectively the use of a password. The sysadmin who still wants to block a user in this manner uses pw lock or passwd --lock:

```
bsd# pw lock dimitri
bsd# pw unlock dimitri

linux# passwd --lock dimitri
linux# passwd --unlock dimitri
```

The advantage of lock and unlock over changing the password is that after the account has been unlocked, the user can continue to use the same password as before.

A more effective method is to mark the account as expired; this renders the account unusable, making it inaccessible to SSH keys as well. On FreeBSD, the pw command is used to expire an account; Linux uses chage.

```
bsd# pw -e 1 dimitri
bsd# pw -e 0 dimitri

linux# chage --expiredate 1 dimitri
linux# chage --expiredate -1 dimitri
```

Blocking an account does not automatically disconnect the user from the system; open sessions remain open until they are closed explicitly. To forcefully log off the user by sending a SIGTERM to all their processes, the pkill command can be used; the companion command pgrep can be used to display all processes for a user without terminating them.

```
# pgrep -l -U dimitri
2380 sshd
2381 bash
2400 bash
2419 grep
# pkill -U dimitri
# pgrep -l -U dimitri
#
```

If pkill does not terminate all processes, a SIGKILL can be sent to the processes instead of the standard SIGTERM:

```
# pkill -KILL -U dimitri
```

More information about processes and signals can be found in Chapter 2, "Unix and POSIX in a Few Words."

Chapter 7, "Secure Shell (SSH)", explains how access over SSH (ssh, scp, sftp) can be blocked, or explicitly granted, for individual users and for groups.

The section "Lightweight Directory Access Protocol (LDAP)" in Chapter 11, "Databases", explains how to change the password in an LDAP user database, preventing the user from sending and receiving email.

It may also be desirable to delete the user's *cron* and *at* jobs; more information about this can be found in Chapter 8, "Task Scheduling".

Other subjects to consider are Subversion, Git, Mercurial, or Bazaar repositories where the user may have access. These are not discussed in this book.

And finally, it may be desirable to bar the user from fora and chat rooms. These are also not discussed in this book. It is important to keep in mind that these applications often allow the user to simply create a new account under a different name.

If the intention is to bar the user from connecting over SSH, but to keep FTP accessible, for example, the login shell can be changed to `/usr/sbin/nologin` (FreeBSD) or `/sbin/nologin` (Linux). With this setup, some FTP servers require that `nologin` has been added to `/etc/shells`.

The last section of this chapter gives some hints that may be practical when a system administrator leaves the department or the company.

Account Deletion

Before a user is removed from the system, it is advisable to note down the UID and GID. After the account has been deleted, these may be used to search the system for files and directories that belonged to the deleted user.

```
# id -u dimitri
1003
# id -g dimitri
1004
```

After the account has been deleted, any left-behind files can be found with the help of the `find` command:

```
# find / -uid 1003 -print > /tmp/dimitri.user
# find / -gid 1004 -print > /tmp/dimitri.group
```

Subsequently, the files `/tmp/dimitri.*` can be analyzed to decide what must be done with each found file or directory. The execution of those `find` commands may take quite some time, as they search the entire system. In an ideal world, only few files will be found, because the user has only stored files in their home directory.

FreeBSD

The FreeBSD administrator only needs a single command to delete an account:

```
bsd# rmuser dimitri
```

This command removes the user's account and home directory, but also all group memberships, scheduled tasks, active processes, and so on. The command asks for confirmation before changes are made to the system.

If the user's files must be backed up, this must be done before the preceding command is executed.

Debian and CentOS

For the Linux administrator, the deletion of an account is a bit more work.

In order to delete an account, the user in question cannot be logged in. It is therefore recommended to start with the procedure for blocking and forcefully disconnecting a user, as explained in a previous section.

Subsequently, all scheduled tasks can be removed. Two applications for scheduling tasks exist, *cron* and *at*; these will be discussed in detail in Chapter 8, "Task Scheduling". However, to prevent the system administrator from having to go back and forth in this book when deleting a user account, the commands for the deletion of scheduled tasks can be found here.

The *cron* tasks are simple to delete:

```
linux# crontab -u dimitri -r
```

Since *at* is not always installed, its presence must be verified first:

```
linux# which at
/usr/sbin/at

linux# which at
/usr/bin/which: no at in (/sbin:/bin:/:/usr/sbin:/usr/bin)
```

If *at* is installed, the following command can be used to remove the *at* tasks:

```
linux# find /var/spool/cron/atjobs \
        -type f \
        -user dimitri \
        -delete
```

And finally, the userdel command can be used to remove the group memberships, the account, and the home directory:

```
linux# userdel -r dimitri
```

On Debian, the alternative command deluser can be used; contrary to userdel, this command can back up the home directory before it is deleted.

```
debian# deluser --backup --remove-home dimitri
```

User Information

Several commands exist to obtain information about users and their processes.

The commands users, who, and w all display a list of logged in users; some are a bit more detailed than others.

```
$ users
diane dimitri

$ who
diane      tty1        2019-11-23    12:21
dimitri    pts/1       2019-11-24    15:26

$ w
19:11:35 up 1 day, 6:50, 2 users, load average: 0.00, 0.01, 0.05
USER      TTY     FROM      LOGIN@   IDLE    JCPU    PCPU    WHAT
diane     tty1              Sat12    7.00s   0.07s   0.00s   w
dimitri   pts/1   gateway   15:26    3.38m   0.01s   0.01s   -bash
```

In Chapter 2, "Unix and POSIX in a Few Words", when processes were treated, the commands top and ps have already been mentioned to obtain detailed information about processes. These commands both recognize the -U command-line parameter that limits the output to the processes of the specified user.

```
$ top -U dimitri
```

```
$ ps -U dimitri
```

To obtain a list of the most recent user logins, the last command can be used. This command accepts a username as a command-line argument to limit the output to a specific user.

```
$ last
dimitri   pts/1   gateway   Sun Nov 24 15:26    still logged in
dimitri   pts/0   gateway   Sun Nov 24 15:12 - 15:34 (00:21)
diane     tty1              Sat Nov 23 12:21    still logged in
```

```
...
$ last diane
diane     tty1                  Sat Nov 23 12:21    still logged in
diane     pts/0  gateway  Thu Nov 21 21:18 - 23:50 (02:31)
diane     pts/0  gateway  Thu Nov 21 15:43 - 17:22 (01:39)
...
```

The id command is one of the commands that can be used to obtain information about the UID, the primary group, and the additional groups. Without arguments, this command displays information about the user executing the command. This command accepts several arguments, for example, to limit the output to only the UID or only the additional groups.

```
$ id diane
uid=1002(diane) gid=1002(diane) groups=1002(diane),0(wheel)
```

The groups command displays the groups that the user is a member of. The Linux variant accepts multiple usernames as arguments.

```
bsd$ groups diane
diane wheel

linux$ groups diane dimitri
diane : diane wheel
dimitri : dimitri wheel
```

The observant reader has noticed that none of these commands require *root* privileges.

Group Creation and Deletion

Groups are a practical tool for extending and limiting user privileges. Groups can be created based on the departments of an organization, like web development or marketing, but also based on functionality, like users who have access to certain printers. The system administrator is completely free in the organization of the groups; there is no limit to the number of groups that can exist, nor is there a limit to the number of users per group or to the number of groups that a user can be a member of.

As indicated in the section about the creation of user accounts, it is customary to create a personal group for each user. This group is used, for example, to protect the confidentiality of the files in the users' home directories.

It is also customary to create a group for the system administrators. This group is called *wheel* on most systems and *sudo* on Debian and its derivatives. The name of this group is not really important; for the systems, it is a group like all others. The difference with other groups is in the privileges that the system administrators assign to the group that all system administrators are members of. More information about this follows later in this chapter.

Groups can be password protected, allowing users to become members of groups without the intervention of a system administrator and to temporarily change their effective group membership. However, this possibility is rarely exploited and therefore not discussed in this book. An argument against the use of such a system could be that it would allow users to share group passwords between them, "to facilitate the job," making the system administrator lose control of group memberships and thus of system access.

FreeBSD

On FreeBSD, the `pw` command is used to create, delete, and modify groups. In their most simple forms, the commands for creation and deletion of groups are self-explanatory:

```
freebsd# pw groupadd webdev
```

```
freebsd# pw groupdel webdev
```

The command for the creation of groups accepts a command-line argument for the immediate addition of users to the new group.

```
freebsd# pw groupadd webdev -M diane,dimitri
```

Debian

The Debian command for the creation of groups is `addgroup`:

```
debian# addgroup webdev
```

This command does not accept a command-line parameter to immediately add users to the newly created group. Instead, the commands for the modification of group memberships are used, as described later in this chapter.

The command for the deletion of groups is `delgroup`:

```
debian# delgroup webdev
```

Since `addgroup` and `delgroup` are interfaces to `groupadd` and `groupdel`, respectively, the `groupadd` and `groupdel` commands can also be executed directly. These commands are discussed in the following section "CentOS".

CentOS

CentOS uses the `groupadd` command for the creation of new groups:

```
centos# groupadd webdev
```

This command does not accept a command-line parameter to immediately add users to the newly created group. Instead, the commands for the modification of group memberships are used, as described later in this chapter.

The `groupdel` command is used for the deletion of groups:

```
centos# groupdel webdev
```

Changing Group Memberships

The different systems also have their own approaches for the management of group memberships.

FreeBSD

The `pw` command can be used in two different manners to add users to groups. The first of these is user centered:

```
freebsd# pw usermod diane -G wheel,webdev
```

The preceding command adds user *diane* to the groups *wheel* and *webdev*. Attention: the user will be removed from all groups that are not mentioned; if *diane* was a member of the group *marketing*, she no longer is after the execution of the preceding command.

The second way to add users to a group is group centered:

```
freebsd# pw groupmod webdev -M diane,dimitri
```

```
freebsd# pw groupmod webdev -m diane,dimitri
```

The first of the two preceding commands replaces the member list of the group *webdev* with *diane* and *dimitri*; if *robert* was a member of this group, he no longer is after the execution of this command.

The second of those commands adds *diane* and *dimitri* to the member list of the group *webdev*; if *robert* was a member of this group, he still is after the execution of this command.

Another way to cancel a user's group membership is the -d parameter to the pw groupmod command:

```
freebsd# pw groupmod marketing -d diane,dimitri
```

After this command has been executed, *diane* and *dimitri* are no longer members of the group *marketing*. Nothing changes for the other members of this group, and nothing changes for *diane*'s and *dimitri*'s other group memberships.

Debian

The adduser command, which was used earlier to create new users, is also used to add users to groups:

```
debian# adduser diane webdev
debian# adduser dimitri webdev
```

This can only be done with the combination of an existing user and an existing group, and a single user can be added to a single group at a time. If many users must be added to the same group and the Bash shell is used, the following code block might somewhat simplify this process:

```
bash# for user in {diane,dimitri,robert}; do
        adduser ${user} webdev
    done
```

And obviously, this loop can be modified to add a single user to multiple groups:

```
bash# for group in {wheel,webdev,marketing}; do
        adduser diane ${group}
    done
```

Other shells have similar functionalities.

The `deluser` command, which was described earlier for the deletion of user accounts, can also be used to end a user's group membership:

```
debian# deluser marketing diane
debian# deluser marketing dimitri
```

Only a single user can be removed from a single group with this command; here too, a `for` loop could be of use if a user must be removed from multiple groups or if multiple users must be removed from a single group.

Since `adduser` and `deluser` are, in this case, interfaces to the `usermod` and `gpasswd` commands, the `usermod` and `gpasswd` commands can also be executed directly. More about this in the next section "CentOS".

CentOS

CentOS uses the `usermod` command to add users to a group. This command can be used to add a user to multiple groups at the same time:

```
centos# usermod --append --groups wheel,webdev diane
```

If the `--append` parameter is omitted, the group list replaces the current group list; the user will no longer be a member of groups that are not mentioned.

The `gpasswd` command is used to remove a user from a group.

```
centos# gpassword --delete diane marketing
```

This command can also be used to add users to a group and to set a password for a group. However, as mentioned before, it may be undesirable to set a password for a group and thus enable users to become members of groups without the intervention of a system administrator.

Group Information

The `id` command, discussed earlier to obtain user information, can be used to display all the groups a certain user is a member of:

```
$ id -Gn diane
diane wheel webdev
```

On BSD, the pw command, also described earlier, can be used to list the members of a group. However, this command only shows the users who have this group as a secondary group.

```
freebsd$ pw groupshow webdev
webdev:*:1019:diane,dimitri
```

Linux does not have a command to display the members of a group. But obviously, this information can be extracted from the group database. In fact, this is the same as the preceding BSD command does, and here too, only users are listed that have the group as a secondary group.

```
$ grep '^webdev:' /etc/group
webdev:*:1019:diane,dimitri
```

The online addendum for this book contains a script that lists all members of a group, both the users that have the group as their primary group and users that have the group as a secondary group.

Permissions

When access or user permissions on Unix are discussed, the subject is generally the traditional system: a file or application belongs to a single user and a single group, a user can be a member of several groups, and the system administrator can juggle these to obtain the desired read, write and execution permissions for each user.

However, since longtime (*FreeBSD 4.0-CURRENT* and *Linux kernel 2.5.46*, both released in 2002), a system exists to extend the somewhat limited traditional system: *Access Control Lists* (*ACL*). This system was first described in *POSIX 1003.1e draft 17*, which was never promoted to standard, but did assure that *ACL* were implemented in Unix kernels and that *ACL* support is enabled by default.

Anyone who works with Unix, whether as an administrator or as a user, cannot escape mastering the traditional system of access rights: this system still forms the basis of authorization on Unix systems. ACL can introduce a welcome extension and simplification of this system; but it is impossible to implement them without a thorough knowledge and understanding of the traditional system.

It is important to keep in mind that access rights are always relative in the sense that if a user has the correct privileges to access a file, but does not have access to the directory that contains the file, they will still not be able to open the file in question.

The permissions for a file can only be changed by the file's owner and by *root*.

Traditional

In the traditional Unix privilege system, each file or each application belongs to a single user and a single group, and each user is a member of one or more groups. The system administrator can then grant three different access levels (read, write, and execute) to the owner, the group, and other users.

The three access levels—read, write, and execute—are often abbreviated to *r*, *w*, and *x*. The user levels—user, group, and other users—are often abbreviated to *u*, *g*, and *o*; the other users are also called *world*, a term that is not strictly correct, because even if a file is accessible to other users, these users must still have an account on the server, so the file is not accessible to the entire world.

As an example, here is the directory listing for an imaginary directory:

```
$ ls -l
total 12
drwxr-xr-x 3 diane wheel 4096 Oct 19 16:07 dir
lrwxrwxrwx 1 diane wheel   18 Oct 19 16:09 link -> ./text.txt
-rwxr-x--- 1 diane wheel 1712 Oct 19 16:06 script.sh
-rw-r--r-- 1 diane wheel 1240 Oct 19 16:04 text.txt
```

The first line of the output (`total 12`) indicates how many blocks on the hard disk are occupied by the contents of this directory. The other lines display a single directory entry per line; these lines consist of the following fields:

- **File type + permissions**

  The first character of the line indicates the file type: - (dash) indicates a regular file, d is a directory, and l means link; the other possibilities are less common and can be found in the `ls` man page.

The rest of this field indicates the permissions: the first group of rwx indicates the permissions for the file owner, the second group of rwx are the permissions for the group, and the third group of rwx are the permissions for other users; a - (dash) indicates that the permission in question is not granted.

If this field ends in a . (dot, only Linux), this means that alternative authorization methods are available, but not in use; a + (plus, both BSD and Linux) means that one or more alternative authorization methods are in use. One of these methods, *Access Control Lists*, is discussed later in this chapter.

- **The number of *hard links***

The second field in the output of ls indicates the number of hard links for this file. Hard links were discussed in Chapter 2, "Unix and POSIX in a Few Words".

The number of hard links for a directory is always the number of sub-directories + 2:

- The identifier for the directory's name in the parent directory

- The identifier . (dot) in the directory itself

- The identifier .. (two dots) in each sub-directory

- **The owner**

The third field contains the username for the owner of the file; in this case, that is *diane*.

- **The group**

The fourth field contains the name of the group that the file belongs to; in this case, that is *wheel*.

- **The size**

The fifth field displays the size of the file in bytes. In the case of a directory, this is not the size of the contents of the directory, but the disk space reserved for the registration of this directory's metadata (like the names of the files in the directory and where these files can be found on the hard disk).

- **Date and time of last modification**

  The sixth, seventh, and eighth fields form the date of the file's last modification. If this is a recent date, the eighth field displays a time, and if the date is less recent, this field displays a year.

- **Filename**

  The last field is the filename. If the file is a soft link, the filename of the link destination is appended to the filename.

With this clarification, the following conclusions can be drawn from the preceding directory listing:

- All files belong to user *diane* and group *wheel*. Note that it is not necessary for user *diane* to be part of the *wheel* group. And even if this is the case, the owner permissions will apply to user *diane* and not the group permissions.

- The `dir` directory only has a single sub-directory, because its number of hard links is 3.

- The `script.sh` shell script can be read, modified, and executed by user *diane*. It can be read and executed, but not modified, by members of the *wheel* group. Other users do not have access to it.

- The file `text.txt` is not executable. User *diane* is allowed to modify the file, and everybody who has a user account on the server can read the file.

- The file `link` is a *soft link* (*symlink*) to the file `text.txt`: a user who opens the file `link` will in reality open the file `text.txt`.

  The permissions for a symlink are always permissive for everybody; the ultimate permissions are determined by the permissions of the file that is the destination of the link.

- The `dir` directory is accessible to everybody, but can only be modified (add/delete files, change permissions) by user *diane*.

Read permissions for a directory are necessary to display its contents and execute permissions for "opening" the directory. It is possible to grant a user access to a file in a directory without permitting them to view the contents of that directory, by only granting this user execute rights (--x) for that directory (plus, obviously, the necessary rights for the file in question); with this configuration in place, the ls command will display an error message for this user and this directory, but the user will still be able to open files within the directory.

Numerical Representation of Permissions

Often access rights are not represented in letters (rwxr-x---), but in digits (750). This is the decimal representation of the binary form of these rights.

An explanation of the binary system is beyond the scope of this book, but in short, it boils down to the following:

The binary system is a base-2 numeral system; the two numerals are usually represented as 0 and 1. A decimal number is represented as a series of 0s and 1s, where each position (*bit*) in the series has a decimal value. The rightmost position in the series has a decimal value of 1, and each next position (to the left) has a value of double the previous value; so the second position from the right has a value 2, the third position has a value 4, and so on. The total decimal value of the series is calculated by adding up the decimal values of the positions that are set to 1; so the binary value 011 has a decimal value of 3 (2+1), and the binary value 101 has a decimal value of 5 (4+1).

To calculate the binary form of the access rights, each of the three access levels is given a numerical value: execute is 1 (binary: 001), write is 2 (binary: 010), and read is 4 (binary: 100).

The different levels can now be seen as switches that can be activated (1) or deactivated (0):

binary	decimal	read	write	execute	rwx
000	0	no	no	no	---
001	1	no	no	yes	--x
010	2	no	yes	no	-w-
011	3	no	yes	yes	-wx
100	4	yes	no	no	r--
101	5	yes	no	yes	r-x
110	6	yes	yes	no	rw-
111	7	yes	yes	yes	rwx

The permissions for the files in the example directory listing in the previous section can now be represented in decimal as follows:

```
dir        : 755
link       : 777
script.sh  : 750
text.txt   : 644
```

Default Permissions

By default, files are created with permissions 666 (rw-rw-rw-); directories get permissions 777 (rwxrwxrwx).

Naturally, it is possible to change the permissions after the creation, but it is also possible to configure the default permissions system wide or on a per-user basis. The term used for this is *umask* (or sometimes *file mode creation mask*), which is both the title of a value and the name of the command that is used to set that value.

The *umask* is a value that is "subtracted" from the default permissions when a file is created. This is best illustrated with examples.

By default, a file is created with permissions 666. If the value of the *umask* is 022 (the default value for the *umask*), in reality, the file will be created with permissions 644; the "write-bits" (value 2) for the group and the other users (the last two positions) have been deactivated.

By default, a directory is created with permissions 777. With a umask of 022, directories will be created with permissions 755.

The *umask* can be set in two ways: by setting the variable *UMASK* in the file /etc/login.defs and with the help of the umask command on the command line.

The variable in login.defs sets the *umask* system wide, and this value is also used to determine the permissions for the home directories for new users. The default value for this variable is 022, but system administrators who feel strongly about privacy could set this to 077 to prevent users from entering each other's home directories.

The umask command can be used to alter the file mode creation mask on an ad hoc per-user basis. This command is often used in /etc/profile to set the default *umask* for logged in users; if the *UMASK* in login.defs was set to 077 to protect the confidentiality of the files in the home directories, the command umask 022 can be executed from /etc/profile to relax the permissions for daily use. This command can also be used in shell scripts, for example, to assure that all files created by the script have the correct permissions.

The umask command can also be used to display the current value of the *umask*:

```
$ umask
0022

$ umask -S
u=rwx,g=rx,o=rx
```

Changing Permissions

Obviously, access rights can be changed after files have been created.

The chown command is used to change the ownership of files:

```
# chown dimitri script.sh
```

The file script.sh now belongs to user *dimitri*.

Since regular users cannot take files from other users nor give files to other users, in practice, only root can change the ownership of files.

The chgrp command is used to change a file's group:

```
$ chgrp wheel text.txt
```

126

The user must be the owner of the file, and a member of the destination group, to be able to change the group ownership of a file.

The chmod command is used to change the access rights for a file:

```
$ chmod 750 dir
$ chmod o+r tekst.txt
$ chmod g-rx script.sh
```

The dir directory now has permissions 750, read permissions for other users (o) have been added (+r) to the file text.txt, and read and execution rights for the group have been revoked from the file script.sh.

To be able to change the access rights for a file, the user must own the file (or be *root*, obviously).

Special Permissions

Apart from the permissions described previously, the access rights have a fourth position (counted from the right, so the leftmost position: special-user-group-other), with the names *set user ID* (binary 100 or decimal 4), *set group ID* (binary 010 or decimal 2), and sticky bit (binary 001 or decimal 1).

The set user ID and set group ID permissions, also simply called SETUID and SETGID, or even SUID and SGID, assure that executable files are executed with the permissions of, respectively, the owner and the group of the executable file, instead of those of the executing user. An example of this usage is the passwd command that permits the user to change their password without granting the user modification rights for the password database.

If the SUID and the GUID have been set, the x indicator in the ls output is replaced with an s:

```
$ ls -l script.sh
-rwxr-x--- 1 diane wheel 1712 Oct 19 16:06 script.sh
$ chmod u+s script.sh
$ ls -l script.sh
-rwsr-x--- 1 diane wheel 1712 Oct 19 16:06 script.sh
$ chmod 6775 script.sh
$ ls -l script.sh
-rwsrwsr-x 1 diane wheel 1712 Oct 19 16:06 script.sh
```

If SETGID is set on a directory, new files in this directory will get the same group as the directory.

```
$ ls -ld testdir
drwxrwsr-x 2 dimitri webdev 4096 Oct 20 17:35 testdir
$ whoami
dimitri
$ groups
users dimitri
$ touch testdir/test.html
$ ls -l testdir
-rw-r--r-- 1 dimitri webdev 0 Oct 20 17:36 test.html
```

The use of SETUID on a directory, and the use of SETUID and SETGID on non-executable files, is ignored on most systems.

On most systems, the sticky bit only has a function on directories. If the sticky bit is set on a directory, files in that directory can only be renamed or removed by their respective owners, even if the file and the directory are writable for all users. This option is often used for the /tmp directory, which is writable for everybody, to prevent users and processes from deleting each other's files.

If the sticky bit is set, the last character in the permissions field of the output of the ls command is replaced with a t:

```
$ chmod +t dir
$ ls -ld dir
drwxr-xr-t 3 diane wheel 4096 Oct 19 16:26 dir
$ chmod 1777 dir
$ ls -ld dir
drwxrwxrwt 3 diane wheel 4096 Oct 19 16:26 dir
```

Access Control Lists

Access Control Lists, or simply ACL, can be considered an advanced subject, which is not vital for the maintenance of an internet server. The reason it is still discussed in this book is that ACL can significantly simplify a Unix administrator's work while at the same time help fine-tune the security of the server.

ACL are an extension to the traditional permission system, allowing the assignment of privileges to users and groups outside a file's traditional user levels of *user*, *group*, and *other*.

If the work is done with a team of administrators, the use of ACL should be discussed thoroughly before their introduction. Even though ACL can definitely extend the possibilities of user and access rights and simplify their organization, it is an undeniable fact that more traditional system administrators often lack knowledge of this subject, and some of them even actively object to them (although no administrator seems to be able to explain this objection).

Access Control Lists are a part of the FreeBSD and Linux kernels since 2002. They have been introduced to make the rigid Unix privilege system (one user, one group, and the rest) more flexible. ACL allow the system administrator to assign different privileges to additional groups or individual users.

Preparation

Even though the functionality has been enabled in the kernel, some action must be taken on FreeBSD and Debian before the ACL can effectively be used.

On FreeBSD, ACL are not necessarily enabled for all mounted file systems. This can be easily verified with the help of the following command:

```
freebsd# mount | grep '^/'
/dev/ada0s1a on / (ufs, local, journaled soft-updates, acls)
```

The output of this command may differ somewhat on each system: multiple partitions may exist, the naming of the partitions may differ, and the mount options (in parentheses) may differ. However, if the option acls is not present in the parentheses, it must be added in the file that defines the mounted file systems.

```
freebsd# nano /etc/fstab
```

# Device	Mountpoint	FStype	Options	Dump	Pass#
/dev/ada0s1a	/	ufs	rw,acls	1	1
/dev/ada0s1b	none	swap	sw	0	0

The option acls must be added to all partitions that will allow the use of ACL (which in practice means all partitions with a *mountpoint*).

After the file has been saved, all partitions are remounted using the following command:

```
freebsd# mount -a
```

On Debian, the *acl* package must be installed; this package contains the user space utilities setfacl and getfacl that are used to manipulate the ACL.

```
debian# apt install acl
```

Usage

As an example, these are the directories and files for an imaginary website:

```
─ srv
  └ www
    └ www.example.com
      ├ *.php
      ├ config
      │  └ *.php
      ├ docs
      │  └ *.pdf
      ├ download
      │  ├ *.exe
      │  └ *.zip
      ├ html
      │  └ *.html
      ├ images
      │  ├ *.jpg
      │  └ banners
      │     └ *.jpg
      ├ script
      │  └ *.js
      └ style
         └ *.css
```

The access limitations for this directory tree could be as follows:

- The senior web developers (group *webdev*) have access to all files and directories.

- The junior web developers (group *jwebdev*) also have access to all files and directories, except the `config` directory.

- The user interface developers (group *uidev*) have access to the `html`, `images`, `script`, and `style` directories.

- The graphic designers (group *design*) have access to the `images` and `style` directories.

- The software developers (group *cdev*) have access to the `download` directory.

- The help desk (group *support*) has access to the `docs` directory.

- The marketing department (group *marketing*) has access to the `docs` and `banners` directories.

- And the web server (user *httpd*) obviously has (read) access to all directories and files, to allow it to serve the website to the internet.

The realization of the preceding requirements using solely the traditional privilege system would be tricky at the least and would probably involve users being in groups where they should not be and scripts that periodically move files to other directories and/or change file permissions. Using ACL, however, all permissions can be made very restrictive to begin with (using the traditional system), after which specific privileges can be assigned to specific users and groups for specific directories and files.

```
# cd /srv/www
# chown -R webdev:webdev ./www.example.com
# chmod -R 771 ./www.example.com
# find ./www.example.com -type f -exec chmod -x {} \;
```

The preceding commands assign execute rights to all directories for everybody. This is necessary to allow users that do not have access to the files in the base directory to still reach the deeper directories. If, for example, the members of the *marketing* group need to edit files in the www.example.com/images/banners directory, they need to be able to open the www.example.com and images directories to reach the banners directory. By making these directories executable, but not readable, the users can traverse these directories without being able to edit, or even see, the other content.

The setfacl (*set file access control list*) command is used to set the ACL. An ACL entry consists of three fields, separated by colons:

```
user/group/other:name:rights
```

These fields have the following meanings:

- user/group/other

  The word user or the letter u if this entry concerns a user; the word group or the letter g if this entry concerns a group; the word other or the letter o if this entry concerns the other users.

- name

  The name of the user or group affected by this entry. If the first field is other, this field is empty. If the first field is user or group and this field is empty, the name of the user or group of the file in question is used.

- rights

  The assigned privileges in the rwx format described before.

A few example ACL entries:

- user:diane:rw

  Read and write privileges for user *diane*.

- group:wheel:rwx

  Read, write, and execute privileges for the members of the *wheel* group.

- other::r

  Read privileges for other users.

These privileges are assigned *in addition* to the existing traditional privileges for owner, group, and others.

To create or modify an ACL entry, the -m (or also --modify on Linux) parameter is used in conjunction with the setfacl command. The -R (or also --recursive on Linux) parameter indicates that the entry should also be recursively applied to all child files and directories.

```
# setfacl -R -m group:jwebdev:rwx ./www.example.com
```

If ACL have been applied to a file or directory, the output for the ls -l command displays a + sign at the end of the permissions field:

```
# ls -l
totaal 4
drwxrwx---+ 9 webdev webdev 4096 Oct 27 14:37 www.example.com
```

According to the traditional system, the directory for this site is accessible only to user *webdev* and group *webdev*. These are the senior web developers who have access to all directories and files; ideally, this user and this group have been created especially for editing the websites (or even for editing only a single website) and have no other privileges on the server.

The + that follows the access rights indicates that ACL have been applied; these can be displayed with the help of the getfacl (*get file access control list*) command:

```
# getfacl ./www.example.com
  file: ./www.example.com
  owner: webdev
  group: webdev
  user::rwx
  group::rwx
  group:jwebdev:rwx
  mask::rwx
  other::---
```

In the preceding example, the privileges for the *jwebdev* group have been assigned recursively, so they are valid for all directories and files in /srv/www/www.example.com. To revoke the privileges for this group for the config sub-directory, the -x (or also --remove on Linux) parameter is used in conjunction with the setfacl command:

```
# setfacl -R -x group:jwebdev ./www.example.com/config
```

Multiple ACL entries can be specified at the same time, separated by commas. Multiple files or directories can be specified at the same time by appending them at the end of the command line.

```
# setfacl -R -m group:uidev:rwx,group:design:rwx \
   ./www.example.com/images ./www.example.com/style
```

The online addendum for this book contains an example that shows all the commands needed to create the directory tree described at the beginning of this section, including all permissions.

Even though in the preceding examples the *root* account was used to set the Access Control Lists, these commands can also be used by regular users (provided that they have the required privileges for changing permissions on the files and directories in question, of course).

Default ACLs

A special form of the ACL is the *default ACL*. A *default ACL* can be set on a directory to determine which permissions will be assigned to new files and sub-directories created in this directory.

On Linux, a default ACL is defined by prepending the ACL entry with the `default` keyword. The following command assigns read, write, and execute permissions for members of the *support* group to all files that will be created in the www.example.com/docs directory from now on:

```
linux# setfacl -m default:group:support:rwx ./www.example.com/docs
```

On FreeBSD, the `-d` parameter is used in conjunction with the `setfacl` command. However, before default ACLs can be defined for specific users and groups, the general default ACLs must be defined.

```
freebsd# setfacl -d -m u::rwx,g::r-x;o::--- ./www.example.com/docs
freebsd# setfacl -d -m g:support:rwx ./www.example.com/docs
```

A default ACL will only be applied to newly created files and sub-directories and to files and directories that are copied in from another file system or another host. Files that are copied from another location on the same file system bring their own permissions.

Limiting Root Access

A typo is easily made, and software sometimes contains bugs. This can be inconvenient if this causes files to disappear or become inaccessible. However, the consequences can be disastrous if it happens to the *root* user; after all, the *root* user has write access everywhere and thus the potential to render the system inaccessible or unusable. This is why daemons are executed under their own username instead of the *root* account.

On top of that, the *root* user's username is always the same on Unix systems, giving potential hackers already half of the information necessary to gain administrator privileges on the system.

It is therefore a good habit to limit the use of the *root* account as much as possible and to entirely disable direct *root* access.

sudo

Before the *root* account can be blocked, some measures must be taken to allow authorized users to execute *root* tasks. To this end, the *sudo* (*superuser do*) application is used. With this application, specific users can be granted the right to execute specific commands under the name of specific other users; this allows for a very precise definition of which users have administrator rights for which commands.

The which command can be used to verify whether *sudo* has been installed:

```
freebsd$ which sudo
freebsd$

debian$ which sudo
debian$

centos$ which sudo
/bin/sudo
centos$
```

On CentOS, *sudo* has been installed, and on FreeBSD and Debian, it hasn't.

```
freebsd# pkg install sudo

debian# apt install sudo
```

Users' privileges are defined in /usr/local/etc/sudoers (FreeBSD) or /etc/sudoers (Linux). However, even though this is a regular text file, it should only be modified using the visudo command. This command opens the configuration file in the text editor that was set as the default.

```
# visudo
```

For the server that is configured in this book, only a single line is important, and that is the line that grants full administrator privileges to the members of the *wheel* group (or the *sudo* group on Debian). The following line should be added to the file sudoers, if it doesn't exist yet:

```
%wheel    ALL=(ALL:ALL)    ALL
```

On Debian, the word wheel must be replaced with the word sudo (or, more in line with the Unix tradition: the sudo group should be renamed to wheel).

An explanation for the preceding line:

- **%wheel**

  The name of the group that will receive the specified privileges; the percent sign indicates that this concerns a group. To assign privileges to a specific user, the username is specified here without a percent sign.

- **ALL** (*first*)

  Before the = sign, the host is indicated for which this line is applicable; this is mainly important if the *sudo* configuration is shared between multiple machines. For the server discussed in this book, the keyword ALL can safely be used, which means every host.

- **ALL** (*second*)

  In parentheses and before the colon, the username under which the specified commands may be executed is specified. Since the *wheel* group should have full administrator privileges, the ALL keyword is used here, allowing the members of this group to execute the specified commands under any desired username.

- **ALL** (*third*)

  In parentheses and after the colon, the name of the group is specified under which commands can be executed. The rules are the same as for the username in the previous point.

- **ALL** (*fourth*)

  The last field of the line specifies the commands that may be executed. Since the *wheel* group should be able to execute any command, the ALL keyword is used here.

Once the sudoers file has been saved with the preceding line, the members of the *wheel* group can execute commands under the *root* username by prepending the command with sudo:

```
$ sudo mkdir /root/test
```

If a password is requested, it is the user's password, not *root*'s password.

If multiple commands must be executed as *root*, it may be practical to open a shell as *root*; commands can then be executed as usual without having to prepend each command with sudo. To leave the *root* shell, the exit command is used as usual.

```
$ sudo bash
# mkdir /root/test
# touch /root/test/file
# exit
$
```

Commands can also be executed under other usernames by adding the username in question as a command-line parameter:

```
$ sudo -u diane mkdir ~diane/test
```

The *sudo* command writes a message to the system logs each time it is executed, making it easy to analyze which user executed which command under which username at what moment.

The *sudo* package allows for a much more fine-grained control of the privileges for users and groups to execute certain commands than described here. The system administrator wanting to fully take advantage of the possibilities of *sudo* should consult the documentation that comes with it.

It is important, however, to not complicate the configuration more than absolutely necessary; the more exceptions are added, the more difficult it becomes to maintain the system.

Locking the Root Account

Now that *sudo* has been configured, the *root* account can be locked down.

Of course, it makes sense to verify first that the *wheel* group has at least one member:

```
$ grep '^wheel:' /etc/group
wheel:*:10:diane,dimitri
```

On Debian, wheel should be replaced with sudo.

The last field of the output of this command contains the usernames of the group members (diane,dimitri). If the group does not have any members, they should obviously be added; this is described earlier in this chapter.

Root access can be blocked in different ways. The most secure and simple way is to completely block all access to the account. The ways to do this have been discussed extensively in the section "Locking an Account"; in short, the following options are available:

```
bsd# pw lock root
bsd# pw -e 1 root

linux# passwd --lock root
linux# chage --expiredate 1 root
```

However, it may feel a bit uncomfortable to entirely block the *root* account (*"What if I accidentally delete the last user from the wheel account..."*). In that case, it could be an option to permit *root* login on the remote console and only block *root* access over SSH; this already reduces immensely the risks of a hacked *root* account. Blocking *root* access over SSH is discussed in Chapter 7, "Secure Shell (SSH)".

If the *root* account is not blocked entirely, it is important to at least change its password. Several password generators exist that can help generate a secure password. It is recommendable to generate a long password of at least 16 random characters. This password is only used in emergencies, so it does not need to be easy to remember. And since this password allows *root* access to the server, it must not be easily guessable, not by humans and not by computers.

setuid

Another way to grant additional privileges to users is to install the application *setuid*. This means that the user executing the application temporarily receives the privileges of the owner of the application.

The `passwd` command, which allows users to change their password, is one of the applications that use this technique, to allow the user to write the new password to a file where the user normally does not have access; the user receives *root* privileges for this single action. Obviously, the necessary security measures have been integrated into the application to prevent the user from abusing the temporarily elevated privileges to make additional modifications to the system.

It is important that a system administrator knows the concept of *setuid*; however, its details will not be discussed here.

Accounts for Other Users

Other users, who never need to log in directly to the server, but who do need to be able to authenticate to read and send mail, will not receive a local server account, but will be stored in a directory service. This is discussed in the section "Lightweight Directory Access Protocol (LDAP)" of Chapter 11, "Databases".

Departure of a System Administrator

Changing a server's root password when a system administrator leaves is not a sign of distrust; it is a sign of good system administration.

Blocking access cuts both ways: on the one hand, it assures that the remaining system administrators, now and in the future, keep a clear image of all persons who have access to the server; on the other hand, it clears the former system administrator of any suspicions if anything unpleasant should happen to the server in the future. A professional system administrator will therefore always remind their colleagues to take terminating measures after their departure.

It is advisable to create a checklist of things that must be arranged and organized when a system administrator leaves. The online addendum for this book contains a file that can be used as an example when creating such a checklist.

Summary

This chapter discussed user management and file permissions. After an explanation of the concept of users and user groups, the format of the files that store the user account and group information was discussed. Since direct manipulation of these files is discouraged, a thorough explanation was then given of the tools that are available for the management of users and groups. The second half of this chapter focused on access permissions; first, the traditional permission system was discussed and then the Access Control Lists that complement the traditional system. Lastly, *sudo* was installed and configured, so that direct root access can be disabled, which greatly enhances the server's security.

In the next chapter, the *Domain Name System* will be discussed, and a DNS server will be installed and configured.

CHAPTER 6

Domain Name System (DNS)

Domain names and hostnames are not required for the functionality of the network; IP addresses are sufficient to enable communication. However, as names are easier to remember for people than number sequences, a system was invented to attach names to these addresses: *DNS* (*Domain Name System*). Thanks to this system, network nodes (servers, workstations, printers, routers, etc.) can be represented by names; the DNS translates these names into the IP addresses that are used for the actual communication and vice versa.

The Domain Name System is hierarchical: the *second-level* domain name **example.com** is a subdomain of the *top-level* domain name **com**; the hostname **green.example.com** is a subdomain of **example.com**; and so on. For a server as described in this book, these three levels are sufficient, but for a large multinational firm, it would not be unthinkable to have a workstation named *pc23.workstations.london.europe.example.com* or a printer named *hp06.printers.washington.namerica.example.com*; clearly, these names would be easier to remember (and locate) than *172.21.243.115* and *192.168.154.98*. The system administrator can freely distribute and assign names as they see fit within the domain name (*zone*) that was assigned to them.

The DNS is not case sensitive; the hostname *green.example.com* is the same as the hostname *GrEeN.ExAmPlE.CoM*. The convention is to always write host and domain names in lowercase letters. In 2009, a standard was approved for the registration of internationalized domain names (IDN), domain names in other character sets than ASCII; nowadays, most network software and many registrars support this standard.

As indicated in the first chapter, the server in this book uses *example.com* as its primary domain name, with *green.example.com* as its primary hostname. The domain names *example.edu* and *example.org* are also handled by this server. The *registrar*

© Robert La Lau 2021
R. La Lau, *Practical Internet Server Configuration*, https://doi.org/10.1007/978-1-4842-6960-2_6

(the company where the domain names have been registered, usually the provider) delegates the domains to this server, and changes to the structure within those domains can be made without the help of the provider.

If the server to be configured is an internal server (office or home server), it is recommended to use domain names that end in *.lan* (*Local Area Network*) to prevent clashing of these domain names with domain names used on the internet. Even though *.lan* has not been officially reserved for internal use, this extension is used in so many local networks, that there is little chance of it ever being reserved for other purposes.

As also indicated in the first chapter, the IP address for *green.example.com* is *198.51.100.156*.

If the server to be configured is an internal server (office or home server), it is advisable to use IP addresses from the IP ranges reserved for private networks:

- **10.0.0.0/8** (*10.0.0.0–10.255.255.255*)

- **172.16.0.0/12** (*172.16.0.0–172.31.255.255*)

- **192.168.0.0/16** (*192.168.0.0–192.168.255.255*)

To guarantee redundancy, a domain name usually has at least two *name servers* active. For this, it is not required to own multiple servers: usually the provider will propose to maintain the *secondary DNS*. If needed, more suppliers can be found on the internet that provide secondary DNS as a free or paid service. Multiple secondary servers can be active at the same time for a single domain name. These *secondary DNS servers* are notified by the *primary DNS server* when changes are made to the domain, and they then copy the new information; such a copy is called a *transfer*.

For the purposes of this book, the provider proposes the server *dns2.example.net*, with IP address *203.0.113.145*, as a secondary DNS server for the domain names *example.com*, *example.edu*, and *example.org*.

By default, the DNS server listens on port 53. This means that port 53 needs to be opened in the firewall for both UDP and TCP and for both incoming and outgoing traffic; UDP is used for "ordinary" DNS requests (*lookups*) and TCP for transfers. Chapter 4, "Network Basics and Firewall", gives more information about the maintenance of the firewall.

In the configuration of the DNS, one speaks of *zones*. Even though *domain* and *zone* do not necessarily have the same meaning, the terms can be used interchangeably in the context of this book. In the example of the large multinational firm earlier, *example.com* would be both the domain and a zone, and *namerica.example.com*, *washington.namerica.example.com*, and *printers.washington.namerica.example.com* are zones, but not domains.

Several DNS server programs exist, but the de facto standard is *BIND* (*Berkeley Internet Name Domain*), developed by *ISC* (*Internet Systems Consortium*). This is the software that is discussed in this book.

BIND has two more or less separate configurations: on the one hand, there is the configuration of the server, defining topics like log files and directories to use, and on the other hand, there is the configuration of the zones in so-called *zone files*.

BIND's executable file is called named for *name daemon*.

Apart from the name server itself, ISC also develops and publishes some applications for analysis and maintenance of DNS. By default, these applications are part of the same package, but some distributions have chosen to separate them from BIND and publish them as one or two separate packages; this enables users who have not installed BIND to use these applications anyway.

Installation

BIND is part of the software repositories of all Linux distributions and BSD systems, which eases the installation.

FreeBSD

The FreeBSD repositories contain several versions of BIND, and the naming of the packages is a bit unfortunate: the version numbers (*9.11* and *9.14* at the time of this writing) have been integrated in the names of the packages, but the descriptions of the packages say nothing about their differences. The BIND website states that both versions are stable releases, but *9.11* is a so-called *Extended Support Version*: this version will be supported longer by ISC. Since *green.example.com* will be updated regularly, version *9.14* can be selected; software updates will automatically replace this version with newer versions when they are published.

The administrative applications are published in the package *dns/bind-tools*. This package is installed alongside *dns/bind914* as a dependency.

```
freebsd# pkg search bind
freebsd# pkg install bind914
```

The configuration for BIND is installed in /usr/local/etc/namedb, and the startup script is /usr/local/etc/rc.d/named. The zone files are installed in the directory /usr/local/etc/namedb/master. To be able to start the name server, the following line must be added to /etc/rc.conf:

```
named_enable="YES"
```

This also guarantees that the name server starts automatically when the server (re)boots.

Debian

The BIND package for Debian, *bind9*, is installed by default. The package *dnsutils*, which contains commands to query the DNS, is not installed by default.

```
debian# apt install dnsutils
```

BIND's configuration and the zone files are installed in /etc/bind.

CentOS

The CentOS developers have chosen to split the name server and the administrative applications into two packages that are installed separately:

```
centos# yum install bind bind-utils
```

The configuration files are installed, a bit disorderly, directly into the /etc directory: /etc/named.*, /etc/rndc.*, and /etc/sysconfig/named; a directory /etc/named is created, but not used. The zone files are installed in /var/named.

To make sure BIND starts automatically when the server boots, the following command must be executed:

```
centos# systemctl enable named
```

Configuration

BIND is configured mainly through the file named.conf. Comments in this file are formatted in *JavaScript style* (double slashes for single-line comments; multi-line comments captured between slashes and asterisks).

```
freebsd# cd /usr/local/etc/namedb
```

```
debian# cd /etc/bind
```

```
centos# cd /etc
```

Before the configuration is created, a cryptographic key is generated; this key will be used to instruct the daemon to reload the configuration without restarting the server.

```
# rndc-confgen -a -r /dev/urandom
```

This generates a file named rndc.key in the configuration directory. This file will be included in the configuration later.

The example configuration file that can be downloaded from the online addendum for this book is a good starting point for the new configuration. It is also wise to conserve the original file as a reference.

```
# mv named.conf named.conf.orig
# nano named.conf
```

The example file starts with the definition of two lists, *secondaries* and *loopback*. These lists can contain IP addresses and IP ranges, separated by semicolons. The first list contains the IP addresses for all secondary servers; in this case, there is only one. The second list contains the loopback addresses for the server; this list is used to limit the initial permissions. The names for the lists may be chosen freely, with the exception of four reserved names:

- **any**

  Matches any hostname

- **none**

  Does not match any hostname

- **localhost**

  Matches the IP addresses (IPv4 and IPv6) of all the server's network interfaces

- **localnets**

  Matches all hosts in all the networks (IPv4 and IPv6) that the server is part of

The next block defines general options for named. The *directory* option specifies the directory that is used as the base directory for all relative paths in the configuration files, and the *pid-file* option specifies the location of the PID file.

The *listen-on* statement specifies all IP addresses where the name server should reply to *lookups* (DNS queries). Normally, these are the loopback address and the server's public IP address, but if the server has multiple IP addresses, the choice can be made to only have the name server listen on a single or some of these IP addresses.

The default access permissions for the name server are restrictive: only the server itself is granted access.

The *forwarders* statement contains a list of IP addresses of DNS caches that should be consulted when the server does not have the answer to a request, before the server sends the request to the root DNS servers to try and find the answer in the DNS hierarchy. Using *forwarders* reduces the load on the root DNS servers and the number of DNS requests sent over the internet. In this case, the Cloudflare/APNIC DNS cache is used.

The logging is kept simple. All log messages are sent to the same file, and this file may never grow larger than 50MB. The five most recent log files are conserved, and older files are deleted automatically.

BIND supports so-called *dynamic DNS updates*; named can also be instructed to reload the configuration without restarting. For these manipulations, the application rndc is used. The *controls* statement determines the conditions for the use of rndc. In this case, the statement determines that rndc can only be used from the server itself and only by means of the key that was generated at the beginning of this section. Dynamic updates are more relevant for home and office networks and are not treated in this book. However, rndc is still used to reload the configuration when changes have been made.

The final statements in the file are the *zone* statement for the zone ".·" (dot), which tells named where to find the root DNS servers, and the *zone* statement for the zone localhost.

The example configuration is a minimal but functional configuration for BIND. However, dozens of other options exist. The system administrator who wants to take things further will find links to the *BIND Administrative Reference Manual* (*ARM*) and other information in the online addendum for this book.

Before the name server can be started, the log directory must be created.

```
# mkdir -p /var/log/named
# chmod 770 /var/log/named

freebsd# chgrp bind /var/log/named

debian# chgrp bind /var/log/named

centos# chgrp named /var/log/named
```

Adding Domains

A configuration as described in the preceding section creates a DNS server that can reply to requests (*lookups*) for the "domain name" *localhost* (and reverse lookups for the IP address *127.0.0.1*) and that can forward lookups for other domains and IP addresses to DNS servers elsewhere in the DNS hierarchy. To be able to handle the registered domain names *example.com*, *example.edu*, and *example.org*, so-called *zone files* must be created for these domains, after which named, the executable file from the BIND package, must be told where these files can be found and what their names are.

No rules exist for the naming of zone files, but obviously, it is a good idea to keep the name recognizable. One of the conventions used for the naming of zone files is *domain-dot-zone*, for example, example.com.zone. Some distributions have chosen to use the extension .db, but this could incorrectly suggest that it concerns a database that needs a specialized application for modification; the zone files can be edited using a regular text editor.

Zone File

For now, the zone file for *example.com* looks as follows:

```
$ORIGIN example.com.
$TTL 2d
@     IN  SOA  ns.example.com. sysadmin.example.com. (
              2020011502  ; Serial
              24h         ; Refresh
              2h          ; Retry
```

```
                        1000h          ; Expire
                        2d             ; TTL
                    )
@       IN  NS   ns
@       IN  NS   dns2.example.net.
@       IN  MX   10 mx.example.com.
@       IN  A    198.51.100.156
green   IN  A    198.51.100.156
ns      IN  A    198.51.100.156
mx      IN  A    198.51.100.156
```

Zone files use *assembly-style* comments: everything from a semicolon to the end of a line is considered a comment and is not interpreted by the server.

On FreeBSD, this file could be saved as
`/usr/local/etc/namedb/master/example.com.zone`, on Debian as
`/etc/bind/example.com.zone`, and on CentOS as `/var/named/example.com.zone`.

The first line indicates the zone to which this file applies. In the example of the large multinational firm given before, the *$ORIGIN* could be `london.europe.example.com`, allowing the local system administrators to manage the DNS for the London-based branch. The value of this field ends in a dot.

The second line, *$TTL* (*Time To Live*), indicates how long by default a client can store the received data. After this time limit, a new lookup must be made (or a new transfer, if the client is a secondary server). If this is a numerical value, it is interpreted as a number of seconds. For readability, units may be used, like `1d` for *1 day*; the accepted units are `s` (*seconds*), `m` (*minutes*), `h` (*hours*), `d` (*days*), and `w` (*weeks*). It is possible to specify a different *TTL* for each record.

The other lines in the zone file are called *resource records*, or simply *records*. In these records, the name of the zone (*$ORIGIN*) may be abbreviated to the at sign (@). Hostnames that do not end in a dot will have the *$ORIGIN* appended internally.

Resource records consist of five fields:

- **Hostname or domain name**

    This is the requested hostname, the key that BIND looks for when the server receives a lookup for *www.example.com*, for example. This field is optional, and if it is not specified, the record inherits the hostname from the previous record in the file.

- **TTL**

    This field is also optional, and if it is not specified, the *$TTL*
    specified in the second line of the file will be used. In the example
    file, none of the records have an explicitly specified *TTL*, so all
    records use the default *TTL*.

- **Class**

    This value is practically always IN (for *internet*). In order not to
    complicate things unnecessarily, the other possible values will not
    be discussed here.

- **Type**

    The record type. An NS record defines a name server, an MX record
    defines a mail server, and so on. A list of record types follows.

- **Data**

    The data for the record. This varies by record type.

SOA Record

The first record is the *SOA* (*Source of Authority*) *record*. In the example, this record is
spread over multiple lines to allow for the comments. The record can also be put on
a single line without the semicolons (because a semicolon would turn the rest of the
line, including the values, into a comment). If the record is put on a single line, the
parentheses are optional.

This mandatory record specifies the primary name server for this domain
(ns.example.com) and the email address for the person or service responsible for
this zone (sysadmin@example.com; the at sign has been replaced by a dot because
of the special meaning of the at sign in this file). If these two values did not end in a
dot, BIND would internally append the *$ORIGIN* and interpret them as, respectively,
ns.example.com.example.com and sysadmin@example.com.example.com.

It is advised to note down the email address; this address needs to be created when
the email server is configured in a following chapter.

The SOA record also contains some numerical values between the parentheses:

- **Serial**

  Each time changes are made to the zone file, this serial number must be incremented; this tells the secondary servers that a new configuration is available. No mandatory format exists for this field, but most system administrators follow the convention YYYYMMDDnn (*year, month, day, sequence number*); thus, the preceding example file is the result of the second change made on January 15, 2020. Using this format, one can always be sure that the next number is higher than the previous and that 99 changes per day can be made.

- **Refresh**

  After this amount of time, secondary servers are expected to request the serial number for the zone from the primary server to determine whether any changes have been made in the meantime.

- **Retry**

  If the primary server is unavailable to a secondary server when it is supposed to refresh its configuration, the secondary server is supposed to retry after this delay.

- **Expire**

  If the primary server is unavailable to a secondary server for an extended period, the secondary server is supposed to consider its configuration out of date after this delay.

- **TTL**

  This is the *Time To Live* that is sent with negative responses (*hostname not found*).

The values as given in the preceding example are the values for smaller, stable zones, as recommended by *RIPE* (*Réseaux IP Européens; European IP Networks*), an international organization located in Amsterdam dedicated to the technical development of the internet since 1989 and responsible for the distribution and registration of IP addresses in Europe, West Asia, and the former USSR.

NS Record

The next two records are *NS* (*Name Server*) *records*. These records define the name servers for this zone, the primary and secondary servers. Since the data for the first of these two records does not end in a dot, BIND will interpret this as `ns.example.com`—the given value with the *$ORIGIN* appended.

An *NS record* refers to a hostname and not an IP address. The hostname referred to by an *NS record* must have an *A record*; a *CNAME record* is not sufficient (the *A* and *CNAME* records will be discussed next). A domain should have at least two name servers and thus also at least two *NS records*.

MX Record

The next record is an *MX* (*Mail eXchange*) *record* that indicates the server that handles the email for this zone. The data for an *MX record* starts with a number: the *preference* (*priority*). Multiple mail servers may be defined with different priorities; if the server with the lowest *preference* is unavailable, the client will try to deliver the mail to a server with a higher *preference*.

An *MX record* refers to a hostname and not an IP address. The hostname referred to by an *MX record* must have an *A record*; a *CNAME record* is not sufficient.

During the configuration of a new server, it is recommended to have the MX record refer to a different server that has been configured to handle mail for this zone until the new server is ready to handle mail. This prevents the loss of emails.

A Record

An *A* (*Address*) *record* links a hostname to an IP address. The *A records* in the example file indicate that DNS lookups for *example.com*, *green.example.com*, *ns.example.com*, and *mx.example.com* should all have the IP address of this server as a result.

Obviously, an *A record* always refers to an IP address and not to a hostname.

AAAA Record

An *AAAA record* serves the same purpose as an *A record*, but for IPv6 addresses. This record probably thanks its name to the fact that an IPv6 address has four times the number of bits of an IPv4 address (128 bits instead of 32). IPv6 is not discussed in this book.

Obviously, an *AAAA record* refers to an IPv6 address and not to a hostname.

CNAME Record

A *CNAME* (*Canonical Name*) *record* defines an *alias*, or alternative name. For example, in the chapter about the email server, the "hostnames" *imap.example.com* and *smtp.example.com* will be created as alternative names for *mx.example.com*. The advantage of this is that, if necessary, the functionality for receiving (*imap*) or sending (*smtp*) email can be moved to a different server without requiring any changes in the users' email clients; if the system administrator changes the reference for the *CNAME record*, the users will be automatically redirected to the new server.

A *CNAME record* refers to a hostname and not to an IP address. *CNAME records* can be chained: a *CNAME record* can refer to another *CNAME record* that can refer to another *CNAME record*, and so on.

TXT Record

The *TXT* (*Text*) *record* is a generic record that can serve multiple purposes.

The data for a *TXT record* depends on the purpose of the record.

SSHFP Record

The *SSHFP* (*Secure Shell fingerprint*) *record* can be used by the SSH server and SSH clients to verify the identity of the SSH server.

An *SSHFP record* contains a hexadecimal representation of a digital fingerprint (and indicators for the algorithms used).

PTR Record

The *PTR* (*Pointer*) *record* enables reverse DNS lookups: the translation of an IP address to the primary hostname. *Reverse DNS* is discussed later in this chapter.

A *PTR record* refers to a hostname and not to an IP address.

Other Records

Several other DNS record types exist, but these are not discussed in this book. More information about these less commonly used types can be found on the internet.

The Other Zone Files

The zone files for *example.edu* and *example.org* are a bit more limited, because these domains use the *example.com* NS and MX servers. Also, the server has no hostname in these domains.

This is the zone file for *example.edu*:

```
$ORIGIN example.edu.
$TTL 2d
@  IN  SOA  ns.example.com. sysadmin.example.com. (
                2020011501   ; Serial
                24h          ; Refresh
                2h           ; Retry
                1000h        ; Expire
                2d           ; TTL
             )
   IN  NS   ns.example.com.
   IN  NS   dns2.example.net.
   IN  MX   10 mx.example.com.
   IN  A    198.51.100.156
```

This file can be copied for *example.org*; only the first line will need to be edited (and clearly the serial number for both).

Adding Zones to the Configuration

Now that the zone files have been created, BIND must be informed. To do this, the following lines are appended to named.conf:

```
zone "example.com" {
    type master;
    file "/usr/local/etc/namedb/master/example.com.zone";
    allow-query { any; };
```

```
    allow-transfer { secondaries; };
    notify yes;
};
```

The first line (zone) tells BIND that this server handles DNS for the domain *example.com* and opens the configuration block for this zone.

The second line (type) indicates that this server is the primary server for this domain.

Line number three (file) specifies the path to the zone file. The path in the preceding example is valid for FreeBSD; on a Debian server, the file is installed as /etc/bind/example.com.zone and under CentOS as /var/named/example.com.zone.

The fourth line (allow-query) allows everybody to do DNS lookups for this domain on this server.

Line five (allow-transfer) allows the secondary servers to execute the zone transfers needed to be able to function as secondary DNS. The group secondaries has been defined before in the top of the configuration file.

The sixth line (notify) ensures that the secondary servers are notified when the serial number of a zone file is incremented. This enables the secondary servers to update their data immediately, instead of waiting for the next *Refresh*.

The last line closes the block.

These lines can be copied for *example.edu* and *example.org*.

Loading the Configuration

When changes have been made to named.conf or the zone files, named must be instructed to reread its configuration.

The following commands are used to start named:

```
freebsd# service named start

debian# systemctl start bind9

centos# systemctl start named
```

If named had already been started and the configuration for a running server was changed, it is not necessary to restart the name server; BIND can reread its configuration without stopping the server.

```
freebsd# service named reload

debian# systemctl reload bind9

centos# systemctl reload named
```

If the file `rndc.key` has changed, the server should be restarted instead of reloaded.

The DNS server will now be able to reply to all lookups for the zones that were just configured. Also, a signal was sent to the secondary servers to notify them of the availability of a new configuration.

To make sure that the server sends DNS lookups to its own name server before consulting other name servers, the loopback address (*127.0.0.1*) must be prepended to `/etc/resolv.conf`:

```
nameserver 127.0.0.1
nameserver 1.1.1.1
nameserver 1.0.0.1
```

Clients (workstations, routers, other servers) may now be configured to use this server as their DNS server, but that is not required: as the *registrar* has recorded that this server is responsible for the DNS for the registered domains, lookups for these domains will always end up at this server, even for clients that have not set their primary DNS to this server. The server could thus be spared by **not** setting it as the primary DNS for clients; this way, the server does not need to spend memory and processor time on the redirection of requests for domains that are not handled by this server.

Reverse Resolution

In the previous section, the *forward DNS resolving* has been configured: the translation of a hostname to an IP address. However, it can also happen that a client does a lookup for an IP address to find its hostname. This is called *reverse resolving* or *reverse lookups*, sometimes abbreviated to *rDNS* (*reverse DNS*).

This reverse DNS is normally handled by the provider. To link a hostname to the IP address of the server, the system administrator logs on to the provider's web interface and enters the primary hostname, *green.example.com* in this case, in the form provided for that purpose.

Since many mail servers reject messages from hosts without a reverse DNS, this is a crucial setting. If you cannot find a setting for reverse DNS in your provider's web interface, contact them.

For completeness and because this information is necessary for the configuration of an internal server, this is the zone file that enables reverse DNS for the domain *example.com*, using the IP range *198.51.100.152/29* (*198.51.100.152–198.51.100.159*):

```
$ORIGIN 100.51.198.in-addr.arpa.
$TTL 2d
@    IN  SOA  ns.example.com. sysadmin.example.com. (
                2020011502   ; Serial
                24h          ; Refresh
                2h           ; Retry
                1000h        ; Expire
                2d           ; TTL
              )
@    IN  NS   ns.example.com.
@    IN  NS   dns2.example.net.
153  IN  PTR  blue.example.com.
154  IN  PTR  yellow.example.com.
155  IN  PTR  red.example.com.
156  IN  PTR  green.example.com.
157  IN  PTR  pink.example.com.
158  IN  PTR  purple.example.com.
```

This zone file closely resembles the zone file described before: this file also contains a *$ORIGIN*, a *$TTL*, and *SOA* and *NS* records.

To enable reverse DNS, the "domain name" *in-addr.arpa* was invented; the "subdomains" for this domain are the different parts of the IP address in reverse order. For IPv6, this domain is *ip6.arpa*.

According to the preceding example, the host with IP address *198.51.100.153* is called *blue.example.com*, and the host with IP address *198.51.100.157* is called *pink.example.com*. For completeness, these hosts should have *A records* in the zone file for *example.com*, with the IP addresses mentioned here.

To include this zone file in the BIND configuration, the following lines must be added to `named.conf`:

```
zone "100.51.198.in-addr.arpa" {
    type master;
    file "/usr/local/etc/namedb/master/198.51.100.zone";
    allow-query { any; };
    allow-transfer { secondaries; };
    notify yes;
};
```

(Obviously, the path to the zone file should be corrected on Debian and CentOS.)

After named's configuration has been reloaded, the server will be able to reply to reverse lookups.

Consulting and Debugging

To test, and possibly debug, the DNS configuration, the commands host and dig can be used, some of the administrative tools that come with BIND.

```
# host green.example.com
green.example.com has address 198.51.100.156

# host 198.51.100.156
156.100.51.198.in-addr.arpa domain name pointer green.example.com.

# host -t MX example.com
example.com mail is handled by 10 mx.example.com.
```

The output for dig is a bit more vast than that of host.

Clearly, when solving DNS problems, it is important to ensure that a received response originates from the server to be investigated and not from a secondary server or a DNS cache. To ensure this, the address of the server to be consulted can be specified when executing the command; the host command accepts it as the last parameter, and the dig command expects the address to be prepended with an at sign.

To send a lookup to the local DNS server, to discover the IP address for *yellow.example.com*:

```
# host yellow.example.com 127.0.0.1
```

To send a request to *green.example.com*, to find the MX server for the *example.com* domain:

```
# dig @198.51.100.156 -t MX example.com
```

Summary

This chapter discussed the Domain Name System and the configuration of the BIND DNS server. Both forward and reverse DNS were explained, and the meaning of the most commonly used zone types was clarified. Lastly, some tools for the analysis of the DNS configuration were discussed.

The next chapter will focus on SSH, a protocol for making secure encrypted connections, that may well be the most commonly used tool the system administrator has.

CHAPTER 7

Secure Shell (SSH)

Secure shell is a network protocol for the creation of encrypted connections. In its original and purest form, it is used to open a remote terminal and execute commands. However, the protocol can also be used for file transfer (*SCP*, *SFTP*); as an encrypted transport protocol for other, possible less strongly secured protocols; and for port forwarding—the redirection of requests for certain ports to ports on other servers—a technique often used to allow machines on different sides of a firewall to communicate.

To the Unix administrator, SSH is an essential tool for remote administration, and SSH clients and servers are available for practically all operating systems and installed by default on practically all Unix systems.

The SSH daemon is called `sshd` and the client `ssh`; the clients for file transfer are called `scp` and `sftp`.

To allow SSH connections to the server, inbound traffic on TCP port 22 must be admitted in the firewall configuration.

Installing and Configuring the SSH Server

Several SSH servers exist. The most commonly used by far is *OpenSSH*, a package developed by a number of OpenBSD developers, that consists of an SSH server and client and tools for file transfer and SSH key management. The *OpenSSH Portability Team* follows *OpenSSH* development and ports it to a large number of other operating systems.

Installation on FreeBSD

Even though *OpenSSH* packages and ports exist, it is part of the base system and does not need to be installed separately.

© Robert La Lau 2021
R. La Lau, *Practical Internet Server Configuration*, https://doi.org/10.1007/978-1-4842-6960-2_7

If the package or port is ever installed as a dependency for another package, for instance, this will not pose a problem: the original version is installed in /usr/bin, and the package or port will be installed in /usr/local/bin; the versions can coexist without any problem. If no other changes are made, the version from the base system will continue to be used by default.

If the intention is to replace the version from the base system with the package or port, for example, to take advantage of the patches available in the Ports Collection, these are the steps to be followed:

1. Install port.

2. Stop SSH daemon

   ```
   freebsd# service sshd stop
   ```

3. Change or define two variables in /etc/rc.conf:

   ```
   sshd_enable="NO"
   openssh_enable="YES"
   ```

4. Start OpenSSH daemon

   ```
   freebsd# service openssh start
   ```

5. Start a new SSH session WITHOUT closing the existing connection.

6. If the new connection works, the first connection can be closed.

When the (Open)SSH daemon is stopped, existing connections are not interrupted. It is important to test the functionality of the newly installed daemon before ending the connection with the old daemon; if the new daemon does not start well, the old connection is often the only chance to repair the problem. When the functioning of the new daemon has been verified, the old connection must be ended to ensure that all connections use the newly installed daemon.

However, for daily use, the OpenSSH version from the base system suffices; it is usually unnecessary to replace it.

The configuration for the original version is installed in /etc/ssh. The package and the port install their configuration in /usr/local/etc/ssh; if the original version is replaced, it is recommended to add a text file to /etc/ssh, explaining the switch and referring to the new directory, to avoid confusion.

Installation on Debian

The Debian developers have chosen to split OpenSSH into several packages, the most important of which are *openssh-server* and *openssh-client*. Normally, these packages have both been installed. This can be verified with the following command:

```
debian# apt list --installed "openssh*"
```

If openssh-server is not installed, this command will take care of that:

```
debian# apt install openssh-server
```

The configuration is installed in /etc/ssh. After its installation, the daemon is started automatically.

Installation on CentOS

On CentOS, OpenSSH has also been split into multiple packages. The most important of these—the server, the client, and a package which contains code that is shared between the server and the client—have already been installed, and the server has been started. In the unthinkable case that the provider used an installation image without OpenSSH, this can be repaired with the help of yum:

```
centos# yum install openssh-server openssh-clients
```

On CentOS, the configuration is also installed in /etc/ssh.

Configuration

The configuration file for the SSH server is sshd_config (attention: that is with a d; the file ssh_config, without a d, contains the default configuration for the client). This file contains one option per line. Almost all available options are contained in the file with their default values. To change an option, the hash sign at the beginning of the line is removed, and the value is changed.

The names of the options are very descriptive, and sshd_config(5) contains extensive documentation. It is therefore unnecessary to describe each option here. A few important options are highlighted, with their recommended values:

- **PermitRootLogin no**

  This option determines whether the *root* user should be allowed to log in directly using SSH. All three systems have a different default setting here: FreeBSD says no, Debian chose prohibit-password, and CentOS selected yes.

  If *root* is allowed to log in directly, this enables an attacker to try and break the security for the *root* account by launching a brute-force attack, an attack that uses a script or application to try and "guess" the password by trying hundreds or thousands of passwords. Obviously, such an attack is without chance if sshd unconditionally blocks each *root* login attempt.

  Furthermore, it is impossible to find out later who has been logged in as *root*, if *root* is allowed to log in directly. If users log in with their own usernames and then use sudo to gain root privileges, the username and time will be recorded.

  Since sudo has been configured in a previous section to allow system administrators to traceably gain root privileges, there is no reason to allow direct root access to the server.

- **StrictModes yes**

  Users' personal SSH settings are stored in ~/.ssh. If this option is activated, sshd will verify that only the user has write access to this directory and to the files therein.

- **PubkeyAuthentication yes**

  This option permits the use of SSH keys. These will be discussed extensively in a later section.

- **Subsystem sftp /usr/...**

  This server will not host an *FTP* server; in its stead, *SFTP* will be used, the encrypted alternative based on SSH. This option activates the *SFTP* server. More about *SFTP* in a following section.

- **AllowGroups wheel sudo webdev**

  This is not an option for daily use, but it is good to be aware of its existence.

  If this option has been defined, only the members of the specified groups can log in using ssh (or scp, sftp, etc.). This is a simple and effective way to, temporarily or permanently, unconditionally deny access to certain groups of users; for example, it may sometimes be desirable that only system administrators have access to the server. Related options are **AllowUsers**, **DenyUsers**, and **DenyGroups**.

Some more options will be modified in the section about SSH keys. When the configuration has been modified, sshd must be restarted.

Starting and Stopping

On all three systems, the SSH daemon is automatically started on system boot. Sometimes, however, it can be desirable to restart the daemon in the interim, for example, when the configuration has changed.

When the SSH daemon is restarted, existing connections are not disconnected. This is due to the fact that the daemon, as soon as a connection is established, starts a child process and transfers the connection to that child process. The daemon can then be restarted without it affecting the child processes. In some cases—after important configuration changes, for example—it might therefore be necessary to manually terminate all connections, forcing the users to re-log in, and thus submit them to the new configuration.

FreeBSD

These are the commands for starting, stopping, and restarting the SSH daemon that was installed with the base system:

```
freebsd# service sshd start
```

```
freebsd# service sshd stop
```

```
freebsd# service sshd restart
```

If OpenSSH was replaced with the version from the Ports Collection, the name of the service has changed to openssh:

```
freebsd# service openssh start
```

If the SSH daemon should not start at boot time, the variable *sshd_enable* (or *openssh_enable*) should be set to NO in /etc/rc.conf. The service command can also be used for this:

```
freebsd# service sshd disable
```

This command does exactly the same as manually editing rc.conf. This command does not stop the daemon. The following command is used to undo that action and reconfigure the daemon to be automatically started at boot time:

```
freebsd# service sshd enable
```

If a service has been disabled in rc.conf, it cannot be started or stopped manually either.

Debian and CentOS

Debian and CentOS both use systemctl for starting and stopping services; however, on Debian the service is called ssh and on CentOS sshd.

```
debian# systemctl start ssh
centos# systemctl start sshd
```

```
debian# systemctl stop ssh
centos# systemctl stop sshd
```

```
debian# systemctl restart ssh
centos# systemctl restart sshd
```

To prevent the daemon from starting at boot time, systemctl also has a disable sub-command:

```
debian# systemctl disable ssh
centos# systemctl disable sshd
```

This command does not stop the daemon. To reconfigure the daemon to start again at boot time, the `enable` sub-command is used:

```
debian# systemctl enable ssh
centos# systemctl enable sshd
```

Starting a Session

The next sections explain how to start an SSH connection from a Unix or Windows computer. No matter which system is used as the client, the first time a user connects to a server, they are asked to accept a so-called *host key fingerprint*. This "fingerprint" is a unique string of characters that allows to verify the server's identity (or actually the identity for the encryption key the server uses to encrypt the connection). Even though it is not simple to verify this fingerprint—it is a long string of seemingly random characters—it is important to perform this verification to be sure the server is who it says it is. This verification needs to be performed only once, unless the server changes its hostname/IP address or its key; the SSH client stores the combination of IP address and fingerprint in the file `~/.ssh/known_hosts`.

The server's administrator can provide the fingerprints used by the server; system administrators are advised to send them to all new users. The list of used fingerprints can be generated by executing the following command on the server:

```
$ for f in /etc/ssh/*.pub; do ssh-keygen -lf ${f}; done
```

Obviously, on FreeBSD, this path must be corrected to `/usr/local/etc/ssh/*.pub`.

It is not necessary to keep these fingerprints a secret; they can be distributed freely and could even be published in an online help desk system.

Linux, BSD, and macOS

On Unix systems, `ssh` is a command-line application. Even though the `ssh` command accepts a large number of command-line arguments, the hostname of the machine to connect with usually suffices:

```
$ ssh green.example.com
```

If no username is specified, `ssh` will use the username with which the user is logged in locally. The remote username can be added to the hostname:

```
$ ssh dimitri@green.example.com
```

For even more convenience, the hostname and username can be stored in the configuration file `~/.ssh/config`.

```
Host grn
 HostName green.example.com
 User dimitri
```

The indentation is optional.

The user can then use the following command to connect to the server:

```
$ ssh grn
```

This will be translated by `ssh` to

```
$ ssh -l dimitri green.example.com
```

which is the same as the previously shown command with the at sign.

Multiple `Host` definitions can be stored in `~/.ssh/config`; each line that starts with the keyword `Host` begins a new definition, which then continues until the next `Host` keyword. It is therefore important to put general settings at the top of the file and host-specific options below.

If necessary, the options stored in `~/.ssh/config` can be overwritten on the command line:

```
$ ssh diane@grn
```

See `ssh(1)` for more command-line options and `ssh_config(5)` for more configuration options.

Several graphical SSH clients also exist for Unix.

Windows

The most commonly used SSH client for Windows is called *PuTTY*.

PuTTY is a mature project—more than 20 years—and open source. Moreover, *PuTTY* is very comprehensive and well-documented. The online addendum for this book contains links to the *PuTTY* website and documentation.

The settings for *PuTTY* may seem a bit overwhelming at first, but the only three settings that are necessary to establish an SSH connection are the hostname of the machine to connect with, the port, and the type of connection. If needed, *PuTTY* will ask for the username and password. *PuTTY* allows the storage of profiles, which prevents the settings from needing to be made again and again.

Most, if not all, other open source SSH clients for Windows are based on *PuTTY*. For security reasons, great caution is advised with closed source clients; after all, the SSH client is used as a system administration tool, which potentially gives it access to many servers and passwords.

PuTTY also runs on Unix and is available in the software repositories of virtually all Linux and BSD variants.

File Transfer via an SSH Connection

Except as a protocol for a remote terminal, SSH can also be used as a protocol for file transfer. *SCP* and *SFTP* are two file transfer protocols based on SSH.

SFTP

In its use, *SFTP* (*SSH File Transfer Protocol*) can be compared to *FTP*: a client connects to a server, and the user can interactively manage files on the server, and between the client and the server, until the connection is cut.

As indicated before, the option Subsystem sftp must be activated in the sshd configuration to be able to use *SFTP*.

```
$ sftp dimitri@green.example.com
sftp> pwd
Remote working directory: /home/dimitri
sftp> ls
bin  Documents  Downloads  logo.png  todo.txt
sftp> get logo.png
Fetching /home/dimitri/logo.png to logo.png
/home/dimitri/logo.png        100%    621    6.2KB/s    00:00
sftp> exit
$
```

The `sftp` command also loads the SSH configuration, so if the user's `~/.ssh/config` contains the previously described `Host` definition, the following command will also establish the connection:

```
$ sftp grn
```

Windows users can use *SFTP* on the command prompt with the help of *PSFTP* that is part of *PuTTY*:

```
C:\Users\Dimitri> psftp dimitri@green.example.com
```

The available *SFTP* commands are listed, respectively, in `sftp(1)` and on the PuTTY website; these sources also list the available command-line parameters.

Clearly, graphical clients also exist for *SFTP*. Virtually all graphical file managers for Unix support the *SFTP* protocol; instead of a local path, a URL as the following can then be given to connect to the `/srv/www` directory on the server *green.example.com* using the username *dimitri*:

```
sftp://dimitri@green.example.com/srv/www
```

WinSCP is an open source graphical client for Windows, which is partially based on *PuTTY*'s source code. A link to the website can be found in the online addendum for this book.

SCP

SCP (*Secure Copy Protocol*) is a one-shot application: for each file or directory that is sent or retrieved, the command is executed again. The following command will send the file `logo.png` to user *dimitri*'s home directory on server *green.example.com*; the connection is established with the username *dimitri*, and obviously, the transaction is aborted if there is no account named *dimitri* on the server or if the user does not provide the correct password for that account.

```
$ scp ./logo.png dimitri@green.example.com:/home/dimitri
```

The hostname and the name of the directory on the host are separated by a colon. If the name of the directory does not begin with a slash, it is considered to be relative to the user's home directory on the server.

The same command is used to copy a file from the server to the client:

```
$ scp dimitri@green.example.com:Documents/Contract.odt .
```

Since the `scp` command also loads the SSH configuration, the preceding commands can be abbreviated as follows, if the user has included the previously described `Host` definition in the file `~/.ssh/config`:

```
$ scp ./logo.png grn:
```

```
$ scp grn:Documents/Contract.odt .
```

The OpenSSH developers have indicated in April 2019 that they feel that *SCP* is an obsolete and inflexible protocol, and they advise to replace its use with *SFTP*. However, because of *SCP*'s one-shot approach for file transfer, this command is very suited for the use in scripts, especially when combined with the SSH keys that are described in a next section.

The `scp` command can also be used to copy files between two external servers:

```
$ scp green:/tmp/packages.txt blue:/tmp/packages.green.txt
```

Obviously, this requires an account on both servers.

The Windows SFTP client *WinSCP* began its life as an SCP client and still supports this protocol.

rsync

The *rsync* package allows the synchronization of entire directory trees. By default, *rsync* uses SSH as its transport protocol, combining *rsync*'s speed with *ssh*'s encryption.

Since both the possibilities and the documentation for *rsync* are very extensive, the system administrator is referred to `rsync(1)` for more information.

SSH Keys Instead of Passwords

Good passwords are often hard to remember. And bad passwords, obviously, are a security risk. A way for SSH to circumvent these problems is the use of cryptographic key pairs.

A cryptographic key pair consists of two (virtual) keys, one of those is to be kept secret (*private key*) and the other is not (*public key*). Messages that have been encrypted with the public key can only be decrypted with the private key; anyone in possession of the public key can send a message to the owner of the private key, and the owner of the private key is the only person who can read the message. And the other way around, a message can be signed with the private key, after which the public key can be used to verify the identity of the private key and thus of the sender; the public key can also be used to verify that the message has not been modified between the sending and the verification. Clearly, the owner of the private key is expected to store the private key in a safe place and to protect it with a password. This system of a private and a public key is called *public-key cryptography* or *asymmetric cryptography*.

SSH can make use of this form of cryptography for authentication. The user generates a key pair and installs the public key in their home directory on the server (or asks the system administrator to do so). When the user connects to the server, instead of a password, the SSH client sends a message that was signed with the *private key*; if the signature matches the *public key* that was installed on the server, access is granted. Even though the user must still enter a password—the one for the private key—this password does not leave the client, minimizing the chances that it will be cracked.

It is possible to generate key pairs without a password, but it is recommended to not do so unless there is no other choice, such as for use in scripts. In this case, it is advised to change the permissions for the key file to make it accessible only to a single user.

A user can generate multiple key pairs, which allows the user to have a different key for each server. And multiple public keys per user can be installed on a server, which allows the user to have a different key pair for the same server on each client machine.

Generating a Key Pair

The key pair is generated on the client machine.

Unix

On Unix systems, the tools for key management are installed with the SSH client. The ssh-keygen command is used to generate a key pair. Even though ssh-keygen accepts a large number of command-line parameters, the default settings generate keys that suffice largely in most situations; ssh-keygen will ask for information that is needed to complete the generation of the key pair.

```
$ ssh-keygen
Generating public/private rsa key pair.
Enter file in which to save the key (/home/dimitri/.ssh/id_rsa):
Enter passphrase (empty for no passphrase):
Enter same passphrase again:
Your identification has been saved in
    /home/dimitri/.ssh/id_rsa.
Your public key has been saved in
    /home/dimitri/.ssh/id_rsa.pub.
The key fingerprint is:
SHA256:GTo+RWvlJ+LZZNMZpXB5oZWV8dzOgz7sdYH1phDQ/yM dimitri@dimpc
The key's randomart image is:
+---[RSA 3072]----+
|          o...+=+|
|           +o=ooo|
|         o . =o .+|
|        o * . +=o.|
|       o S * =o +=|
|      . = * +oE ++|
|       o o .  +o.o|
|        .    . o .|
|             .   |
+----[SHA256]-----+
```

In the preceding example, the user has accepted the name for the key as suggested by ssh-keygen (id_rsa). However, the user is entirely free in the choice of name, and if they have multiple keys to log in to multiple servers, for example, it is recommended to use recognizable key filenames (like key-green-dimitri); for organization and oversight, it is advisable to always store the keys in the ~/.ssh directory.

The *fingerprint* and *randomart image* should be sent to the system administrator who is charged with the installation of the key on the server for easy validation of the public key. Obviously, the *fingerprint* and *randomart image* are not sent in the same email as the public key; they could be sent in a chat message (the fingerprint and randomart image do not need to be kept secret) or in a separate email. If both were sent in the same email and an attacker would manage to intercept that email, it would be relatively easy to replace both and trick the system administrator into the installation of an alternative key.

The system administrator then regenerates a *fingerprint* and *randomart image* for the received public key and compares those to the data received in the chat. The fingerprint and the ASCII image have the same meaning and value, but for humans images are easier to compare than long strings of seemingly random characters.

```
# ssh-keygen -lvf ./rcvd-keys/key-green-dimitri.pub
```

Windows

The *PuTTYgen* application, which is part of the *PuTTY* installation, is used to generate key pairs on Windows.

WinSCP, the graphical *SFTP* client for Windows, can also make use of the key pairs generated by *PuTTYgen*.

PuTTY cannot make use of key pairs generated using the Unix `ssh-keygen` command. The Unix version of `puttygen` (lowercase and command line only) can be used to generate key pairs that can be used by the OpenSSH client, but those keys cannot be used by *PuTTY* itself.

Installing the Key on the Server

After validation of the received public key and the user's identity, the system administrator copies the contents of this text file to the file `~/.ssh/authorized_keys` (in the home directory of the user in question); the entire content is put on a single line. Empty lines in this file are ignored, and comments start with a hash sign (#); furthermore, the last field of the line can be modified freely. It is advised to make use of these possibilities to organize the data in this file, because public keys alone are difficult to distinguish.

Normally, the user also has write privileges for this file, so once the user has access to the server, they can also add and delete keys. Obviously, apart from the user (and *root*) nobody should have write privileges for this file.

Instead of SCP/SFTP and then copy/paste, the `ssh-copy-id` command can alternatively be used to copy the public key to a server and install it in the `authorized_keys` file. This prevents copy/paste errors; however, it also prevents the addition of comments in the file for the organization of the keys.

```
$ ssh-copy-id -i ~/.ssh/key-green-dimitri.pub dimitri@grn
```

It is obvious that for this to work, the user should already have a key (or a password) on the server.

Using a Key to Connect

Once the public key has been installed on the server, the private key can be used to log in.

To not have to repeatedly enter the password for the private key, applications have been developed that keep the keys in memory, so that a user only needs to enter the password for the first use of a key.

Unix

The OpenSSH command-line client's -i parameter is used to refer to the private key to be used:

```
$ ssh -i ~/.ssh/id_rsa dimitri@green.example.com
```

It is also possible to define the *IdentityFile* option in ~/.ssh/config:

```
Host grn
  HostName green.example.com
  User dimitri
  IdentityFile /home/dimitri/.ssh/id_rsa
```

The key's password is asked when logging in:

```
$ ssh grn
Enter passphrase for key '/home/dimitri/.ssh/id_rsa':
```

The ssh-agent application, which was installed together with the SSH client, can be used to keep the keys in memory, so that the user only has to enter the password once. More information about this application can be found in ssh-agent(1).

Windows

To use an SSH key with PuTTY, the key is simply selected through **Connection ➤ SSH ➤ Auth ➤ Private key file for authentication**.

PuTTY also includes an application that keeps unlocked keys in memory for reuse. The online PuTTY documentation explains how to start this application, *Pageant*, and how to add keys.

The graphical SFTP client for Windows, *WinSCP*, can also make use of *Pageant*.

Rejecting Password-Based Authentication

Now that authentication with the help of SSH keys has been configured, the authentication with the help of passwords can be disabled; this will force users to use keys, which is more secure. Clearly, only password authentication for SSH is disabled, retaining the possibility for password authentication on the (remote) console in case of an emergency.

To disable password-based authentication in OpenSSH, only a single parameter in /etc/ssh/sshd_config needs to be modified:

```
PasswordAuthentication no
```

On FreeBSD, this is the default value.

After a restart of the sshd service, authentication will only be allowed with the use of SSH keys.

Summary

This chapter introduced the reader to SSH, arguably the Unix administrator's most important tool. The installation and configuration of the SSH server were discussed, and the reader learned to start a remote terminal over SSH, as well as to transfer files over the encrypted protocol; the client side of the matter was discussed for both Unix and Windows. Secure cryptographic keys were generated to replace the less secure passwords, after which the authentication with the help of passwords was disabled on the server, forcing the users to use SSH keys only.

The next chapter will discuss the synchronization of the system clock and the scheduling of both recurring and unique tasks.

## CHAPTER 8

Task Scheduling

To keep the work interesting and to save time, it is important to automate repetitive and recurring tasks as much as possible. The most important and most commonly used application to do this on Unix systems is *cron*.

Network Time Protocol (NTP)

To reliably schedule tasks, it is important that the system clock is precise. *NTP* (*Network Time Protocol*) prevents the clock from deviating too much by periodically synchronizing it with other, more precise clocks on the network. These clocks do not need to be in the same time zone: *NTP* servers and clients use UTC standard time to synchronize, and the client corrects the time for the configured time zone. A client can synchronize with multiple clients; this is even recommended to enhance reliability.

The package that provides an NTP daemon and client is simply called *ntp*. A popular alternative is *OpenNTPD*, which was developed for OpenBSD and is available in the FreeBSD Ports Collection and the Debian software repositories.

To allow the synchronization of the server's clock with external NTP servers, UDP port 123 must be opened in the firewall for outbound traffic. If the server should also serve as an NTP server for other computers, UDP port 123 must also be opened for inbound traffic. This latter functionality is not discussed in this book, but can be easily enabled with the help of the man page for the configuration file.

Normally, no changes need to be made to the configuration file except if, for privacy or other considerations, the server should synchronize with other NTP servers or the server must also function as an NTP server.

More information is available in `ntpd(8)` and the man pages that that man page refers to.

© Robert La Lau 2021
R. La Lau, *Practical Internet Server Configuration*, https://doi.org/10.1007/978-1-4842-6960-2_8

FreeBSD

On FreeBSD, *ntp* is part of the base system, so it is already installed. To be able to start the ntpd daemon, the following line must be added to /etc/rc.conf:

```
ntpd_enable="YES"
```

This will make the NTP daemon start at boot time. A manual start is done as with other daemons:

```
freebsd# service ntpd start
```

The configuration file is /etc/ntp.conf.

Debian

On Debian, the *openntpd* package is installed by default. It is not necessary to replace this with the *ntp* package.

The configuration file is /etc/openntpd/ntpd.conf, and the openntpd service is started automatically.

CentOS

On CentOS, none of the packages are installed by default; the *ntp* package is available in the default software repositories.

The service is not started automatically after its installation.

```
centos# yum install ntp
centos# systemctl enable ntpd
centos# systemctl start ntpd
```

The configuration file is /etc/ntp.conf.

Cron

Cron is a daemon that checks every minute to see whether there are tasks to be executed and executes them if there are. The name *cron* comes from χρόνος (*chronos*), the Greek word for time.

A task that is scheduled with *cron* is called a *cronjob*, and the file where *cronjobs* are stored is called a *crontab* (*cron table*). Examples of common cronjobs are the creation of backups, checking for available updates, periodic scans for viruses and *rootkits*, sending mailings, and so on.

In principle, each user can have their own crontab, but the system administrator can limit the access to *cron* using so-called `allow` and `deny` files. If an `allow` file exists and the name of a certain user does not appear in this file, this user cannot make use of *cron*. If no `allow` file exists, but a `deny` file exists and the name of a certain user appears in this file, this user cannot make use of *cron*. If neither an `allow` file nor a `deny` file exist, all users can make use of *cron*. On FreeBSD, the `allow` file is called `/var/cron/allow`, and the `deny` file is called `/var/cron/deny`; on Linux, they are `/etc/cron.allow` and `/etc/cron.deny`, respectively.

The command to display and edit the crontab is called `crontab`. To display the crontab, the `-l` (*list*) switch is used, and to edit the crontab, the `-e` (*edit*) switch is used. The *root* user can also add the `-u` argument to display or edit other users' crontabs.

```
$ crontab -e
```

```
# crontab -l -u diane
```

A crontab can contain cronjobs and definitions of variables, one cronjob or definition per line. Empty lines and lines beginning with a hash sign (#) are ignored. By default, cronjobs are executed with only three environment variables: *SHELL*, *LOGNAME*, and *HOME*. The values for the variables *LOGNAME* and *HOME* are taken from the cronjob owner's `/etc/passwd` entry, and the *SHELL* variable is set to `/bin/sh`; the *LOGNAME* variable cannot be overwritten in the crontab. For the rest, the owner of the crontab can define any variable necessary for the execution of the cronjobs. One special variable can be defined: *MAILTO*; if this variable is defined, all output for the cronjobs in the crontab will be sent to this email address.

The line for a cronjob consists of six whitespace-separated fields: the first five fields determine the time at which the cronjob must be executed, and the rest of the line is the command to be executed. These are the five fields that determine the time in this exact order:

- **Minute**

  Allowed values: 0–59

- **Hour**

  Allowed values: 0–23

- **Day of the month**

  Allowed values: 1–31

- **Month**

  Allowed values: 1–12

- **Day of the week**

  Allowed values: 0–7 (0 and 7 are both Sundays)

The 24-hour clock is used for the time specification.

In addition to single values, also series (1-5), sets (1,3,5), and combinations thereof (0,2-5,7,9-11) can be specified. A special value is *, which represents any allowed value; a cronjob with an asterisk in the *day-of-the-month* field will be executed every day of the month (unless the execution is prevented by the value in one of the other fields). More ways to define the execution time of cronjobs are described in crontab(5).

An example crontab could look as follows:

```
# Send possible output to Dimitri.
MAILTO=dimitri@example.com

# Search for commands in these three directories.
PATH=/bin:/usr/bin:/usr/local/bin

# Back up the accounting records every night at 3:15.
15 3 * * * tar -cf /data/backup.$(date +%F) /data/accounting

# Send a mail to everybody, each Friday at 4:30 pm.
30 16 * * 5 echo "Have a good weekend!" | mail all@example.com

0 7 1,15 * * echo "Day 1 and 15 of each month, at 7:00 am"

0 13 1 1,5,9 * echo "1 January, May, September at 1:00 pm"

15 8 13 * 5 echo "Every Friday the 13th at 8:15 am"
```

In addition to user crontabs, there are also system crontabs. These crontabs are stored in the file /etc/crontab and the directory /etc/cron.d.

The format for system crontabs resembles that of user crontabs. However, since the system crontab does not contain cronjobs for a single user, but can contain those of multiple users, an additional field is added between the time specification and the command to execute; this field contains the username for the cronjob's owner. The system crontab could contain cronjobs like the following:

```
15 12 5 * * diane echo "5th of each month at 12:15 pm, for Diane"
30 8 * * 1-5 root echo "Each working day at 8:30 am, for root"
```

The system crontabs are not modified with the help of the crontab command, but with a regular text editor.

Linux also provides the directories /etc/cron.daily, /etc/cron.hourly, /etc/cron.monthly, and /etc/cron.weekly, where scripts can be installed to be executed daily, hourly, monthly, and weekly, respectively.

In this same manner, FreeBSD provides the directories /etc/periodic and /usr/local/etc/periodic and their respective sub-directories. The scripts in these directories can be enabled and disabled; the file /etc/defaults/periodic.conf shows which scripts are enabled by default. To enable additional scripts, the corresponding variables should be defined in the file /etc/periodic.conf, which can be created if it doesn't exist yet (/etc/defaults/periodic.conf may be overwritten with software updates). The variables to be defined can be found in the scripts in question.

Anacron

A *cron* variant that should also be mentioned is *anacron*. This daemon functions on the same principle as *cron*, but does not assume that the server is always powered on. If a cronjob was not executed because the server was switched off, *cron* will not execute it at all; *anacron* will still execute it as soon as the server is powered on again.

Since the server described in this book is supposed to always be powered on, *anacron* is not discussed further here.

at

The at command is used to schedule non-recurring tasks. This application is not installed by default on Debian and CentOS; on Debian, the daemon is started automatically after the installation.

```
debian# apt install at
```

```
centos# yum install at
centos# systemctl enable atd
centos# systemctl start atd
```

To schedule the execution of a command, the command is sent to the at command's *STDIN* in text form; the time and date can be specified as command-line parameters. The following command, for example, schedules a reboot for next Saturday morning at half past three:

```
# echo "reboot" | at 03:30 Saturday
```

The command that will be executed on Saturday morning at 3:30 is not echo reboot, but reboot; the echo is only used to send the command to at. Another practical example is this one:

- The system administrator has redefined the firewall rules, but is not entirely sure of their correctness.

- Before loading the new rules into the firewall, the system administrator creates an at job that will reload the old, functioning rules back into the firewall in five minutes.

  ```
  # echo "nft -f /root/rules.good" | at now + 5 minutes
  ```

- The new rules can now be loaded into the firewall with confidence, knowing that even if the system administrator gets locked out, the old rules will be effective again in five minutes, allowing the administrator back in.

The atq (*at queue*) command displays the scheduled *at jobs* for the user who executes the command or for all users if the command is executed by *root*.

The atrm command is used to delete *at jobs*; the argument for this command is the *job id* from the output of atq.

The system administrator can use the at.deny and at.allow files to specify which users can or cannot make use of at. More information about this and other details can be found in the miscellaneous man pages.

On Debian and CentOS, *at* is a daemon (atd) that executes scheduled commands every minute. However, on FreeBSD at is a command that is executed by cron every five minutes; it is therefore possible that *at jobs* on FreeBSD are executed a few minutes later than scheduled.

Summary

In this chapter, the reader learned to schedule jobs, both recurring and non-recurring. To do this effectively, the server was also configured to synchronize its time with time servers on the internet.

The next chapter will explain the basics of web server configuration, and a first virtual host will be created.

CHAPTER 9

Web Server Part 1: Apache/Nginx Basics

The web server is the software that makes the website(s) accessible. The web server does this by listening on the ports 80 and 443 and serving the files in certain directories as responses to requests received on those ports. Port 80 is the default port for HTTP (*Hypertext Transfer Protocol*), and port 443 is the port for the encrypted HTTPS variant (the *S* meaning *Secure*). Even though web servers can usually be configured to listen on other ports, a client like a web browser or a web crawler will always send HTTP and HTTPS requests without an explicit port indication to ports 80 and 443, respectively; if the user does not specify a protocol, clients will usually fall back to HTTP.

The configuration as described in this book ensures that all requests to port 80 are always redirected to port 443, assuring that all communications are always encrypted. However, in some parts of the world cryptography and/or encryption are forbidden or regulated. The system administrator who is subject to such regulations can easily adapt the configuration to a non-encrypted setup; the given configuration examples will speak for themselves.

The messages sent between the client and the web server consist of two components: the headers and the body or payload. The headers are used for the communication between the client and the web server and are not shown to the user; the body comprises the information that is presented to the user (the website) and any information the user may send to the web server, like the data from a web form.

The client can use several different methods to send requests to the web server. The most commonly used methods for "regular" websites are GET and POST. A GET request consists solely of headers, without a body; limited data can be included with the request as part of the URL (*Uniform Resource Locator*), the requested file's address. A POST

© Robert La Lau 2021
R. La Lau, *Practical Internet Server Configuration*, https://doi.org/10.1007/978-1-4842-6960-2_9

request consists of both headers and a body, which allows for the inclusion of more data; this so-called request body can contain entire files. Some other methods are described in Chapter 13, "Web Server Part 2: Advanced Apache/Nginx", when WebDAV is discussed.

This is an example of the communication that takes place for the request of *www.example.com*:

> **User ➤ Web browser**:
>
> Types *www.example.com* into the location bar + `Enter`.
>
> **Web browser ➤ DNS server**, port 53:
>
> What is the IP address for host *www.example.com*?
>
> **DNS server ➤ Web browser**:
>
> The IP address for *www.example.com* is `198.51.100.156`.
>
> **Web browser ➤ 198.51.100.156**, port 80:
>
> Send me the page "/" for host *www.example.com*.
>
> **Web server ➤ Web browser**:
>
> Send that request to *www.example.com*'s port 443.
>
> **Web browser ➤ 198.51.100.156**, port 443:
>
> Send me the page "/" for host *www.example.com*.
>
> **Web server ➤ Web browser**:
>
> Here is the encrypted page *www.example.com/index.html*.
>
> **Web browser ➤ User**:
>
> Displays the page and changes the protocol in the location bar to `https`.

Obviously, this is a very simplified representation of the reality.
A few important points to keep in mind with this example:

- Even though the final result, the `index.html` page, is encrypted before it is sent, this is not the case for the communication transcribed previously. A party who manages to intercept this traffic may not be able to discover the contents of the response, but they will know the address that was requested.

- Generally, a web page is not a single entity, but consists of multiple files; images, for example, are usually requested and sent separately from the initially requested (HTML) page. These additional files may originate from different sources and are not necessarily encrypted as well.

- The preceding (simplified) communication concerns a GET request. When a POST request is sent to port 443, its payload will also be encrypted. However, if the communication takes place with a redirect on port 80, as in the given example, the payload will not be encrypted for the initial request to port 80.

Most web servers can be extended with functionalities like authentication and authorization and the integration or interpretation of programming languages for serving dynamically generated content.

Web servers can also generally be configured to host multiple websites for multiple domains and/or subdomains. This is called virtual hosting, which means that the server presents itself under multiple hostnames.

The two most commonly used web servers are Apache and Nginx (pronounced as engine x). This book describes the configuration for both. Since normally only a single server listens on a certain port, it is up to the system administrator to select one. Because this decision is mainly subjective and depends on personal requirements and wishes, this book does not discuss this choice; many websites exist that compare the different web servers and their functionalities. In short, the list of differences mostly boils down to Nginx being a bit faster and needing less memory and processing power, while Apache provides more documentation and more modules for added functionalities. Both web servers serve about 30% of the internet's websites/servers.

If so desired, both web servers can be installed at the same time for testing purposes, for example. However, to be able to start one server, the other must be stopped, or the web servers must be configured to listen on different ports; without other modifications, such as a reverse proxy, no more than a single daemon can listen on a port at the same time.

The following pages describe the installation and initial configuration for both Apache and Nginx and for some modules that extend their functionality. The web servers will be configured to allow serving multiple websites on a single server. This technique is called virtual hosting, and the websites are called virtual hosts. A first virtual host will also be created. In a following chapter—after the SSL/TLS certificates have been installed for encryption of web and email traffic—the web server configuration will be extended further.

Apart from the web servers themselves, PHP will also be installed. PHP is by far the most commonly used programming language for the development of websites and web applications, and if the server is being configured to serve websites, it is very probable that these will be developed in PHP.

To serve websites on the default ports, the inbound TCP ports 80 (HTTP) and 443 (HTTPS) must be opened in the firewall. Even if only HTTPS sites are served, it is recommended to open both ports in the firewall. This allows the web server to be configured to redirect all requests for port 80 to port 443.

Directory

Even though all operating systems and web servers seem to have their own preference as to the directory from which the websites should be served, this book follows the Filesystem Hierarchy Standard that was described in Chapter 2, "Unix and POSIX in a Few Words".

```
# mkdir -p /srv/www
```

In this directory, a sub-directory will be created for each website that will be served.

To prevent unauthorized access to the files of the websites, it is recommended to create a user and a group specifically for the development of websites and to make the new directory accessible only to this user and group; obviously, all web developers should be members of this group. The examples in this book assume that this user and this group exist, and both have the name webdev; the webdev user's home directory is /srv/www. Chapter 5, "User Management and Permissions", explains how to create users and groups.

```
# chown webdev:webdev /srv/www
# chmod 0771 /srv/www
```

The permissions for this directory are 0771, which is all permissions for the user and group, and only execute rights for other users. This allows other users to "traverse" this directory to reach its sub-directories, without being able to see the other contents of this directory. This is used to allow the web server and the PHP-FPM instances to access the websites.

Apache

Apache is the oldest of the two selected web servers and has been the common standard for a long time. A web server administrator will not be able to avoid Apache, especially with companies that have been around for some time.

The actual name for this web server is Apache HTTP server. The HTTP server is only one of over 200 projects managed by The Apache Software Foundation.

Installation on FreeBSD

At the moment of writing, the only version available for FreeBSD is Apache 2.4.

```
freebsd# pkg search apache
freebsd# pkg install apache24
```

The configuration files are installed into /usr/local/etc/apache24.
Apache is not started automatically.

```
freebsd# service apache24 enable
freebsd# service apache24 start
```

The most important Apache modules are installed together with the web server. The names of the Apache modules all start with mod_, so more modules can be found with the following command:

```
freebsd# pkg search mod_
```

If Apache was installed from the Ports Collection, the most practical way to (un)install modules is to check and uncheck the desired modules in the Apache installation options and reinstall the web server.

```
freebsd# portsnap fetch update
freebsd# cd /usr/ports/www/apache24
freebsd# make config
freebsd# make reinstall clean
```

After reinstallation, Apache must be restarted.

Installation on Debian

On Debian, Apache has been split up into several packages and is called apache2 (the 2 indicating the version number: 2.4).

```
debian# apt install apache2 apache2-data apache2-utils
```

Apache's configuration files are installed into /etc/apache2.

If no other web server is active, Apache is started automatically after installation.

Many Apache modules are installed by default. More modules can be found with this command:

```
debian# apt search "libapache2-mod"
```

Apache must be restarted after modules have been installed or removed.

Installation on CentOS

Apache is called httpd (HTTP daemon) on CentOS and has been split up into two separate packages.

```
centos# yum install httpd httpd-tools
```

The configuration is installed into /etc/httpd.

Once installed, Apache must be started manually.

```
centos# systemctl enable httpd
centos# systemctl start httpd
```

A large number of Apache modules is installed by default. More modules can be found with the help of the following command:

```
centos# yum search apache mod_
```

First Test

If the installation succeeded, a first web page can be requested using Lynx on the command line:

```
$ lynx localhost
```

The default test page for Apache is very simple and only contains the text "It works!". Debian and CentOS have added some more text to this. Terminate Lynx by tapping *q* and then *Enter*.

If Apache does indeed say that it works, it is a good idea to verify that this page is also available from elsewhere on the internet (home, work). Obviously, the address to use is then *http://green.example.com/* and not *localhost*.

If the page is accessible from the command line, but not from the internet, the cause for this can probably be found in the DNS configuration or in the firewall configuration.

Note that the test page is not installed in /srv/www, but in /usr/local/www/apache24/data (FreeBSD), /var/www/html (Debian), or /usr/share/httpd/noindex (CentOS).

Configuration

Just like all the systems have their own username for the Apache daemon (*www* on FreeBSD, *www-data* on Debian, and *apache* on CentOS), they also have their own organization for the configuration files. It is impossible and unnecessary to discuss all configuration directives here—they are all discussed extensively on the Apache website—so only the most important ones, which are crucial to the functioning of the web server, will be highlighted.

A few important changes that will be made to the configuration:

- Switch from the default prefork *MPM* (*Multi-Processing Module*) to the event MPM. The Multi-Processing Modules are responsible for the reception of the requests and the transfer of these requests to the child processes. By changing the MPM, Apache will be able to process more connections while at the same time requiring less memory.

- Enable the *proxy_fcgi_module*. This module will enable Apache to communicate with the PHP interpreter; this will be discussed later in this chapter.

The initial configuration file loads additional configuration files with the help of the Include and IncludeOptional directives. Files loaded in this fashion are sorted alphanumerically per directory. This is why some of the filenames start with a number: this forces the web server to load the configuration files in a certain order.

Comments in the Apache configuration files start with a hash sign (#); text from a hash sign until the end of a line will not be interpreted by Apache.

FreeBSD

The configuration is installed in /usr/local/etc/apache24. The main configuration file in this directory is httpd.conf; this is the file that is loaded when the web server is started, and other configuration files are loaded from this file.

The most important directives in httpd.conf:

- **LoadModule**

    This directive appears multiple times, be it with a hash sign at the beginning of the line or not. This is used to enable and disable the modules: if there is no hash sign at the beginning of the line, the module is activated.

    All modules are discussed extensively on the Apache website, including their individual configuration options.

    Modules that must be enabled in any case:

    - mpm_event_module

    - proxy_module

    - proxy_fcgi_module

    - rewrite_module

    Modules that must be disabled in any case:

    - mpm_prefork_module

    - mpm_worker_module

- **User www**

    Group www

    The username and group name under which the web server daemon is run. These are not the same as the username and group name under which PHP scripts are executed. Normally, these need not be changed, but if they are, the user and group must exist prior to the web server being (re)started.

- **ServerAdmin www-admin@example.com**

  This address is displayed on some error pages. This address should be noted down; when the mail server is configured in a later chapter, this alias must be created.

- **DocumentRoot "/usr/local/www/apache24/data"**

  A hash sign should be placed at the beginning of this line, as well as on the lines below this line, from `<Directory>` up to and including `</Directory>`.

  This block defines the installation directory for a website, but the configurations for the websites will be placed in separate files in a dedicated directory.

- **ScriptAlias /cgi-bin/ "/usr/local/www/apache24/cgi-bin/"**

  This directive should be disabled as well, together with the `<Directory> </Directory>` block a few lines below, which refers to the same directory.

  A cgi-bin is a directory where scripts are installed that can be served by the web server, like a contact form or a forum; these scripts and directories will be configured per website, if needed.

- **Include etc/apache24/extra/httpd-mpm.conf**

  This line should be enabled. This file defines how Apache manages child processes.

- **Include etc/apache24/extra/httpd-default.conf**

  This line should also be enabled. This file defines some default values.

- **IncludeOptional etc/apache24/virtual-hosts/*.conf**

  This line must be added at the end of the file. It instructs Apache to load any configuration files in the `virtual-hosts` directory; this directory will contain the configuration files for the websites hosted by this server.

And clearly, the directory mentioned in that last point must be created.

```
freebsd# mkdir /usr/local/etc/apache24/virtual-hosts
```

All files in the configuration directory and its sub-directories can be freely modified, as long as the documentation and some common sense are used.

After the configuration has been modified, Apache must be instructed to load the new configuration:

```
freebsd# service apache24 reload
```

Debian

The configuration files have been installed in /etc/apache2. The main configuration file in this directory is apache2.conf; this file is loaded when the web server is started, and additional files are loaded from this file. A number of variables are used in apache2.conf and other files; these variables are defined in the file envvars.

A single parameter can be added to apache2.conf:

- **ServerAdmin www-admin@example.com**

  This address is displayed on some error pages. This address should be noted down; when the mail server is configured in a following chapter, this alias must be created.

  This directive can be added anywhere in the file.

On Debian, additional configuration files are loaded by creating a symlink in the conf-enabled directory to the actual file in the conf-available directory; Apache loads all files for which a link exists in the conf-enabled directory.

In the file conf-available/security.conf, the following block should be enabled; hence, the hash signs at the beginning of these lines should be removed. This blocks the web server's access to the entire file system by default. The comments in the file indicate that this might prevent certain web applications from functioning, but this can never be more important than the server's security. If necessary, it will be evaluated on a case-by-case basis how to work around this limitation without compromising security.

```
<Directory />
    AllowOverride None
    Require all denied
</Directory>
```

The link `conf-enabled/serve-cgi-bin.conf` must be deleted. A cgi-bin is a directory where scripts are installed that can be served by the web server, like a contact form or a forum; these scripts and directories will be configured per website, if needed.

```
debian# rm /etc/apache2/conf-enabled/serve-cgi-bin.conf
```

Modules are enabled and disabled in the same manner: if a symlink exists in the `mods-enabled` directory to a file in the `mods-available` directory, the module is enabled. Modules that must be enabled in any case:

- mpm_event_module
- proxy_module
- proxy_fcgi_module
- rewrite_module
- socache_shmcb_module
- ssl_module

Modules that must be disabled in any case:

- mpm_prefork_module
- mpm_event_module

```
debian# cd mods-enabled
debian# for m in {mpm_event,proxy,proxy_fcgi,rewrite,socache_shmcb,ssl}; do
        for s in {conf,load}; do
          if [ ! -e "./${m}.${s}" ]; then
            if [ -f "../mods-available/${m}.${s}" ]; then
              ln -s "../mods-available/${m}.${s}" .
            fi
          fi
        done
      done
debian# for m in {prefork,worker}; do
        for s in {conf,load}; do
          if [ -e "./mpm_${m}.${s}" ]; then
            rm "./mpm_${m}.${s}"
```

```
            fi
        done
    done
```

More information about the different modules and the functionalities that they offer can be found on the Apache website.

The configurations for the websites to be hosted are stored in the `sites-available` directory; a symlink in the `sites-enabled` directory, to the file in question, enables a site. The link `sites-enabled/000-default.conf` should be deleted; the server will start with an empty configuration for the. websites to be served.

All files in the configuration directory and its sub-directories can be freely modified with the help of the documentation and some common sense.

After the configuration has been modified, Apache must be instructed to load the new configuration:

```
debian# systemctl reload apache2
```

CentOS

The. configuration has been installed in `/etc/httpd`. The main configuration file in this directory is `conf/httpd.conf`; this file is loaded when the web server is started, and additional configuration files are loaded from this file.

Settings to be made in `conf/httpd.conf`:

- **ServerAdmin www-admin@example.com**

   This address is displayed on some error pages. This address should be noted down; when the mail server is configured in a following chapter, this alias must be created.

- **DocumentRoot "/var/www/html"**

   This line must be disabled, as do the two `<Directory>` `</Directory>` blocks below it that refer to `/var/www` and `/var/www/html`, respectively.

   These lines define the installation directory for a website, but the configurations for the websites will be stored in separate files in a different directory.

- **ScriptAlias /cgi-bin/ "/usr/local/www/apache24/cgi-bin/"**

  This directive should be disabled as well, together with the
  `<Directory>` `</Directory>` block a few lines below, which refers
  to the same directory.

  A cgi-bin is a directory where scripts are installed that can be
  served by the web server, like a contact form or a forum; these
  scripts and directories will be configured per website, if needed.

- **IncludeOptional virtual-hosts/*.conf**

  This line must be added to the end of the file. It instructs Apache
  to load any configuration files in the `virtual-hosts` directory;
  this directory will contain the configuration files for the websites
  hosted by this server.

And clearly, the directory defined in that last point must be created.

```
centos# mkdir /etc/httpd/virtual-hosts
```

The modules are loaded by the files in the directory `conf.modules.d` by means
of the `LoadModule` directive. In the `conf.modules.d/00-mpm.conf` file, the
mpm_prefork_module must be disabled, and the mpm_event_module must be
enabled. In `conf.modules.d/00-proxy.conf`, at least the proxy_module and the
proxy_fcgi_module must be enabled.

More configuration files can be found in the `conf.d` directory. In the
`conf.d/welcome.conf` file, hash signs should be placed at the beginning of all lines.

All files in the configuration directory and its sub-directories can be modified freely,
as long as the documentation and some common sense are used.

After the configuration has been modified, Apache must be instructed to load the
new configuration:

```
centos# systemctl reload httpd
```

.htaccess

Most directives that can be put in the configuration files can also be put in a file named
`.htaccess` in the website directories (the system administrator decides which directives
can and cannot be used in that file). An advantage of this could be that the proprietor
of a website could (partly) configure the web server without needing the assistance of

a system administrator. A disadvantage, however, is that the web server must look for this file with every request and interpret the directives it contains and not only in the directory for the current request but also in all its parent directories. A lot of memory and processing power can therefore be saved by not using the `.htaccess` file, but instead copy its instructions to the virtual host configuration, if possible. This possibility is discussed further in a later chapter.

Nginx

Nginx entered the market in 2004, and its market share has grown enormously since. According to some statistics, Nginx took over the status of market leader from Apache in 2020; according to other statistics, this will probably happen in 2021.

Just like Apache, Nginx can be extended with additional functionality with the help of modules.

Installation on FreeBSD

Several Nginx packages are available. The nginx-full package installs all available modules.

```
freebsd# pkg search nginx
freebsd# pkg install nginx-full
```

The Nginx configuration files are installed into `/usr/local/etc/nginx`.
Nginx is not started automatically.

```
freebsd# service nginx enable
freebsd# service nginx start
```

Installation on Debian

Debian knows three different Nginx packages: nginx-light, nginx-full, and nginx-extras; the differences become clear when the `apt show` output for all three packages is compared. The nginx-full package installs all available modules.

```
debian# apt install nginx-full
```

The Nginx configuration is installed into /etc/nginx.

If no other web server is active, Nginx is started automatically when the installation is finished.

Installation on CentOS

Nginx is not available in the default CentOS software repositories; before the web server can be installed, Fedora *EPEL* (*Extra Packages for Enterprise Linux*) must be added. EPEL is a software collection containing additional packages for distributions like CentOS, Red Hat Enterprise Linux, and Oracle Linux; the collection is maintained by members of the Fedora community.

```
centos# yum install epel-release
```

Once EPEL has been added, Nginx can be installed. The nginx package installs all available modules as dependencies.

```
centos# yum install nginx
```

The Nginx configuration is installed in /etc/nginx.

After the installation has finished, Nginx must be started manually.

```
centos# systemctl enable nginx
centos# systemctl start nginx
```

First Test

Once the installation is completed, a first web page can be requested using Lynx on the command line:

```
$ lynx localhost
```

Terminate Lynx by pressing *q*, followed by *Enter*.

If the test page is available from the local machine, it is a good idea to verify that it is also reachable from elsewhere on the internet (home, work). Obviously, the address to request would then be *http://green.example.com/*.

If the test page is available from the command line, but not from the internet, the cause is probably in the DNS configuration or in the firewall configuration.

Note that the test page is not installed in /srv/www, but in /usr/local/www/nginx-dist (FreeBSD), /var/www/html (Debian), or /usr/share/nginx/html (CentOS).

Configuration

On FreeBSD

- Nginx is executed under the username www.

- The configuration is installed in the /usr/local/etc/nginx directory.

- The modules are installed in the /usr/local/libexec/nginx directory.

On Debian

- Nginx is executed under the username www-data.

- The configuration is installed in the /etc/nginx directory.

- The modules are installed in the /usr/share/nginx/modules directory.

On CentOS

- Nginx is executed under the username nginx.

- The configuration is installed in the /etc/nginx directory.

- The modules are installed in the /usr/lib64/nginx/modules directory.

Since the documentation on the Nginx website is extensive and complete, only the most important directives, which are crucial to the functioning of the web server, are discussed here.

The main configuration file is nginx.conf; other configuration files are loaded from this file.

Nginx's configuration is divided into contexts. A context is a collection of directives, captured in curly brackets; directives that are not in any curly brackets are said to be in the main context. Contexts can be nested. Directives end in a semicolon. Comments start with a hash sign; comments can start in the middle of a line.

A very simple but functional configuration could look like the following:

```
user nginx;
http {
    server {
        listen 80;
        location / {
            root /srv/www/website;
        }
    }
}
```

This configuration defines a web server (`http`) that is executed under the username `nginx` and that listens on port 80 for a single virtual server (`server`) to serve static content (HTML, CSS, JavaScript, images, etc.) from the directory `/srv/www/website`.

This example also shows the most important contexts for the configuration of a web server:

- **main**

  The context for directives that are not in curly brackets. In this example, the `user` directive and the `http` context are in the `main` context.

- **http**

  The `http` context contains all directives and contexts needed for the configuration of a web server. The `http` context is defined in the `main` context.

- **server**

  The `server` context contains all instructions needed for the configuration of a virtual server (a website). Multiple `server` contexts can be defined in a single `http` context.

  Debian places these contexts in separate configuration files in the `/etc/nginx/sites-available` directory. The system administrator then symlinks the files for the sites that must be activated to the `/etc/nginx/sites-enabled` directory, and these symlinks are then included in the `http` context in `nginx.conf`.

- **location**

  A `location` context defines the configuration for a URL or for a collection of URLs that all match the same pattern. The `location` context can appear in a `server` context or in another `location` context. Multiple `location` contexts can be defined for a single virtual server.

Additional configuration files can be included with the `include` directive. This directive accepts a single filename, as well as a pattern matching a collection of files (e.g., `/path/to/dir/*.conf`). If a collection of files is loaded, the files are loaded in alphanumerical order; to force the web server to load the files in a certain order, the filenames can be prepended with a number. The `include` directive can appear in any context, and the configuration from the included file will be loaded into the context in question.

These are the most important directives for the configuration of a web server:

- **load_module "/path/to/modules/module.so";**

  The `load_module` directive can only be used in the `main` context and loads a module when the web server is started.

  Debian places these directives in separate configuration files in the `/etc/nginx/modules-available` or `/usr/share/nginx/modules-available` directories. The system administrator then symlinks the needed files to the `/etc/nginx/modules-enabled` directory, and the symlinks are included in `nginx.conf`.

- **worker_processes auto;**

  The `worker_processes` directive defines the number of child processes that is spawned to process requests. The `auto` value instructs Nginx to calculate the optimal number of worker processes to be spawned.

  This directive can only be used in the `main` context.

- **sendfile on;**

  If `sendfile` is enabled, the web server uses a more efficient way of processing requests. This optimization only concerns static content like HTML pages, images, style sheets, and JavaScripts;

this directive does not have any influence on dynamic content like PHP scripts.

This directive can only be used in the http, location, and server contexts.

- **listen 80;**

  listen 198.51.100.156:80;

  The listen directive defines the IP address and/or the port on which the server expects to receive requests. The IP address only needs to be added if the server has multiple IP addresses, and the web server should not listen on all IP addresses.

  This directive can only be used in the server context.

- **server_name www.example.com example.com;**

  The server_name directive defines the name or names under which this website is served; the first name following this directive is the primary name.

  This instruction can only be used in a server context.

- **index index.html index.php index.htm;**

  The index directive defines the file that will be sent if no file is requested explicitly, but only a directory. In most instant web applications, this file is called index.html or index.php.

  This directive can be used in the http, server, and location contexts. It is practical to define the preceding line in the http context and then overwrite it in "deeper" contexts where needed.

- **error_page 404 /404.html;**

  error_page 500 502 503 504 /50x.html;

  The error_page directive defines a page that is displayed if an error occurs. The last parameter is the page to display, and all other parameters are the HTTP status codes for which the page must be displayed. A few examples of HTTP status codes are 200 for OK (no problem encountered), 404 for File Not Found, and

500 for Internal Server Error; the complete list can be found on Wikipedia, among other websites. Obviously, error pages should not be created for all HTTP status codes: a code 200, for instance, should result in the requested page being sent, and a status code starting with 3 should redirect the client to an alternative for the requested page; these are standard behaviors for the web server that should not be altered by creating an error_page.

This directive can be used in the http, server, and location contexts.

To serve the same error pages for all websites, a configuration like the following could be included in the http context:

```
http {
    error_page 404 /error/404.html;
    error_page 500 502 503 504 /error/50x.html;
    location /error/ {
        root /srv/www;
    }
}
```

The shared error pages can then be installed in the /srv/www/error directory.

- **include "/usr/local/etc/nginx/virtual-servers/*.conf";**

  include "/etc/nginx/sites-enabled/*.conf";

  include "/etc/nginx/virtual-servers/*.conf";

  This line should be added to the end of the http context (but inside of it, not after it). This directory will contain the configurations for the hosted websites. The first of the preceding lines is for FreeBSD, the second for Debian, and the third is for CentOS.

  On FreeBSD and CentOS, this directory must be created. Debian uses the same system as for the modules: website configurations are installed in the sites-available directory, and to enable a website, a symlink to its configuration file is created in the sites-enabled directory.

If the `http` context already contains a `server` context, this `server` context may be deleted, so that the main configuration file does not contain any `server` contexts.

On Debian, the `/etc/nginx/sites-enabled/default` symlink can be deleted.

The syntax of the configuration files can be verified with the help of the `-t` switch for the `nginx` command.

```
# nginx -t
```

mod_php

Many Apache web servers make use of the mod_php Apache module for the execution of PHP scripts. In a way, mod_php loads the PHP interpreter directly into the web server.

However, PHP-FPM, discussed in the following section, offers a number of important advantages over mod_php, including reduced use of memory and processing power (and therefore faster websites), and the fact that the PHP scripts for each website can be run under their own username (which can simplify security and monitoring). Furthermore, mod_php is only available for Apache; other web servers already use PHP-FPM.

For these reasons, this book only discusses the configuration of PHP-FPM and not that of mod_php.

The system administrator who is ready to switch from mod_php to PHP-FPM will find some pointers at the end of this chapter.

PHP-FPM

PHP-FPM is short for PHP FastCGI Process Manager. FastCGI (*Fast Common Gateway Interface*) is a protocol that allows web servers to call external interpreters for the execution of scripts. PHP-FPM is a FastCGI implementation that was developed especially for PHP.

PHP-FPM is a separate daemon that waits for requests from the web server and interprets these requests with the help of the PHP interpreter. The daemon starts one or more so-called pools, and each pool listens on a certain address, which may be a TCP socket (IP address + port) or a Unix socket. Each pool can be executed under its own username, and each pool can have its own limits and logging configured.

Since PHP-FPM can listen on a TCP port, the web server and the PHP daemon could be installed on different servers, if desired.

Installation on FreeBSD

PHP-FPM is part of the PHP installation, so the interpreter is installed at the same time.

At the moment of this writing, PHP 7.4 is the most recent available PHP version for FreeBSD. The PHP installation follows the usual procedure.

```
freebsd# pkg search php
freebsd# pkg install php74
freebsd# service enable php-fpm
```

Installation on Debian

Debian moved PHP-FPM to a separate package that in turn installs PHP as a dependency. Two different packages exist for the installation of PHP-FPM: php7.0-fpm and php-fpm. The former explicitly installs PHP version 7.0, and the latter installs the most recent version and will thus be updated when a more recent version becomes available in the official Debian software repositories.

```
debian# apt search "php.*-fpm"
debian# apt install php-fpm
```

Installation on CentOS

On CentOS, the PHP-FPM package is simply called php-fpm. If the intention is not to use PHP in combination with mod_php or on the command line, there is no need to install the php package. The yum info command shows that CentOS is the most prudent or conservative concerning new PHP versions: at the moment of this writing, the current version is 5.4.

```
centos# yum info php-fpm
centos# yum install php-fpm
centos# systemctl enable php-fpm
```

Configuration

As indicated before, PHP-FPM can listen on TCP sockets and on Unix domain sockets. These are the most important differences:

- If TCP sockets are used, the use of the entire network stack is required, which means that each packet must be wrapped up as a TCP packet, for subsequently being unwrapped again, even if the web server and the FPM are running on the same server. Unix sockets do not require the use of the entire network stack. A Unix socket will therefore require less memory and less processing power than a TCP socket. However, this difference is minimal in most setups.

- A TCP socket can process more connections than a Unix socket; a Unix socket will therefore sooner hit its limits and generate error messages.

- If Unix sockets are used, the web server and the FPM must run on the same server; Unix sockets cannot be used over the network. If the FPM listens on TCP sockets, the web server and the FPM can be separated.

- Web server functionalities like Alias, which allow parts of websites to be installed elsewhere in the file system, cannot be combined with Unix sockets.

In short, it could be said that the use of Unix sockets makes more sense for smaller and simpler sites, and the use of TCP sockets is more appropriate for larger, busier, and more complex sites. Since a separate pool can be started for each site and a separate address can be configured for each pool, this choice can be made individually for each website; it is even possible to configure the web server to use a local FPM for some websites and a remote FPM for others.

Since the configuration with TCP sockets has more possibilities and modern servers can be expected to be powerful enough to be able to handle a bit of extra overhead for the use of the network stack, this book will only discuss the configuration based on TCP sockets.

PHP-FPM spreads its configuration over multiple files: a file for the general configuration and a configuration file for each pool. The documentation included in these files is extensive and clear. Even though it obviously won't hurt to have a look at the general configuration, it is generally unnecessary to modify it.

```
freebsd# less /usr/local/etc/php-fpm.conf
```

```
debian# less /etc/php/7.0/fpm/php-fpm.conf
```

```
centos# less /etc/php-fpm.conf
```

One of the lines in this file looks a bit like the following:

```
include=/path/to/directory/*.conf
```

This line assures that all files with a name ending in `.conf` in said directory are loaded as well; these are the configuration files for the different pools. An example file is included in that directory; it is recommended to rename this file and put it aside to make sure that there is always an unmodified original, where default settings can be looked up.

```
freebsd# cd /usr/local/etc/php-fpm.d
```

```
debian# cd /etc/php/7.0/fpm/pool.d
```

```
centos# cd /etc/php-fpm.d
```

```
# mv www.conf www.conf.orig
```

The name of the new file is not important, as long as it does not end in `.conf`; after all, the FPM loads all files of which the name ends in `.conf` as additional configuration files.

Even though these sub-configurations contain a lot of information, only a few settings are mandatory. These are the most important ones, in short:

- **[www.example.com]**

  Each pool configuration begins with the name of the pool in square brackets. The system administrator is free in the choice of names, but it is recommended to keep them recognizable: commands like ps display the name of the pool in question for each PHP-FPM process, so a recognizable pool name facilitates the calculation of memory and CPU usage per website.

- **user = w-ex-com**

  group = w-ex-com

  The user and group name under which the process (and thus the interpreted PHP scripts) must be executed. Essentially, this could be any valid user with read privileges for the PHP scripts, but it is recommended to create a dedicated user for each pool; this user should only have read privileges for the files in the pool in question. In a shared web hosting setup, the pool could run under the username of the customer who owns the website.

- **listen = 127.0.0.1:9000**

  The address on which php-fpm listens for this pool, in the format IP_address:port. If the web server and PHP-FPM are installed on the same server, the IP address is 127.0.0.1. If the web server and PHP-FPM run on different servers, the IP address of the network interface of the server running PHP-FPM is used. Conventionally, the first php-fpm listens on port 9000, and subsequent instances listen on subsequent ports, but this is not mandatory.

- **listen.allowed_clients = 127.0.0.1**

  The IP addresses of the servers that are allowed to connect to this pool. Multiple IP addresses should be separated by commas. If the web server and PHP-FPM run on the same server, this address is 127.0.0.1 (website visitors send requests to the web server, but only the web server sends requests to the FPM). If the web server and PHP-FPM run on separate servers, the IP address(es) of the web server(s) should be listed.

- **pm = static**

  pm = ondemand

  pm = dynamic

  This parameter determines how child processes are managed; the abbreviation pm stands for process manager. A value of static will start a fixed number of processes for the pool. A value of ondemand will not start any processes until requests arrive. A value of

dynamic will start a certain number of processes when the pool is
started, and this number will be augmented when requests arrive.

For a busy website, dynamic is often the best choice; this option
will make sure that there are always running child processes
waiting to answer incoming requests. For a quiet site (up to a few
hundred visitors per day), ondemand is often the best choice; this
option prevents child processes from reserving memory when
in fact there is nothing to do, with as additional cost that a new
child process must be spawned each time a new request comes in,
which slightly raises the response times.

To save memory and improve response times at the same time, it
could be an idea to move multiple quiet websites from ondemand
pools to a single dynamic pool.

- **pm.max_children = 20**

  This parameter determines how many child processes are
  spawned (static) or how many child processes are spawned at
  most (dynamic and ondemand). This is a mandatory parameter.

- **pm.min_spare_servers = 5**

  pm.max_spare_servers = 10

  These parameters are only used if the pm parameter has a value
  of dynamic, in which case they are also mandatory. These
  parameters determine how many unused child processes should
  be spawned, at least and at most, to wait for incoming requests.

Especially those last parameters—pm.max_children and pm.*_spare_servers—
depend heavily on variables like the server's capacity, the number of hosted websites,
the size and load for these sites, the number of visitors, other processes that run on
the server and also need memory, and so on. The PHP-FPM settings suggested in this
book should be seen as examples and acceptable starting values, but it is the system
administrator's responsibility to optimize them for their specific situation. Tools that
can be used for this optimization are the log files for PHP-FPM and the web server and
commands like top. Furthermore, the online addendum for this book contains a list
of links to a number of open source load testing tools that can help study the server's
behavior under increasing numbers of website visitors.

Especially if the server hosts a large number of websites, it is recommended to maintain separate log files for each pool. The parameters `access.log`, `slowlog`, and `php_admin_value[error_log]` can be set to achieve this.

The per-pool configuration will be discussed in more detail later in this chapter when the first virtual host (website) is created.

PHP

Since PHP-FPM has been installed to serve PHP scripts, it is probably a good idea to also briefly discuss the configuration for the PHP interpreter. However, this is not a book about website development, so for more in-depth documentation, please refer to available books and websites about PHP.

Configuration

The main configuration for PHP is called `php.ini`. FreeBSD comes with two example files, of which one must be selected. Debian also has two versions: one for use with PHP-FPM and the other for use with the PHP cli. CentOS comes with a single version. Even though it clearly won't hurt to have a look at the file, it is usually not necessary to make any changes; the file is provided with extensive and clear documentation.

```
freebsd# cp /usr/local/etc/php.ini-production \
         /usr/local/etc/php.ini
freebsd# nano /usr/local/etc/php.ini

debian# nano /etc/php/7.0/fpm/php.ini
debian# nano /etc/php/7.0/cli/php.ini

centos# nano /etc/php.ini
```

PHP extensions, discussed in the next section, have a configuration file each in a separate directory. The configuration of extensions is generally limited to enabling or disabling the extension.

```
freebsd# ls /usr/local/etc/php

debian# ls -l /etc/php/7.0/fpm/conf.d
debian# ls -l /etc/php/7.0/cli/conf.d

centos# ls /etc/php.d
```

When the PHP configuration has been modified, the PHP-FPM must be restarted.

Extensions

PHP extensions (sometimes also called modules) add functionalities to PHP to extend its possibilities. Examples of such possibilities are communication with databases, generation and modification of images, and cryptographic functions.

A number of PHP extensions are installed by default; which extensions those are depends on the operating system. All systems also publish additional extensions in their respective software repositories.

On FreeBSD, additional PHP extensions can be installed through the package *php<version>-extensions*. Obviously, it is important to select the same version as for the previously installed php package (php74).

```
freebsd# pkg info | grep '^php'
freebsd# pkg search php.*-extensions
freebsd# pkg install php74-extensions
```

Debian does not use unambiguous names for PHP extensions. The most practical way to find them is the command

```
debian# apt search php
```

On CentOS, the name for all available PHP modules begins with php-; additional extensions can therefore be found with the command

```
centos# yum search php-
```

Apart from the extensions available in the software repositories for the different systems, there are also *PEAR* and *PECL*.

PECL (*PHP Extension Community Library*) contains PHP extensions that are developed in C and add functionalities to the PHP interpreter.

PEAR (*PHP Extension and Application Repository*) contains PHP code that can be used in PHP applications.

The application for management of PEAR and PECL extensions is installed as follows:

```
freebsd# pkg install php74-pear
```

```
debian# apt install php-pear
```

```
centos# yum install php-pear
```

Subsequently, these commands can be executed to obtain help with the management of the extensions:

```
# pear help
```

```
# pecl help
```

PECL extensions, just like the default PHP extensions, must be enabled after they have been installed; this is done by creating a file in the directory containing the configuration files for PHP extensions, following the example of the already existing files in that directory.

Links to the PHP, PEAR, and PECL websites are available in the online addendum for this book.

A First Virtual Host or Virtual Server

The server hosts multiple domain names and hostnames; this is called virtual hosting. For the web server, this means that multiple websites must be hosted; such a website is called a virtual host by Apache and a virtual server by Nginx.

In the following sections, the default website will be created: the website that will be displayed if a request arrives for an address for which no website has been configured explicitly. Examples are requests for *http://green.example.com/*, *http://198.51.100.156/*, *http://ns.example.com/*, and *http://mx.example.com/*, but also *www.example.com* and *www.example.edu*, as long as those websites have not been installed yet. For all these addresses, the requests are sent to this server based on their DNS records; instead of replying with the message "Website does not exist", the web server will be configured to serve a default website at these addresses.

A lot of what is discussed in these sections could easily be turned into a script, which can be especially practical for servers that host multiple websites with comparable configurations. The creation of such a script is left as an exercise for the reader.

DNS

Normally, the first step in the creation of a virtual host or virtual server is the addition of the new hostname to the DNS configuration. However, since it concerns the default website here, this is not necessary: this website is meant to be served for hostnames that are present in DNS already, but that have no website created explicitly.

Names

Once the hostname has been defined, the name for other items can be derived from it. Since this is the default website and the name of this server is *green.example.com*, the following names will be used:

Directory for the website	`/srv/www/green.example.com`
Configuration file Apache/Nginx	`000-green.conf`
Access log file Apache/Nginx	`/var/log/www-green.log`
Error log file Apache/Nginx	`/var/log/www-green.error`
Configuration file PHP-FPM	`green.conf`
Pool name PHP-FPM	`green.example.com`
Username PHP-FPM	`www-green`
Port number PHP-FPM	`9000`

User

The user will have a group with the same name and no login shell; the home directory will be the website directory, and the user will not be added to any additional groups.

```
freebsd# adduser
debian# adduser --gecos "green.example.com" \
        --home /srv/www/green.example.com \
        --no-create-home \
        --disabled-login \
        --shell /usr/sbin/nologin \
        www-green

centos# useradd --comment "green.example.com" \
        --home-dir /srv/www/green.example.com \
        --no-create-home \
        --user-group \
        --shell /sbin/nologin \
        www-green
```

Directories

The next step is the creation of the directories from where the website is served. The `/srv/www/www.example.com` directory will contain several sub-directories. Even though not all of these directories will be used for all websites, it can be practical to maintain a certain uniformity for all website directories:

- **alias**

  It may sometimes be desirable to install certain functionalities separate from the actual website. If, for example, a forum is served at the address `www.example.com/forum`, it is best to keep this package separated from the rest of the website to make sure that an upgrade of the forum software will not damage the website. Web servers can be configured to serve certain parts of a website from a different part of the file system—a different directory; Apache and Nginx call this an alias.

  The sub-directory named `alias` could be used to harbor such packages.

  Aliases are discussed in more depth in Chapter 13, "Web Server Part 2: Advanced Apache/Nginx".

- **bin**

  Some websites come with shell scripts for the execution of cronjobs, for example. To keep oversight, it is practical to install these scripts with the website; this directory could be used for those scripts.

- **cgi-bin**

  A cgi-bin is a directory where scripts are installed that can be executed by the web server; this is mainly used to add some interactivity to mostly static websites. Examples of such scripts are a contact form or a visitor counter.

  The scripts in the cgi-bin are executed by the web server and not by the FastCGI Process Manager that executes the PHP scripts. CGI scripts are discussed in more depth in Chapter 13, "Web Server Part 2: Advanced Apache/Nginx".

- **conf**

  Some web applications expect (and rightly so) that the
  application's configuration, like database passwords, is stored
  away from the actual website to make sure that this data can never
  be visible to the website's visitors. This sub-directory could be
  used to store such data.

- **htdocs**

  This sub-directory will contain the actual website.

  A website's base directory is also called the document root.

- **tmp**

  This sub-directory will contain all temporary files, like session
  data, uploads while they are being processed, and so on.

Obviously, the system administrator is completely free to add directories to this list
or to remove certain directories. In some setups, like web hosting for customers, it may
be practical to add a directory for log files; it is usually not a good idea to grant customers
access to the /var/log directory, where also other, more confidential log files can be found.

These directories are all property of user webdev and group webdev. ACL will be
used to grant read privileges to the web server and the PHP-FPM; this is done before the
sub-directories are created, so that the sub-directories can inherit the base directory's
ACL. The following set of commands clearly shows that differences most certainly exist
between the different Unices.

```
# cd /srv/www
# mkdir green.example.com
# setfacl -m user:www-green:rx ./green.example.com
```

The default ACL are created differently on BSD and Linux.

```
bsd# setfacl -d -m user:www-green:rx ./green.example.com
```

```
linux# setfacl -m default:user:www-green:rx ./green.example.com
```

The username for the web server is different on all systems.

```
freebsd# setfacl -m u:www:rx ./green.example.com
freebsd# setfacl -d -m u:www:rx ./green.example.com
```

```
debian# setfacl -m u:www-data:rx ./green.example.com
debian# setfacl -m d:u:www-data:rx ./green.example.com

centos+apache# setfacl -m u:apache:rx ./green.example.com
centos+apache# setfacl -m d:u:apache:rx ./green.example.com

centos+nginx# setfacl -m u:nginx:rx ./green.example.com
centos+nginx# setfacl -m d:u:nginx:rx ./green.example.com
```

The creation of directories is the same everywhere.

```
# mkdir green.example.com/{alias,bin,cgi-bin,conf,htdocs,tmp}
# setfacl -m u:www-green:rwx green.example.com/tmp
```

More default ACL.

```
bsd# setfacl -d -m u:www-green:rwx green.example.com/tmp

linux# setfacl -m d:u:www-green:rwx green.example.com/tmp
```

And finally, the traditional permission set and a test page.

```
# chown -R webdev:webdev green.example.com
# chmod -R 2770 green.example.com
# echo "It works!" > green.example.com/htdocs/index.html
```

The web server and PHP-FPM have been granted read privileges with the help of ACL. Furthermore, PHP-FPM has been granted write privileges for the tmp sub-directory, so it can store things like session data.

If objections against the use of ACL exist within the organization, everybody will need read privileges for all directories, and PHP-FPM will need to be the owner of the tmp sub-directory (to avoid having to grant write privileges to everybody).

```
# chmod -R 2775 /srv/www/green.example.com
# chown www-green /srv/www/green.example.com/tmp
```

If the web server would also need write privileges for the tmp directory, for example, for CGI scripts that store data, the most practical solution would be to create a group that both the web server and PHP-FPM are members of and then grant write privileges to this group for the tmp directory.

However, this is all overly complicated and less secure than the use of Access Control Lists.

PHP-FPM

The next thing to configure is the FastCGI Process Manager.

```
freebsd# nano /usr/local/etc/php-fpm.d/green.conf
```

```
debian# nano /etc/php/7.0/fpm/pool.d/green.conf
```

```
centos# nano /etc/php-fpm.d/green.conf
```

A minimal version of that file could look like the following:

```
; The name for the pool.
; Amongst other things, this name is displayed in `ps' output.
[green.example.com]

; The user and group.
; PHP scripts will be executed under these names.
user = www-green
group = www-green

; The network socket.
; Only accept requests from the server itself.
listen = 127.0.0.1:9000
listen.allowed_clients = 127.0.0.1

; Process manager options.
; Since this site will not get many visitors, 'ondemand' suffices.
; For this same reason, only a few child processes are spawned.
pm = ondemand
pm.max_children = 3

; Environment variables.
env[TMP] = /srv/www/green.example.com/tmp
env[TEMP] = /srv/www/green.example.com/tmp
env[TMPDIR] = /srv/www/green.example.com/tmp

; PHP configuration variables.
php_flag[short_open_tag] = off
```

```
php_admin_value[open_basedir] = /srv/www/green.example.com:/usr/share
php_admin_value[upload_tmp_dir] = /srv/www/green.example.com/tmp
php_admin_value[session.save_path] = /srv/www/green.example.com/tmp
```

If the PHP configuration variable *open_basedir* is defined to limit the directories to which PHP has access (which usually is a good idea), the directory /usr/local/share (FreeBSD) or /usr/share (Debian and CentOS) should always be added to the list. PHP modules and some web applications are installed in this directory, so PHP should have read privileges here. Multiple directories are separated with colons.

To check the configuration for typos and similar errors, php-fpm can be executed with the -t parameter:

```
freebsd# php-fpm -t
```

```
debian# php-fpm7.0 -t
```

```
centos# php-fpm -t
```

When the configuration has been modified, the php-fpm daemon must be reloaded, but since this is the first pool, the service has not been started yet on FreeBSD and CentOS.

```
freebsd# service php-fpm start
```

```
debian# systemctl reload php7.0-fpm
```

```
centos# systemctl start php-fpm
```

Apache

A separate configuration file is created for each virtual host. The name of this file should end in .conf. Since the files are loaded in alphanumerical order, the filenames begin with a number; the virtual host for which the configuration is loaded first is automatically the default virtual host.

```
freebsd# cd /usr/local/etc/apache24/virtual-hosts
```

```
debian# cd /etc/apache2/sites-available
```

```
centos# cd /etc/httpd/virtual-hosts
```

```
# nano 000-green.conf
```

217

No TLS certificates have been installed yet, so for now, a virtual host will only be created for port 80. In the next chapter, where TLS is discussed, this configuration will be modified to serve the website on port 443.

```
<VirtualHost *:80>

  # The name for the virtual host.
  ServerName green.example.com

  # Log files.
  CustomLog /var/log/www-green.log combined
  ErrorLog /var/log/www-green.error

  # The website directory.
  # Everybody has access.
  DocumentRoot /srv/www/green.example.com/htdocs
  <Directory /srv/www/green.example.com/htdocs>
    Require all granted
  </Directory>

  # The page that will be sent if a non-existing file is
  # requested.
  # Attention: this directive prevents an 'Error 404' message
  # from being displayed, but at the same time it hinders
  # the debugging of errors 404.
  FallbackResource /index.html

  # The cgi-bin.
  # This makes CGI scripts available through addresses like
  # http://green.example.com/cgi-bin/myscript.pl
  ScriptAlias /cgi-bin/ /srv/www/green.example.com/cgi-bin/
  <Directory "/srv/www/green.example.com/cgi-bin">
    Require all granted
  </Directory>

  # Files that have a name ending in .php
  # will be sent to the PHP-FPM listening on port 9000.
  ProxyPassMatch "^/(.*\.php(/.*)?)$" \
  "fcgi://127.0.0.1:9000/srv/www/green.example.com/htdocs/$1"

</VirtualHost>
```

The asterisk (*) in the `VirtualHost` address means "Every possible IP address". If the server has multiple IP addresses, the web server can be configured to host a different website on each IP address. For the setup described here, this is not relevant.

Especially if the server will be hosting multiple websites, it makes sense to move all log files to a designated directory. Debian uses the `/var/log/apache2` directory for this purpose and CentOS the `/var/log/httpd` directory; it may be practical to create a similar directory on FreeBSD. If the server hosts customer websites, it is more practical to store the log files in a directory that is accessible to the client; obviously, customers should not have access to each other's log files. The web server does not need to have write privileges for this directory; root suffices. The paths in the preceding examples can be corrected if such a directory is created.

The `Require all granted` directive grants access to everybody to the concerning directory, but from the point of view of the web server; this has nothing to do with the permissions on the file system level. Access control will be discussed further in Chapter 13, "Web Server Part 2: Advanced Apache/Nginx".

On Debian, a symlink must be created in the `sites-enabled` directory to activate the website.

```
debian# cd /etc/apache2/sites-enabled
debian# ln -s ../sites-available/000-green.conf .
```

To check the syntax of the configuration files, the web server binary can be executed with the `-t` parameter.

```
freebsd# httpd -t
```

```
debian# echo "$(source /etc/apache2/envvars && apache2 -t)"
```

```
centos# httpd -t
```

And finally, the web server must be instructed to reload its configuration.

```
freebsd# service apache24 reload
```

```
debian# systemctl reload apache2
```

```
centos# systemctl reload httpd
```

Nginx

A configuration file is created in the designated directory for each virtual server. The name of this file must end in `.conf`. The filenames begin with a number, because they are loaded in alphanumerical order; the virtual server configuration that is loaded first is automatically the default virtual server.

No TLS certificates have been installed yet, so for now, a virtual host will only be created for port 80. In the next chapter, where TLS is discussed, this configuration will be modified to serve the website on port 443.

FreeBSD

```
freebsd# cd /usr/local/etc/nginx/virtual-servers
freebsd# nano 000-green.conf
```

```
http {
  server {
    # Listen on port 80.
    listen 80;

    # The name for the virtual server.
    server_name green.example.com;

    # Log files.
    access_log /var/log/www-green.log;
    error_log /var/log/www-green.error;

    # Document root and index file.
    location / {
      root /srv/www/green.example.com/htdocs;
      index index.html index.php index.htm;
    }

    # Files with a name ending in .php
    # will be sent to the PHP-FPM listening on port 9000.
    location ~ \.php$ {
      fastcgi_pass    127.0.0.1:9000;
      fastcgi_index   index.php;
      fastcgi_param   SCRIPT_FILENAME $request_filename;
```

```
        include          fastcgi_params;
    }
  }
}
```

```
freebsd# nginx -t
freebsd# service nginx restart
```

Debian

```
debian# cd /etc/nginx/sites-available
debian# nano 000-green.conf
```

```
http {
  server {
    # Listen on port 80.
    listen 80;

    # The name for the virtual server.
    server_name green.example.com;

    # Log files.
    access_log /var/log/www-green.log;
    error_log /var/log/www-green.error;

    # Document root and index file.
    location / {
      root /srv/www/green.example.com/htdocs;
      index index.html index.php index.htm;
    }

    # Files with a name ending in .php
    # will be sent to the PHP-FPM listening on port 9000.
    location ~ \.php$ {
      include snippets/fastcgi-php.conf;
      fastcgi_pass 127.0.0.1:9000;
    }
  }
}
```

```
debian# cd ../sites-enabled
debian# ln -s ../sites-available/000-green.conf .
debian# nginx -t
debian# systemctl restart nginx
```

CentOS

```
centos# cd /etc/nginx/virtual-servers
centos# nano 000-green.conf
```

```
http {
  server {
    # Listen on port 80.
    listen 80;

    # The name for the virtual server.
    server_name green.example.com;

    # Log files.
    access_log /var/log/www-green.log;
    error_log /var/log/www-green.error;

    # Document root and index file.
    location / {
      root /srv/www/green.example.com/htdocs;
      index index.html index.php index.htm;
    }

    # Files with a name ending in .php
    # will be sent to the PHP-FPM listening on port 9000.
    location ~ \.php$ {
      fastcgi_pass    127.0.0.1:9000;
      fastcgi_index   index.php;
      fastcgi_param   SCRIPT_FILENAME $request_filename;
      include         fastcgi_params;
    }
  }
}
```

```
centos# nginx -t
centos# systemctl restart nginx
```

Common

Especially if the server will be hosting multiple websites, it makes sense to gather all the log files in a single designated directory. Debian and CentOS use the /var/log/nginx directory for this purpose; it may be practical to create a similar directory on FreeBSD. If the server will be hosting customer websites, it is more practical to store the log files in a directory that is accessible to the customer; obviously, customers should not have access to each other's log files. The web server needs write privileges for this directory. The paths in the preceding examples can then be corrected.

Test

The first virtual host or virtual server can now be tested. The following line can be saved as /srv/www/green.example.com/htdocs/info.php to create a simple PHP script:

```
<?php phpinfo(); ?>
```

The addresses *http://green.example.com/info.php*, *http://ns.example.com/info.php*, and *http://mx.example.com/info.php* should now display a page listing the settings and configurations for PHP and all installed PHP modules.

If this is not the case:

- Verify that the web server and PHP-FPM daemons have been started.

- Verify that the web server and PHP-FPM daemons have read privileges for the directory in question.

  ```
  # sudo -u www-green ls /srv/www/green.example.com/htdocs
  ```

- Analyze the web server and PHP-FPM log files.

- Verify the names for files and directories.

- Verify the syntax for all created and modified files, and check them for typos.

- In the worst case, restart from scratch, from the beginning of this chapter.

As long as this virtual host is not functional, there is no use continuing to Chapter 10, "Traffic Encryption: SSL/TLS"; that chapter makes use of this virtual host.

If no filename is requested (`http://green.example.com/`), the web server will look for a file named `index.html` or `index.php` in that same directory.

It Works!

If the test in the previous section is successfull, enough knowledge has been gathered to install a first home-made website:

1. DNS record

2. PHP-FPM user

3. Directories

4. PHP-FPM configuration

5. Apache or Nginx configuration

6. Files (HTML, PHP, images, style sheets, JavaScript) in sub-directory `htdocs`

In the next chapters, TLS certificates will be added to serve the websites over an encrypted connection, databases will be installed to facilitate the storage and modification of the content and the metadata for the websites, and more advanced web server functions will be discussed.

Replacing mod_php with PHP-FPM

Some quick tips for the system administrator who is ready to make the switch from mod_php to PHP-FPM. Administrators who are not in charge of Apache web servers running the mod_php module can safely disregard this section.

It is not necessary to make the switch for all hosted websites at the same time; the switch can be made one site at a time. This means that it is also possible to make a copy of an existing site and switch this copy to PHP-FPM and test it before switching the production site.

To begin, configure a PHP-FPM pool for the site, as described earlier in this chapter.

Make sure the PHP-FPM has read privileges, and write privileges if needed, for the website directory; preferably use ACL for this. In principle, the Apache user will no longer need write privileges for this directory (but it will still need read privileges).

Then add the following lines to the Apache configuration for the `VirtualHost` in question:

```
<FilesMatch "\.(php|php[57]|phtml)$">
    # Stop using mod_php for this virtual host.
    SetHandler None
</FilesMatch>

# Send PHP files to the PHP-FPM.
# This can be put on a single line _without_ the backslash
# between the 2 arguments.
# Correct the port (9000) for the configured PHP-FPM pool.
# Correct the directory for the website.
ProxyPassMatch "^/(.*\.php(/.*)?)$" \
  "fcgi://127.0.0.1:9000/srv/www/www.example.com/htdocs/"
```

Now test the entire website, including forms and other dynamic and interactive elements. Analyze the web server and PHP-FPM log files before accepting the change.

Summary

This chapter treated the installation and basic configuration of the web server. Both Apache and Nginx were discussed, as well as the PHP FastCGI Process Manager that will be serving PHP content. A small detour was made for detailing some basic facts about PHP configuration. Lastly, the first virtual host (Apache) or virtual server (Nginx) was created.

In the next chapter, TLS encryption will be implemented that will be used to encrypt all web and mail traffic.

CHAPTER 10

Traffic Encryption: SSL/TLS

On today's internet, encryption is no longer optional. System administrators want security, users and customers demand privacy and confidentiality, governments and other authorities demand protection of privacy, and web browsers and search engines also insist on encryption.

SSL (*Secure Sockets Layer*) and *TLS* (*Transport Layer Security*) are terms that often pop up in this context, and they are often used interchangeably. The reason for this is twofold: on the one hand, TLS is the successor of SSL and also based on that protocol, so the protocols are related and serve the same purpose; and on the other hand, the protocols use the same types of certificates for the encryption of data. The most important differences are in the way that the connection is set up (the handshake) and in the fact that TLS resolves some SSL vulnerabilities. In popular parlance, the two terms will probably still be used interchangeably for some time to come; the regular internet user, who had just gotten used to the term SSL, will need some time to accept the new name TLS.

TLS can be used to encrypt the communication between a web browser and a web server, but also other network traffic, like email. This encryption functions roughly as follows:

- The owner of the server (or website, or service) obtains a *TLS certificate*, a digital document that contains the server's hostname and a public key. This certificate is digitally signed by a *certificate authority* (*CA*), a certified organization that vouches for the authenticity of the TLS certificate. The private key that accompanies the certificate's public key is stored on the server.

© Robert La Lau 2021
R. La Lau, *Practical Internet Server Configuration*, https://doi.org/10.1007/978-1-4842-6960-2_10

- Clients (web browsers, mail clients, etc.) contain a collection of CA certificates for certificate authorities that are (or at least should be) trustworthy. This collection is generally composed by the developers of the software, but end users can manipulate this list.

- When a client connects to the server, the server sends the TLS certificate to the client. After having verified the server's hostname with the hostname in the certificate, the client then uses the enclosed public key to encrypt a message to the server. If the server manages to decrypt the encrypted message, it has proven that it is the server it claims to be. The client and server then negotiate the keys that will be used for the encryption of the rest of the communication, and the actual communication begins.

To obtain a TLS certificate, the owner must be verified. Three levels of verification exist:

- *Domain Validation*

  For a *Domain Validation* certificate, all that is verified is the applicant's ownership of the domain for which the certificate is requested. While the encryption is the same as with the other certificates, the owner's legitimacy has not been verified, which limits the reliability of these certificates. This type of certificate is considered reliable enough for personal websites and intranets, but not for web shops and public services.

- *Organization Validation*

  For an *Organization Validation* certificate, it is not only verified that the applicant owns the domain but also that the applicant is a legitimate organization. The organization information is included in the certificate. This certificate is considered fit for corporate websites and web shops.

- *Extended Validation*

  For an *Extended Validation* certificate, the applicant must satisfy a long list of criteria. This certificate has the highest level of reliability.

Organization Validation certificates are sold for a few dozens of euros or dollars, and *Extended Validation* certificates are more expensive. These certificates are usually valid for one or two years. A search for *"SSL certificate"* or *"TLS certificate"* should be enough to get started with these. Some vendors install the certificates for their customers, and others provide an installation manual.

Domain Validation certificates can be obtained without cost.

Let's Encrypt

The free certificates can be obtained from many different suppliers, but they all come from *Let's Encrypt*. *Let's Encrypt* is a nonprofit dedicated to the encryption of all internet traffic. *Let's Encrypt's* services are free and completely automated. The certificates are valid for three months, but they can be renewed indefinitely.

Certbot

Many different clients exist for the application and installation of the certificates, but Let's Encrypt recommends the use of *certbot*. *Certbot* functions as follows (somewhat simplified):

1. The system administrator creates a virtual host (Apache) of virtual server (Nginx) for the hostname for which a certificate is to be obtained.

2. The administrator launches `certbot` and answers the few questions that are posed (email address and so forth).

3. Certbot creates a file in the virtual host/server.

4. Certbot sends a message to Let's Encrypt.

5. Let's Encrypt makes an HTTP request to the file that was created in step 3.

6. If Let's Encrypt finds the file, the applicant has proven to be the owner of the domain, and certbot receives the certificate.

7. Certbot installs the received certificate.

8. The system administrator modifies the configuration for the web server or other service to include the certificate.

It is therefore a requirement that the domain name is registered and the DNS is properly configured before the certificate is requested; otherwise, it will be impossible for Let's Encrypt to make the HTTP request.

For FreeBSD, multiple packages named *py*_certbot* exist. Since the *py* prefix usually indicates *python* (the programming language), the installed Python version must be found first.

```
freebsd# pkg search certbot
freebsd# pkg info | grep python
freebsd# pkg install py36-certbot

debian# apt install certbot

centos# yum install certbot
```

It can be practical to create a dedicated directory for the file that is created in step 3. This way, all hosted websites can use the same directory, without the risk of `certbot` clashing with password security that may be configured for a site or with a reverse proxy that doesn't know how to handle `certbot` traffic.

Certbot creates a directory named `.well-known`. This directory is defined in RFC 5785 and is used by other automated web services as well. In this directory, `certbot` creates a sub-directory named `acme-challenge` (*Automatic Certificate Management Environment*) for the application of the certificate. So the full URL for this directory would be *www.example.com/.well-known/acme-challenge*.

```
# mkdir -p /srv/www/rfc5785
# chmod 2770 /srv/www/rfc5785

freebsd# chown www:www /srv/www/rfc5785

debian# chown www-data:www-data /srv/www/rfc5785

centos+apache# chown apache:apache /srv/www/rfc5785

centos+nginx# chown nginx:nginx /srv/www/rfc5785
```

Since `certbot` deletes the created files after the application, this directory will mostly be empty, though.

To make use of this directory, instead of using a directory in each website's document root, a few lines must be added to the web server configuration. For Apache, the following lines can be added to `httpd.conf` (`apache2.conf` on Debian):

```
Alias "/.well-known/" "/srv/www/rfc5785/.well-known/"
<Directory "/srv/www/rfc5785">
    AuthType None
    Require all granted
</Directory>
```

For Nginx, a separate file named `rfc5785` could be created in the configuration directory, with the following contents:

```
location /.well-known/ {
    alias /srv/www/rfc5785/.well-known/;
    auth_basic off;
    allow all;
}
```

This file can then be included in each server context with the following directive (Nginx does not accept `location` contexts within the `main` or `http` contexts):

```
include rfc5785;
```

The URL */.well-known/* now points at the same server directory for all websites.

Aliases will be discussed further in Chapter 13, "Web Server Part 2: Advanced Apache/Nginx".

Installation of the green.example.com Certificate

The first TLS certificate is for the default virtual host/server that was created in the previous chapter—the website that is displayed if a request arrives for a (sub-)domain for which no website was explicitly created.

The directory that will be used for this request is /srv/www/rfc5785. The hostname for this virtual host/server is *green.example.com*, but the site is also displayed for the other names in the DNS, *ns.example.com* and *mx.example.com*.

With this information, the command for requesting the certificate can be assembled:

```
# certbot certonly --webroot \
    -w /srv/www/rfc5785 \
    -d green.example.com \
    -d ns.example.com \
    -d mx.example.com
```

The first time `certbot` is executed, it poses a few questions:

1. **Email address**

   When a certificate is about to expire, a notification is sent to this
   address. It may be practical to assign a dedicated address for this,
   like *tls-certificates@example.com*. Note this address down; in a
   later chapter, this email alias will have to be created.

2. **Conditions**

   The general conditions must be accepted; a link to those
   conditions is given. Since this is a service for the protection of
   the confidentiality of data, possibly even customer data, it is
   recommended to actually read the conditions.

3. **Share email address**

   Let's Encrypt asks permission to share the email address with their
   partner *Electronic Frontier Foundation*.

These questions only have to be answered once; the responses are stored and reused
with subsequent requests.

When `certbot` finishes, it indicates whether the request was successful or not.
If the request did not succeed, the cause can probably be found in the DNS settings
(*Do all the hostnames point at the correct virtual host?*) or in the web server settings
(*Does the .well-known directory for this virtual host refer to the directory mentioned on
the command line?; Does the web server have access to this directory?*).

On FreeBSD, the new certificate is stored in `/usr/local/etc/letsencrypt` and
on Debian and CentOS in `/etc/letsencrypt`. The `archive` sub-directory contains all
certificates—the previous and the current—and the `live` sub-directory contains links to
the currently valid certificates.

The certificate is stored under the hostname that was mentioned first on the command
line when the certificate was requested, which is `green.example.com` in this case.

Apache

In the previous chapter, the first virtual host was created in the file `000-green.conf`.
Until now, this virtual host only listened on port 80. Now that the TLS certificate has
been installed, the existing configuration can be moved to port 443 (HTTPS), and port 80
(HTTP) can be configured to redirect all traffic to port 443.

```
freebsd# nano /usr/local/etc/apache24/virtual-hosts/000-green.conf
```

```
debian# nano /etc/apache2/sites-available/000-green.conf
```

```
centos# nano /etc/httpd/virtual-hosts/000-green.conf
```

The lines in bold must be added:

```
<VirtualHost *:80>
  # The name for the virtual host.
  ServerName green.example.com

  # Redirect all requests to the HTTPS variant.
  # The 'permanent' flag assures that a 301 HTTP status code
  # is sent to the client. If the 'temp' flag would be used
  # instead, a 302 status code would be sent.
  Redirect permanent "/" "https://green.example.com/"
</VirtualHost>

<VirtualHost *:443>
  # The name for the virtual host.
  ServerName green.example.com

  # Enable SSL/TLS.
  SSLEngine on

  # SSL/TLS certificate and key.
  # (Correct these paths for FreeBSD!)
  SSLCertificateFile \
    /etc/letsencrypt/live/green.example.com/fullchain.pem
  SSLCertificateKeyFile \
    /etc/letsencrypt/live/green.example.com/privkey.pem

  # And then the rest of the existing configuration.
  # ...
</VirtualHost>
```

The file now has two VirtualHost blocks: one for port 80, with only a redirect to port 443, and another one for port 443, where all requests will now be processed, using TLS encryption.

If Apache is now instructed to reload its configuration and the site *green.example.com* is then requested in the browser, the well-known padlock in the location bar will indicate that the traffic between the browser and the website is encrypted.

Nginx

In the previous chapter, the first virtual host was created in the file 000-green.conf. Until now, this virtual host only listened on port 80. Now that the TLS certificate has been installed, the existing configuration can be moved to port 443 (HTTPS), and port 80 (HTTP) can be configured to redirect all traffic to port 443.

```
freebsd# nano /usr/local/etc/nginx/virtual-servers/000-green.conf

debian# nano /etc/nginx/sites-available/000-green.conf

centos# nano /etc/nginx/virtual-servers/000-green.conf
```

The lines in bold should be added:

```
server {
    # Listen on port 80.
    listen              80;

    # The name for the virtual server.
    server_name         green.example.com;

    # Redirect all requests to the HTTPS variant.
    return              301 https://green.example.com/;
}
server {
    # Listen on port 443, and enable SSL/TLS.
    listen              443 ssl;

    # The name for the virtual server.
    server_name         green.example.com;

    # Enable session cache and allow multiple requests
    # per session, to spare CPU.
    ssl_session_cache   shared:SSL:5m;
    ssl_session_timeout 10m;
    keepalive_timeout   75s;
```

```
# SSL/TLS certificate and key.
# (Correct paths for FreeBSD!)
ssl_certificate \ /etc/letsencrypt/live/green.example.com/fullchain.pem;
ssl_certificate_key \ /etc/letsencrypt/live/green.example.com/privkey.pem;

# And then the rest of the existing configuration.
# ...
}
```

The file now contains two server contexts: one for port 80, with only a redirect to port 443, and another one for port 443, where all requests will now be processed, using TLS encryption.

If Nginx is now instructed to reload its configuration and the site *green.example.com* is then requested in the browser, the well-known padlock in the location bar will indicate that the traffic between the browser and the website is encrypted.

Automatic Renewal

As indicated, Let's Encrypt certificates have a validity of three months. However, with the help of *cron* and *certbot*, they can be renewed indefinitely.

On FreeBSD, all that is needed to enable automated renewal of the certificates is the addition of a single line to the /etc/periodic.conf file (create the file if it doesn't exist):

```
weekly_certbot_enable="YES"
```

On Debian, a *systemd service* has been installed that is started twice per day by a *systemd timer*. Verify the timer with the following command:

```
debian# systemctl status certbot.timer
```

And use the following command to display when the service was last started:

```
debian# systemctl status certbot.service
```

On CentOS, a *systemd service* and *systemd timer* have been installed as well, but the timer has not yet been started. Enable and start the timer.

```
centos# systemctl enable certbot-renew.timer
centos# systemctl start certbot-renew.timer
```

Restart the Web Server

The web server loads the certificate in memory, so when a certificate has been renewed, the web server must be restarted to load the new certificate. To accomplish this, `certbot` provides so-called *hooks*, actions that are executed at fixed points in the process. The three defined hooks are the *pre-hook*, which executes scripts before certbot checks whether certificates need renewal; the *deploy-hook*, which executes scripts if one or more certificates have been renewed; and the *post-hook*, which executes scripts after verification and possible renewals, regardless of whether certificates have been renewed or not. The web server should therefore be restarted in the *deploy-hook*, as this is only useful if a certificate was actually renewed.

In the `/usr/local/etc/letsencrypt` directory (FreeBSD) or the `/etc/letsencrypt` directory (Debian and CentOS), a sub-directory `renewal-hooks` exists, which in turn contains the sub-directories `deploy`, `post`, and `pre`. Scripts that are installed in these directories (and that are executable) will be automatically executed by the related hooks. In this case, the script can be very simple.

Apache on FreeBSD:

```
#!/bin/sh
/usr/sbin/service apache24 reload
```

Nginx on FreeBSD:

```
#!/bin/sh
/usr/sbin/service nginx reload
```

Apache on Debian:

```
#!/bin/sh
/bin/systemctl apache2 reload
```

Nginx on Debian and CentOS:

```
#!/bin/sh
/bin/systemctl nginx reload
```

Apache on CentOS:

```
#!/bin/sh
/bin/systemctl httpd reload
```

The system administrator is completely free in the choice of a name for this script; as long as it is installed in the correct directory and made executable, it will be executed. Obviously, these scripts can be used for more than just restarting daemons; an example of another use could be the sending of an email after a successful certificate renewal.

These scripts have several environment variables at their disposal, which contain, among other things, the name of the domain(s) for which the certificate was renewed. See the Certbot website for more information about his.

The section "Lightweight Directory Access Protocol (LDAP)" of Chapter 11, "Databases", contains a more elaborate example of the use of these hooks.

Certificate Removal

Certbot can also be used to delete certificates, if this should ever be necessary. For this to work, the virtual host/server in question should first be removed, or at least have SSL/TLS disabled.

The following command displays a menu of all installed certificates:

```
# certbot delete
```

Select the number(s) of the certificate(s) to be deleted, and press *Enter*. Attention: pressing *Enter* without selecting a certificate will delete all certificates.

As long as a certificate is not removed, it will be renewed automatically, even if it is not in use.

Summary

This chapter discussed TLS encryption. It briefly explained the inner workings of this protocol and the different types of certificates. Subsequently, the installation and maintenance of *Domain Validation* TLS certificates was discussed. TLS encryption was also configured for the default virtual web host.

In the next chapter, several *database management systems* will be installed and configured, including web interfaces for easy manipulation of the databases.

CHAPTER 11

Databases

For centuries, humankind has been developing systems that help to store and retrieve data. It is therefore not surprising that the development of the computer and the database go hand in hand and that databases are an inseparable part of almost every automated system.

Some examples of the use of databases on an internet server are

- Users and passwords

- The association of email addresses and users

- Lists of available and installed software

- Content for websites and web applications

- Virus definitions for the virus scanner

A database is a structurally stored collection of data. A database management system, or simply DBMS, is used to retrieve and manipulate this data (CRUD: Create, Read, Update, Delete).

The majority of databases are so-called relational databases, and the language used to communicate with virtually all relational database management systems (RDBMS) is *SQL* (*Structured Query Language*), a standardized language for working with relational databases. This standard is a minimum set of requirements, and most DBMSs have added their own extensions.

Apart from the extensions each DBMS adds to SQL, the differences between DBMSs consist of the type of tables they support, the way the data is structured and stored; the comparison of these differences is beyond the purpose of this book. Later in this chapter, two general-purpose RDBMSs will be installed: MariaDB and PostgreSQL. A system administrator who has requirements that cannot be fulfilled by these two DBMSs will probably have sufficient knowledge to find a DBMS that does fulfill the requirements.

239

© Robert La Lau 2021
R. La Lau, *Practical Internet Server Configuration*, https://doi.org/10.1007/978-1-4842-6960-2_11

Apart from these two RDBMSs, a directory service will be installed (LDAP). This directory service will be used later in this book to store users who do not have a local system account, but still need to access, for example, the email services provided by this server.

MariaDB, PostgreSQL, and LDAP are installed, configured, and started in this chapter, but will not be actually used until later in this book.

db.example.com

Web interfaces will be installed for MariaDB, PostgreSQL, and LDAP to facilitate their management; these are phpMyAdmin, phpPgAdmin, and phpLDAPadmin, respectively. To not overly complicate the configuration, these web interfaces will all be served from the *db.example.com* virtual host.

To set up this virtual host/server, the following steps must be taken:

1. **DNS record**

   The *db.example.com* hostname must be an alias for *green.example.com.*

   ```
   db  IN  CNAME  green
   ```

   (Increment serial number!)

2. **SSL/TLS certificate**

   The certificate is installed with the following command:

   ```
   # certbot certonly --webroot \
       -w /srv/www/rfc5785 \
       -d db.example.com
   ```

3. **User**

   The www-db user must be created for the execution of PHP scripts. This user's primary group is a group with the same name as the username, and the user is not a member of any other groups. This user's home directory is /srv/www/db.example.com (but this directory needs not be created, yet), and the user will not have a login shell.

4. **Directories**

The virtual host will be installed in the /srv/www/db.example.com
directory.

```
# mkdir /srv/www/db.example.com
# cd /srv/www/db.example.com
# chown webdev:webdev .
# chmod 2770 .

freebsd# setfacl -m user:www:rx .
freebsd# setfacl -d -m user::rwx,group::rwx,other::--- .
freebsd# setfacl -d -m user:www:rx .

debian# setfacl -m user:www-data:rx .
debian# setfacl -m default:user:www-data:rx .

centos+apache# setfacl -m user:apache:rx .
centos+apache# setfacl -m default:user:apache:rx .

centos+nginx# setfacl -m user:nginx:rx .
centos+nginx# setfacl -m default:user:nginx:rx .

# setfacl -m user:www-db:rx .

bsd# setfacl -d -m user::rwx,group::rwx,other::--- .
bsd# setfacl -d -m user:www-db:rx .

linux# setfacl -m default:user:www-db:rx .

# mkdir ./{alias,bin,cgi-bin,conf,htdocs,tmp}
# setfacl -m user:www-db:rwx ./tmp

bsd# setfacl -d -m user::r-x,group::r-x,other::--- ./tmp
bsd# setfacl -d -m user:www-db:rwx ./tmp

linux# setfacl -m default:user:www-db:rwx ./tmp

# echo "<p>db.example.com</p>" > ./htdocs/index.html
```

5. **PHP-FPM pool**

A new PHP-FPM pool is created. The following is the minimal configuration for this new pool; this configuration could be stored as db.conf, for example.

```
[db.example.com]
user = www-db
group = www-db
listen = 127.0.0.1:9001
listen.allowed_clients = 127.0.0.1
pm = ondemand
pm.max_children = 3
env[TMP] = /srv/www/db.example.com/tmp
env[TEMP] = /srv/www/db.example.com/tmp
env[TMPDIR] = /srv/www/db.example.com/tmp
php_flag[short_open_tag] = off
php_admin_value[open_basedir] = /srv/www/db.example.com:/usr/share
php_admin_value[upload_tmp_dir] = /srv/www/db.example.com/tmp
php_admin_value[session.save_path] = /srv/www/db.example.com/tmp
```

On FreeBSD, the directory /usr/share in the *open_basedir* definition must be replaced with /usr/local/www; this is the directory where the web interfaces will be installed.

6. **Virtual host (Apache)**

If the Apache web server was selected, this is the minimal configuration for the virtual host:

```
<VirtualHost *:80>
  ServerName db.example.com
  Redirect permanent "/" "https://db.example.com/"
</VirtualHost>

<VirtualHost *:443>
  ServerName db.example.com

  SSLEngine On
  # Correct these paths for FreeBSD!
```

```
   SSLCertificateFile \
"/etc/letsencrypt/live/db.example.com/fullchain.pem"
   SSLCertificateKeyFile \
"/etc/letsencrypt/live/db.example.com/privkey.pem"

   DocumentRoot /srv/www/db.example.com/htdocs
   <Directory /srv/www/db.example.com/htdocs>
     Require all granted
   </Directory>

   ProxyPassMatch "^/(.*\.php(/.*)?)$" \
"fcgi://127.0.0.1:9001/srv/www/db.example.com/htdocs/$1"
 </VirtualHost>
```

The filename should start with a number greater than the number of the configuration file for the default virtual host, 005-db.conf, for example. On Debian, the virtual host is created in the sites-available directory and then linked to the sites-enabled directory.

7. **Virtual server (Nginx)**

   If the Nginx web server was selected, this is the minimal configuration for the virtual server:

```
server {
  listen 80;
  server_name db.example.com;
  return 301 https://db.example.com/;
}

server {
  listen 443 ssl;
  server_name db.example.com;

  ssl_session_cache shared:SSL:5m;
  ssl_session_timeout 10m;
  keepalive_timeout 75s;
  # Correct these paths for FreeBSD!
  ssl_certificate \
/etc/letsencrypt/live/db.example.com/fullchain.pem;
```

```
  ssl_certificate_key \
/etc/letsencrypt/live/db.example.com/privkey.pem;

  location /.well-known/ {
    alias /srv/www/rfc5785/.well-known/;
  }

  location / {
    root /srv/www/db.example.com/htdocs;
  }

  location ~ \.php$ {
    fastcgi_pass 127.0.0.1:9001;
    fastcgi_index index.php;
    fastcgi_param SCRIPT_FILENAME $request_filename;
    include fastcgi_params;
  }
}
```

(Note that the preceding example is valid for FreeBSD and CentOS; see the previous chapter for the small differences on Debian.)

The filename should start with a number greater than the number of the configuration file for the default virtual host, `005-db.conf`, for example. On Debian, the virtual host is created in the `sites-available` directory and then linked to the `sites-enabled` directory.

8. **Welcome page**

   The web interfaces will be available at the respective addresses *https://db.example.com/mariadb, https://db.example.com/postgres,* and *https://db.example.com/ldap.* Other content for the directory `/srv/www/db.example.com/htdocs` may be freely created. Some system administrators or organizations may wish to create a page that links to those three addresses, while others may instead prefer a page that refers visitors to the main website.

MariaDB (MySQL)

The names MySQL and MariaDB are often used interchangeably, even though they are not the exact same product. The original product is MySQL, an open source DBMS that was developed by the company MySQL AB; this company was sold to Sun Microsystems in 2008. When in turn Sun was sold to Oracle Corporation in 2010, the original owner of MySQL AB lost faith in the direction MySQL went and made a copy of the open source code to start a new open source project on the base of that code (such a copy is called a fork). The company behind MariaDB is called Monty Program AB.

The previous paragraph is in no way information that a system administrator should know by heart, but as the terms *my* and *mysql* are still very frequent in MariaDB, even in filenames, it is practical to realize that these two products share their origin.

Many open source projects, including Linux distributions and BSDs, shared the worries about Oracle's MySQL version and have replaced MySQL with MariaDB as the standard DBMS. Oracle publishes several commercial MySQL variants, but the MySQL Community Server is still open source, and most Unices offer it as an optional alternative to MariaDB.

In the vast majority of setups where one of these two DBMSs is used, it could be replaced with the other one without any problems. Since executable files like `mysql` and `mysql-client` have the same name in both projects, it is less practical to run both systems on the same server.

The installation creates a user and a group with the name mysql. The daemon will be executed under this name.

To make MariaDB/MySQL reachable from the internet, inbound TCP traffic on port 3306 must be allowed. However, this is not necessary for sites that are hosted on the server itself (including phpMyAdmin); these sites contact the DBMS through a Unix socket or through the loopback device. For security reasons, it is therefore recommended to not open this port unless there is a compelling reason to do so.

Installation on FreeBSD

At the moment of writing of this book, MariaDB 10.4 is the most recent version. The package that installs the server also installs the client as a dependency; the installation of the client does not automatically install the server.

```
freebsd# pkg install mariadb104-server
```

Configuration files are not installed. If it should ever be necessary to change MariaDB's default settings, a file named /usr/local/etc/my.cnf should be created, and the following line should be added to /etc/rc.conf:

```
mysql_optfile="/usr/local/etc/my.cnf"
```

Documentation for this configuration file is not installed either. For the accepted settings, the MariaDB website should be consulted.

Per default, MariaDB stores the databases in /var/db/mysql. If some other directory was reserved for this purpose, on a separate partition, for example, the following option must be defined in /etc/rc.conf:

```
mysql_dbdir="/path/to/directory"
```

This directory must belong to user and group mysql.

If the databases must be moved when MariaDB is already in use, the files in the original directory must be moved or copied to the new directory; MariaDB must be stopped before this is done.

The installed service is called mysql-server.

```
freebsd# service mysql-server enable
freebsd# service mysql-server start
```

Installation on Debian

The command to install MariaDB is simple:

```
debian# apt install mariadb-server
```

This command also installs the application mariadb-client. The mariadb daemon is started automatically following the installation.

The configuration files are installed in /etc/mysql; for day-to-day use, it is normally not necessary to modify these. The databases are installed in /var/lib/mysql. If some other directory was reserved for this, on a separate partition, for example, these are the steps to follow:

```
debian# systemctl stop mariadb
debian# nano /etc/mysql/mariadb.conf.d/50-server.cnf
    change option datadir
```

```
debian# mysql_install_db --user=mysql
debian# systemctl start mariadb
```

The mysql_install_db command creates the databases that are used by MariaDB internally for setting and user management. If the *datadir* directory must be moved when MariaDB is already in use, the mysql_install_db command is not executed, but instead the files are moved or copied from the original directory to the new directory.

Installation on CentOS

The mariadb-server package will install the mariadb package, which contains the client, as a dependency.

```
centos# yum install mariadb-server
```

The configuration files are /etc/my.cnf and /etc/my.cnf.d/*.

Per default, MariaDB installs the databases in /var/lib/mysql. If some other directory has been reserved for this, on a separate partition, for example, the option *datadir* in /etc/my.cnf must be modified. The *datadir* directory must belong to user and group mysql. If the databases must be moved when MariaDB is already in use, the files must be moved or copied from the original directory to the new directory; MariaDB must be stopped for this.

The installed service is called mariadb.

```
centos# systemctl start mariadb
```

Post-installation

Once the service has been started, it is wise to make the installation a bit more secure:

```
# mysql_secure_installation
```

This application poses a number of questions and adjusts some settings based on the system administrator's responses. When the root password is asked, this is not the system's root password, but MariaDB's root password (the MySQL/MariaDB administrator is traditionally called root as well); if MariaDB has just been installed, no password has been set yet, and Enter suffices. The application will ask to set a new password for the root account; this account will later be used for user management. Just like the system's root account, the MariaDB root account is not meant to be used for daily work.

Once a MariaDB root password has been set, the MariaDB client, simply called `mysql`, can be used to connect to the MariaDB server.

```
# mysql --password
```

With the root user logged in, this is a good moment to create a user that can be used for day-to-day maintenance.

```
> grant all privileges on *.* to mariadb@localhost identified by
'apassword';
> exit
```

This command consists of the following four components:

- **grant all privileges**

  All available privileges are granted to the new user. Actually, this is not entirely true, since the creation of users and the manipulation of user privileges is excluded from `all privileges`; this privilege can be assigned separately, if desired.

- **on *.***

  The assigned privileges are valid for all tables in all databases. The definition before the dot is the database for which the privileges are valid, and the definition after the dot is the table. This means that the following two definitions mean, respectively, "all tables in database db01" and "table tbl01 in database db02":

  ```
  db01.*
  ```

  ```
  db02.tbl01
  ```

- **to mariadb@localhost**

  The privileges are attributed to the user mariadb, who logs in from host localhost. Any other name may be used instead of mariadb. The username needs not exist as a system username, but this is allowed; in any case, the system username and the MariaDB username are not related in any way. The string `@localhost` indicates that the user can only log in from this server. It is relatively rare that a user logs in from another machine; the user will usually connect to the server over SSH and then log in to the database locally.

- **identified by 'apassword'**

    The password with which this user logs in to the database is `apassword`.

A MariaDB or MySQL command always ends in a semicolon (except the `exit` command).

This user now has almost the same privileges as the root user; from now on, the root account is only needed for user management and for some other more specialized tasks.

For security reasons, it is strongly recommended to create a separate MariaDB user for each website or other application, who only has access to the database for the website or application in question. The following command, for instance, would create a user named `web01`, who has access to all the tables of the `website01` database:

```
> grant all privileges on website01.* to web01@localhost identified by
'password01';
```

This user would use the following command to log in to MariaDB on the command line:

```
$ mysql --user=web01 --password website01
```

Information about all other database manipulations can be found on the MySQL and MariaDB websites.

phpMyAdmin

To facilitate the management of the databases, phpMyAdmin is installed.

Installation on FreeBSD

The most recent version available for FreeBSD is phpMyAdmin 5, and obviously, the version must be installed for the PHP version that has been installed already (PHP 7.4).

```
freebsd# pkg install phpMyAdmin5-php74
```

The files are installed in `/usr/local/www/phpMyAdmin`.

Installation on Debian

The package for Debian is simply called phpmyadmin. During the installation, apt offers to configure a web server (Apache or Lighttpd). Since this configuration does not function with PHP-FPM, no web server needs to be selected here. Then, apt also offers to create a database where phpMyAdmin can store its settings; it is practical to reply Yes here.

```
debian# apt install phpmyadmin
```

The PHP files are installed in /usr/share/phpmyadmin and the configuration file in /etc/phpmyadmin.

Installation on CentOS

The CentOS package is called phpMyAdmin.

```
centos# yum install phpMyAdmin
```

The PHP files are installed in /usr/share/phpMyAdmin and the configuration file in /etc/phpMyAdmin.

Configuration Apache

The following lines must be added to the *db.example.com* virtual host that listens on port 443; this means that these lines are inserted between the <VirtualHost *:443> and </VirtualHost> tags.

```
# Installation directories:
#   FreeBSD : /usr/local/www/phpMyAdmin
#   Debian  : /usr/share/phpmyadmin
#   CentOS  : /usr/share/phpMyAdmin

 Alias "/mariadb" "/usr/local/www/phpMyAdmin"
 <Directory "/usr/local/www/phpMyAdmin">
   Options none
   AllowOverride Limit
   Require all granted
 </Directory>

 ProxyPassMatch "^/mariadb/(.*\.php(/.*)?)$" \
   "fcgi://127.0.0.1:9001/usr/local/www/phpMyAdmin/$1"
```

This makes phpMyAdmin available at the URL *https://db.example.com/mariadb*.

The `ProxyPassMatch` line must be inserted before the existing `ProxyPassMatch` line. These lines are tested in the order in which they are defined in the configuration file, and the existing line matches all URLs that end in `.php`. If the new line was inserted after the existing line, URLs that begin with `/mariadb/` would be caught by the first line and thus never reach the newly added line.

The order for the other elements is not important.

If the web interface is only accessed from a single known IP address or a single set of known IP addresses (e.g., home and/or office), it is recommended to replace the line `Require all granted` with a line like

```
Require ip 192.0.2.125 203.0.113.12
```

This instructs Apache to reject requests from all IP addresses except those listed.

Configuration Nginx

The following lines must be added to the configuration for the *db.example.com* virtual server that listens on port 443; this means that these lines are inserted into the second server context:

```
location /mariadb {
    # Installation directories:
    #    FreeBSD : /usr/local/www/phpMyAdmin
    #    Debian  : /usr/share/phpmyadmin
    #    CentOS  : /usr/share/phpMyAdmin

    alias /usr/local/www/phpMyAdmin;
    location ~ \.php$ {
        fastcgi_pass 127.0.0.1:9001;
        fastcgi_index index.php;
        fastcgi_param SCRIPT_FILENAME $request_filename;
        include fastcgi_params;
    }
}
```

This will make the web interface available at the address
https://db.example.com/mariadb.

If the web interface is only accessed from a single known IP address or a single set of
known IP addresses (e.g., home and/or office), it is recommended to add lines like the
following:

```
allow 192.0.2.125;
allow 203.0.113.12;
deny all;
```

This instructs Nginx to reject requests from all IP addresses except for those listed.

Configuration PHP-FPM

The PHP-FPM pool configuration for *db.example.com* defines the php.ini option
open_basedir to limit the number of directories that this pool has access to.

```
php_admin_value[open_basedir] = /srv/www/db.example.com:/usr/share
```

With this, PHP has the correct privileges to read phpMyAdmin's installation
directory. However, to grant PHP the right to read the configuration directory on Debian
and CentOS, a directory must be added to this definition. For CentOS, this would look
like the following:

```
php_admin_value[open_basedir] =
/srv/www/db.example.com:/usr/share:/etc/phpMyAdmin
```

This should be on a single line.

Furthermore, the configuration file config-db.php belongs to the www-data group
(the web server). Since PHP-FPM is not executed with the web server's username, this
must be corrected.

```
debian# find /etc/phpmyadmin \
        -group www-data \
        -exec chgrp www-db {} \;
```

(The combination of backslash and semicolon at the end of that command is
important.)

Configuration phpMyAdmin

Per default, phpMyAdmin's configuration file `config.inc.php` is installed in the installation directory with the rest of the files. However, the Debian package installs it into `/etc/phpmyadmin`, and the CentOS package installs it into `/etc/phpMyAdmin`. As with the configuration of other packages, Debian splits up the configuration into a multitude of files.

The configuration for phpMyAdmin provides extensive comments, and the website offers documentation in multiple languages.

Connecting to phpMyAdmin

The address *https://db.example.com/mariadb* is used to connect to phpMyAdmin. Per default, the root user cannot log in through phpMyAdmin, but the MariaDB user that was created in an earlier section can; the username is entered without the `@localhost` suffix.

PostgreSQL

PostgreSQL, or simply Postgres, descends from Ingres, which started development in the beginning of the 1970s; this makes Postgres about 20–25 years more mature than MariaDB. Contrary to MariaDB, the PostgreSQL project is not managed by a company, but by a community of private individuals and companies. The PostgreSQL license is less restrictive than the GNU General Public License used by MariaDB.

PostgreSQL has been ported to more operating systems than MariaDB. On the other hand, more programming languages have built-in support for MariaDB than for PostgreSQL.

During the installation, a user and group named postgres will be created. The PostgreSQL daemon will be executed with this username.

To make PostgreSQL reachable from the internet, inbound TCP traffic on port 5432 must be allowed. However, this is not necessary for sites that are hosted on the server itself (including phpPgAdmin). For security reasons, it is therefore recommended to not open this port unless there is a compelling reason to do so.

Installation on FreeBSD

At the moment of writing of this book, the most recent available version is PostgreSQL 12. However, the web interface that will be installed in a following section supports PostgreSQL 11 as the most recent version. In this case, the ease of maintenance is more important than having the latest functionalities, so PostgreSQL 11 will be installed.

The server package automatically installs the client as a dependency; the client package does not automatically install the server.

```
freebsd# pkg install postgresql11-server
```

Per default, the databases are stored in /var/db/postgres, which is the home directory for the user account with which the PostgreSQL daemon is executed. If some other directory has been reserved for this purpose, on a separate partition, for example, the home directory for the postgres user must be changed; Chapter 5, "User Management and Permissions," explains how this is done.

When the installation is completed, the daemon must be enabled, after which the initial data structure can be created.

```
freebsd# service postgresql enable
freebsd# service postgresql initdb
```

This creates the databases that are used for settings and user management, as well as the configuration files; all these files are installed in user postgres's home directory.

Then, the daemon may be started.

```
freebsd# service postgresql start
```

If the databases must be moved when PostgreSQL is already in use, this is the procedure to follow:

```
freebsd# service postgresql stop
freebsd# nano /var/db/postgres/data11/postgresql.conf
  modify variable data_directory
freebsd# mv /var/db/postgres/* /path/to/new/directory
freebsd# vipw
  change home directory to /path/to/new/directory
freebsd# service postgresql start
```

The configuration file ~postgres/data11/postgresql.conf is documented with extensive comments. If and when this file has been changed, the daemon must be restarted.

If desired, user postgres's home directory and the directory where the databases are stored can be separated by defining the *postgresql_data* variable in /etc/rc.conf. The postgresql.conf configuration file can normally be found in the data directory; this location can be changed by including a line like the following in /etc/rc.conf:

```
postgresql_flags="-c config_file=/usr/local/etc/postgresql.conf"
```

The HTML documentation can be installed with the postgresql11-docs package; the files will be installed in /usr/local/share/doc/postgresql. Obviously, this documentation is also available at the PostgreSQL website.

Installation on Debian

The postgresql package installs the most recent available version; this is PostgreSQL 9.6 at the time of writing of this book. The package also installs the accompanying client.

```
debian# apt install postgresql
```

The daemon is automatically started when the installation is complete.

The configuration files are installed in /etc/postgresql and /etc/postgresql-common.

The databases are stored in /var/lib/postgresql. If some other directory was reserved for this purpose, on a separate partition, for example, this is the procedure to follow:

```
debian# systemctl stop postgresql
debian# nano /etc/postgresql/*/*/postgresql.conf
  modify variable data_directory
debian# mv /var/lib/postgresql/* /path/to/new/directory
debian# systemctl start postgresql
```

The postgresql-doc package installs the documentation; this installs the man pages and the HTML documentation.

Installation on CentOS

The postgresql-server package installs the PostgreSQL daemon. This package automatically installs the most recent available version, which is PostgreSQL 9 at the time of writing this book. The PostgreSQL client is also installed automatically as a dependency.

```
centos# yum install postgresql-server
```

Subsequently, the initial databases must be created with the following command:

```
centos# postgresql-setup initdb
```

The databases are installed in /var/lib/pgsql/data.
Once the databases have been created, the daemon can be started.

```
centos# systemctl start postgresql
```

If some other directory has been reserved for the databases, on a separate partition, for example, this is the procedure to follow (after the initialization of the preceding databases):

```
centos# systemctl stop postgresql
centos# mkdir /path/to/new/directory
centos# chown postgres:postgres /path/to/new/directory
centos# cp -a /var/lib/pgsql/* /path/to/new/directory
centos# nano /usr/lib/systemd/postgresql.service
  modify the line Environment=PGDATA=/var/lib/pgsql/data
centos# systemctl daemon-reload
centos# systemctl start postgresql
```

Post-installation

Once the postgresql daemon is started, the client, called psql, can be used to connect to the server. However, as long as no other PostgreSQL users have been created, this can only be done through the account of the postgres system user.

```
# sudo -u postgres psql
postgres=# help
postgres=# \q
#
```

For the creation of new users and all other database manipulations, the PostgreSQL documentation should be consulted.

For security reasons, it is strongly recommended to create a separate PostgreSQL user for each website or other application.

phpPgAdmin

To facilitate database management, phpPgAdmin is installed.

Installation on FreeBSD

On FreeBSD, the version should be installed that corresponds to the PHP version that is installed (7.4).

```
freebsd# pkg install phppgadmin-php74
```

The files are installed in /usr/local/www/phpPgAdmin.

Installation on Debian

The Debian phppgadmin package automatically installs the most recent version. The installation scripts insist on configuring Apache, but since this configuration does not function with PHP-FPM, it can be removed immediately afterward.

```
debian# apt install phppgadmin
debian# rm /etc/apache2/conf-enabled/phppgadmin.conf
```

The PHP files are installed in /usr/share/phppgadmin and the configuration file in /etc/phppgadmin.

Installation on CentOS

The CentOS package is called phpPgAdmin.

```
centos# yum install phpPgAdmin
```

The PHP files are installed in /usr/share/phpPgAdmin and the configuration file in /etc/phpPgAdmin.

Configuration Apache

The following lines should be added to the configuration for the virtual host *db.example.com* that listens on port 443; this means that these lines are inserted between the `<VirtualHost *:443>` and `</VirtualHost>` tags:

```
# Installation directories:
#   FreeBSD : /usr/local/www/phpPgAdmin
#   Debian  : /usr/share/phppgadmin
#   CentOS  : /usr/share/phpPgAdmin

Alias "/postgres" "/usr/local/www/phpPgAdmin"
<Directory "/usr/local/www/phpPgAdmin">
  Options none
  AllowOverride Limit
  Require all granted
</Directory>

ProxyPassMatch "^/postgres/(.*\.php(/.*)?)$" \
  "fcgi://127.0.0.1:9001/usr/local/www/phpPgAdmin/$1"
```

This makes phpPgAdmin available at the address *https://db.example.com/postgres*.

The `ProxyPassMatch` line must be inserted before the existing `ProxyPassMatch` line. These lines are tested in the order in which they are defined in the configuration file, and the existing line matches all URLs that end in `.php`. If the new line was inserted after the existing line, URLs that begin with `/postgres/` would be caught by the first line and thus never reach the newly added line.

The order for the other elements is not important.

If the web interface is only accessed from a single known IP address or a single set of known IP addresses (e.g., home and/or office), it is recommended to replace the line `Require all granted` with a line like

```
Require ip 192.0.2.125 203.0.113.12
```

This instructs Apache to reject requests from all IP addresses except those listed.

Configuration Nginx

The following lines should be added to the configuration for the virtual server *db.example.com* that listens on port 443; this means that these lines are inserted into the second server context:

```
location /postgres {
    # Installation directories:
    #   FreeBSD : /usr/local/www/phpPgAdmin
    #   Debian  : /usr/share/phppgadmin
    #   CentOS  : /usr/share/phpPgAdmin

    alias /usr/local/www/phpPgAdmin;
    location ~ \.php$ {
        fastcgi_pass 127.0.0.1:9001;
        fastcgi_index index.php;
        fastcgi_param SCRIPT_FILENAME $request_filename;
        include fastcgi_params;
    }
}
```

This makes the web interface available at the address *https://db.example.com/postgres*.

If the web interface is only accessed from a single known IP address or a single set of known IP addresses (e.g., home and/or office), it is recommended to add lines like the following:

```
allow 192.0.2.125;
allow 203.0.113.12;
deny all;
```

This instructs Nginx to reject requests from all IP addresses except for those listed.

Configuration PHP-FPM

The PHP-FPM pool configuration for *db.example.com* defines the php.ini option *open_basedir* to limit the number of directories that this pool has access to.

```
php_admin_value[open_basedir] = /srv/www/db.example.com:/usr/share
```

With this, PHP has the correct privileges to read phpPgAdmin's installation directory. However, to grant PHP the right to read the configuration directory on Debian and CentOS, a directory must be added to this definition. For Debian, this would look like the following:

```
php_admin_value[open_basedir] =
/srv/www/db.example.com:/usr/share:/etc/phppgadmin
```

This should be on a single line.

Configuration phpPgAdmin

Per default, phpPgAdmin's configuration file `config.inc.php` is installed in the `conf` sub-directory in the installation directory. However, the Debian package installs it into `/etc/phppgadmin`, and the CentOS package installs it into `/etc/phpPgAdmin`.

The configuration for phpPgAdmin provides extensive comments, and the website offers additional documentation.

Lightweight Directory Access Protocol (LDAP)

LDAP is not a database, nor is it a database management system. LDAP is a network protocol that is used to communicate with a directory service; a directory service is comparable to a *DBMS* that is used to access hierarchically structured data. However, the term directory service is also often used to indicate the underlying database, and the term LDAP is also often used to indicate the directory service and the underlying database; it is good to recognize this, but it is also good to know that this is not entirely correct.

The units stored in the database are called entries, objects, or records. A record has one or more attributes; an attribute has one or more values. A Person object, for example, could have First Name, Last Name, Email Address, and Phone Number attributes. Each record always has a Distinguished Name (DN) attribute. This is a unique name that identifies the object in the database.

For exchange, transfer, and modification, the data in the database can be represented as plain text. This text format is called *LDIF* (*LDAP Data Interchange Format*). An LDIF file can consist of one or more records, separated by empty lines; a record consists of one or more attributes, with one attribute per line and no empty lines. Values that cannot be represented in ASCII can be encoded using base64, an encoding system that allows for the representation of binary data as ASCII.

The LDAP installation described here is mainly intended to be used as a user database for the email server. However, many other uses are possible for LDAP.

During the installation, a user and group named ldap (FreeBSD and CentOS) or openldap (Debian) are created. The daemon will be executed under this name.

Another tool that will be installed is phpLDAPadmin. This is a web interface for the directory service, comparable to phpMyAdmin for MariaDB/MySQL and phpPgAdmin for PostgreSQL. Several desktop clients exist for the manipulation of LDAP directory services. These clients are installed on the PC or workstation and connect to server over the network. One of those clients, Apache Directory Studio, will be discussed briefly.

To make LDAP accessible from the internet, inbound traffic on port 636 must be allowed in the firewall; unencrypted LDAP traffic uses port 389, but this is only used over the loopback device in this setup and does not need to be allowed explicitly in the firewall. The encrypted TCP port is used to manipulate the directory service remotely; the IMAP server uses the unencrypted port for user authentication; phpLDAPadmin and command-line applications use the installed Unix socket.

Installation

OpenLDAP is the *de facto* standard open source LDAP server, and moreover, it is available for more operating systems than other LDAP servers. This is the server that will be installed here.

The installation on Debian asks for a password for the LDAP administrator during the installation. Since the existing configuration will be removed after the installation, the password entered here is not important.

```
freebsd# pkg install openldap-server
```

```
debian# apt install slapd ldap-utils
    enter LDAP administrator password
```

```
centos# yum install openldap-servers openldap-clients
```

On FreeBSD the configuration files are installed in /usr/local/etc/openldap, on Debian in /etc/ldap, and on CentOS in /etc/openldap. The daemon is called slapd on all three systems; on Debian the service is started automatically, and on CentOS the service is not started, but a sample database is created.

To avoid surprises later on, it is recommended to delete the existing configuration files and databases and start from scratch.

```
freebsd# rm /usr/local/etc/openldap/slapd.{conf,ldif}
```

```
debian# systemctl stop slapd
debian# rm /var/lib/ldap/*
debian# rm -rf /etc/ldap/slapd.d
```

```
centos# rm /var/lib/ldap/*
centos# rm -rf /etc/openldap/slapd.d
```

TLS Certificate

As the LDAP server may be accessed from the internet (e.g., with the help of Apache Directory Studio), this traffic must be encrypted. A Let's Encrypt certificate, as generated earlier for the hostnames *green.example.com* and *db.example.com*, can be used for this purpose. A new certificate will be generated: the LDAP server will be attributed its own subdomain, and since the certificates are free of charge, there is no need to use a single certificate for all subdomains.

To begin with, a new DNS alias named *ldap.example.com* is added. Only a single line needs to be added to the zone file for *example.com*:

```
ldap    IN   CNAME   green
```

Obviously, the serial number for the file must also be incremented, and named should reload its configuration when the file has been saved.

The certificates can be requested without creating a virtual host first, because in a previous chapter, a default virtual host has been created, which catches all traffic for hostnames that do not have a virtual host configured explicitly.

```
# certbot certonly --webroot \
    -w /srv/www/rfc5785 \
    -d ldap.example.com
```

The new certificate is stored in /usr/local/etc/letsencrypt (FreeBSD) or /etc/letsencrypt (Debian and CentOS). However, user ldap (FreeBSD and CentOS) or openldap (Debian) does not have access to that directory, so the certificate must be copied to OpenLDAP's configuration directory. It is practical to create a small script for

this purpose; save this as /usr/local/sbin/tls-openldap (it can also be downloaded
from the online addendum for this book):

```
#!/usr/bin/env bash

# The name under which the certificate is stored.
dom="ldap.example.com"

# When the script is executed on the command line,
# the system should be passed as an environment variable.
# Example:
#     env system=freebsd tls-openldap
[ -z "${system}" ] && {
  cat <<-EOM
    Usage:
      env system=<os> $(basename $0)

    Where <os> is one of the following possibilities:
      freebsd
      debian
      centos

    Example:
       env system=freebsd $(basename $0)
EOM
  exit 1
}

# Define source, destination and user:group.
case "${system}" in
  freebsd)
    src="/usr/local/etc/letsencrypt/live/${dom}/*.pem"
    dst="/usr/local/etc/openldap/certs"
    ug="ldap:ldap"
    ;;
  debian)
    src="/etc/letsencrypt/live/${dom}/*.pem"
    dst="/etc/ldap/certs"
    ug="openldap:openldap"
    ;;
```

```
  centos)
    src="/etc/letsencrypt/live/${dom}/*.pem"
    dst="/etc/openldap/certs"
    ug="ldap:ldap"
    ;;
  *)
    echo "Unknown system."
    exit 1
    ;;
esac

# Create destination directory, if it doesn't exist.
[ ! -d "${dst}" ] && {
  mkdir "${dst}" \
    && chown ${ug} "${dst}" \
    && chmod 750 "${dst}" \
    || exit 1
}

# Copy the certificates.
cp -L ${src} ${dst}
chown ${ug} ${dst}/*
chmod 640 ${dst}/*
```

Make the script executable (but only for root), and execute it with the system in question as an environment variable.

```
# chown root:root /usr/local/sbin/tls-openldap

# chmod 750 /usr/local/sbin/tls-openldap

freebsd# env system=freebsd tls-openldap

debian# env system=debian tls-openldap

centos# env system=centos tls-openldap
```

The certs sub-directory of the OpenLDAP configuration now contains four files of which the name ends in .pem.

Let's Encrypt certificates have a validity of three months, and it is not quite practical to have to execute this script every three months. However, it is possible to have `certbot` execute certain actions when certificates have successfully been renewed; this functionality can be used to automatically copy new certificates to the OpenLDAP configuration directory.

For this, a second script is created. Save this as `/etc/letsencrypt/renewal-hooks/deploy/copy-certs` (this should be prepended with `/usr/local` on FreeBSD):

```bash
#!/usr/bin/env bash

# Terminate the execution if a command
# terminates unsuccessfully.
 set -e

# Exit function.
 unknown() {
    echo "Unknown system."
    exit 1
}

# Determine what system this is.
uname=$(uname)
case ${uname} in
  FreeBSD)
    system=freebsd
    ;;
  Linux)
    if [ -f /etc/os-release ]; then
      system=$(source /etc/os-release; echo ${ID})
    else
      unknown
    fi
    ;;
  *)
    unknown
    ;;
esac
unset uname
```

```
# Execute this loop for all domains
# that had their certificates renewed.
 for dom in ${RENEWED_DOMAINS}; do
   case ${dom} in
     ldap.example.com)

         # If the domain is ldap.example.com.
         # copy the certificates to the LDAP directory.
         env system=${system} /usr/local/sbin/tls-openldap

         # And restart the LDAP daemon.
         case ${system} in
           freebsd)
             service slapd restart
             ;;
           debian|centos)
             systemctl restart slapd
             ;;
         esac
         ;;
   esac
 done
```

Make this script executable:

```
# chown root:root copy-certs
# chmod 750 copy-certs
```

Scripts in the `renewal-hooks/deploy` sub-directory of the Let's Encrypt configuration directory are executed if and when certificates have been renewed successfully. So the preceding two scripts make `certbot` copy successfully renewed certificates for *ldap.example.com* to the OpenLDAP configuration directory; the names of the certificates do not change, so there is no need to modify the OpenLDAP configuration. Obviously, the preceding two scripts could have been joined into a single script, but that would have made it harder to execute it on the command line.

Daemon Configuration

The OpenLDAP configuration is created in LDIF format first and then converted to an LDAP directory that is used by slapd (the OpenLDAP daemon). This way, most of the settings can be modified using LDAP commands, which means that usually the daemon does not need to be restarted after a configuration change. The configuration file for slapd is called slapd.ldif.

```
freebsd# cd /usr/local/etc/openldap

debian# cd /etc/ldap

centos# cd /etc/openldap

# nano slapd.ldif
```

The following configuration is a solid configuration to begin with. As indicated, empty lines have a meaning in LDIF, so they cannot be randomly added or deleted. For readability, empty lines starting with a hash sign can be inserted; these lines will be ignored as comments and will not influence the format of the file. A line starting with a space is interpreted by OpenLDAP as a continuation of the previous line instead of as a new line. In this case, it is important to know that exactly one space is removed when the lines are joined internally; it may therefore be necessary to start the continuation line with two spaces, if the last characters on the first line and the first characters on the second line must not be joined into a single word.

The strings in bold must be verified and possibly corrected. If the domain name consists of more than two components (*london.europe.example.com*), these components can be added without any problem (dc=london,dc=europe,dc=example,dc=com).

```
# The 'cn=config' DN is hard-coded in OpenLDAP's code,
# and cannot be changed.
 dn: cn=config
 objectClass: olcGlobal
 cn: config
#
# PID file and command line arguments.
# Directories:
#   FreeBSD: /var/run/openldap
#   Debian : /var/run/slapd
#   CentOS : /var/run/openldap
```

```
 olcArgsFile: /var/run/slapd/slapd.args
 olcPidFile: /var/run/slapd/slapd.pid
#
# SSL/TLS certificates + key.
# Directories:
#   FreeBSD: /usr/local/etc/openldap/certs
#   Debian : /etc/ldap/certs
#   CentOS : /etc/openldap/certs
 olcTLSCertificateFile: /etc/ldap/certs/fullchain.pem
 olcTLSCertificateKeyFile: /etc/ldap/certs/privkey.pem
 olcTLSCACertificateFile: /etc/ldap/certs/chain.pem
 olcTLSVerifyClient: never

# The database backend to be loaded.
#
# This section can be omitted entirely on CentOS, where
# back_mdb is built-in, and needs not be loaded as a module.
# This can be verified with the following command:
#    slapd -VVV
#
# Directories:
#   FreeBSD: /usr/local/libexec/openldap
#   Debian : /usr/lib/ldap
#   CentOS : /usr/lib64/openldap
 dn: cn=module,cn=config
 objectClass: olcModuleList
 cn: module
 olcModulePath: /usr/lib/ldap
 olcModuleLoad: back_mdb

# Schema configuration.
 dn: cn=schema,cn=config
 objectClass: olcSchemaConfig
 cn: schema

# Schema to be loaded.
# Directories:
```

```
#    FreeBSD: /usr/local/etc/openldap/schema
#    Debian : /etc/ldap/schema
#    CentOS : /etc/openldap/schema
 include: file:///etc/ldap/schema/core.ldif
 include: file:///etc/ldap/schema/cosine.ldif
 include: file:///etc/ldap/schema/nis.ldif

# The 'frontend' database contains the default settings
# for all the other databases.
dn: olcDatabase=frontend,cn=config
objectClass: olcDatabaseConfig
objectClass: olcFrontendConfig
olcDatabase: frontend
olcAccess: to * by * read
# SHA is the default password hash.
olcPasswordHash: {SSHA}

# Security for the configuration.
# Login credentials:
#    login DN: cn=config
#    password: helloconfig
# Use the `slappasswd' command to generate the password hash.
dn: olcDatabase=config,cn=config
objectClass: olcDatabaseConfig
olcDatabase: config
olcRootDN: cn=Manager,cn=config
olcRootPW: {SSHA}Sn+shDsSKusf6sUdlw2kA2D5v23dHJh2
olcAccess: to * by * none

# The actual database.
dn: olcDatabase=mdb,cn=config
objectClass: olcDatabaseConfig
objectClass: olcMdbConfig
olcDatabase: mdb
olcDbMaxSize: 1073741824
olcSuffix: dc=example,dc=com
#
# The database administrator.
# Login credentials:
```

```
#    login DN: cn=Manager,dc=example,dc=com
#    password: helloldap
# Use the `slappasswd` command to generate the password hash.
olcRootDN: cn=Manager,dc=example,dc=com
olcRootPW: {SSHA}tXOobEm/DqrTwUOtsNcgOlxgS7Fp9/QH
#
# The database directory.
# This directory's path:
#   FreeBSD: /var/db/openldap-data
#   Debian : /var/lib/ldap
#   CentOS : /var/lib/ldap
# This directory must exist, may not have permissions more
# permissive than 0770, and must be owned by the
# slapd user/group (FreeBSD, CentOS: ldap; Debian: openldap).
olcDbDirectory: /var/lib/ldap
#
# Access rights.
# (The continuation lines begin with 2 spaces!)
#
# Passwords can be modified by the user and the LDAP manager.
olcAccess: to attrs=userPassword
  by self write
  by anonymous auth
  by dn.base="cn=Manager,dc=example,dc=com" write
  by * none
#
# The timestamp for the last password change.
olcAccess: to attrs=shadowLastChange
  by self write
  by * read
#
# All other data can only be changed by the Manager.
olcAccess: to *
  by dn.exact="cn=Manager,dc=example,dc=com" write
  by * read
```

To avoid storing passwords as plain text in the configuration, a hash is generated using the slappasswd command.

The directory for the PID file and the Unix socket must be created, if it does not exist yet.

```
freebsd# mkdir -p /var/run/openldap
freebsd# chown ldap:ldap /var/run/openldap

centos# mkdir -p /var/run/openldap
centos# chown ldap:ldap /var/run/openldap
```

Then, the LDIF file is converted to a configuration directory.

```
# mkdir ./slapd.d
# slapadd -n 0 -F ./slapd.d -l ./slapd.ldif
# chmod 750 ./slapd.d

freebsd# chown -R ldap:ldap ./slapd.d

debian# chown -R openldap:openldap ./slapd.d

centos# chown -R ldap:ldap ./slapd.d
```

The sub-directories and files in the new directory should never be modified manually; they are loaded by slapd when the daemon is started, after which the data can be edited using LDAP commands, just like all the other data that is managed through LDAP.

Lastly, before slapd can be started, the command-line parameters for the startup scripts must be modified.

On FreeBSD, these lines must be added to /etc/rc.conf:

```
slapd_enable="YES"

slapd_flags="-F /usr/local/etc/openldap/slapd.d -h
ldap://127.0.0.1/ ld api://%2fvar%2frun%2fopenldap%2fldapi/ ldaps:///"

slapd_sockets="/var/run/openldap/ldapi"
```

(This may not be entirely clear, but these are three lines.)

On Debian, the following options must be modified in /etc/default/slapd:

```
SLAPD_CONF="/etc/ldap/slapd.d"
SLAPD_SERVICES="ldap://127.0.0.1/ ldaps:/// ldapi:///"
```

On CentOS, these settings must be made in /etc/sysconfig/slapd:

```
SLAPD_URLS="ldap://127.0.0.1/ ldaps:/// ldapi:///"
SLAPD_OPTIONS="-F /etc/openldap/slapd.d"
```

The *ldap://127.0.0.1/* URL indicates that unencrypted connections can only be made over the loopback device; the *ldaps:///* URL says that SSL/TLS-encrypted connections can be made from any IP address; and the *ldapi:///* URL references a Unix socket. Note that all URLs contain three slashes.

The daemon can now be started.

```
freebsd# service slapd start
```

```
debian# systemctl start slapd
```

```
centos# systemctl enable slapd
centos# systemctl start slapd
```

Client Configuration

For the local (command-line) LDAP clients, some default settings can be made in the ldap.conf file in the OpenLDAP configuration directory. The system administrator decides, with the help of the accompanying man pages, which settings should or should not be made in this configuration file. However, the following two lines are strongly recommended (and the commands in the following sections will give error messages if these settings have not been made):

```
# nano ldap.conf
```

```
BASE          dc=example,dc=com
URI           ldapi:///
```

More information about the LDAP command-line clients can be found in ldapadd(1) and the man pages referred by that man page.

Container for Users

The LDAP server has been started, and it's time to create the first records. As indicated, the data in a directory service is structured hierarchically. To realize this structure, the first record that is created is of type organization; below this record, a record of type organizationalUnit will be created that will serve as a "container" for the user records. These types (objectClasses) are both defined in the Core schema that was added to the configuration in the preceding LDIF configuration file.

Save the following as, for example, /root/org-unit.ldif:

```
dn: dc=example,dc=com
objectClass: dcObject
objectClass: organization
o: ExampleCom LDAP server
dc: example

dn: ou=users,dc=example,dc=com
objectClass: top
objectClass: organizationalUnit
ou: gebruikers
```

Like dn stands for Distinguished Name (the object's unique name in the hierarchy), o stands for organization and ou for organizationalUnit; dc means Domain Component.

This file is loaded into the LDAP directory with the following command:

```
# ldapadd -D "cn=Manager,dc=example,dc=com" \
    -f /root/org-unit.ldif \
    -W
```

The argument to the -D option is the olcRootDN as specified in the first LDIF file for the database (the second olcRootDN in the file); the last argument is a capital W.

These commands verify that the objects have been loaded correctly:

```
# ldapsearch -x '(objectclass=organization)'
# ldapsearch -x '(objectclass=organizationalUnit)'
```

Users will be added in Chapter 12, "Email Basics".

phpLDAPadmin

The phpLDAPadmin package is a web interface for LDAP, comparable to phpMyAdmin for MariaDB/MySQL and phpPgAdmin for PostgreSQL. This interface is a great tool to make the complex LDAP matter more transparent.

Installation on FreeBSD

On FreeBSD, the installed version should match the installed PHP version.

```
freebsd# pkg info php*
freebsd# pkg search phpldapadmin
freebsd# pkg install phpldapadmin-php74
```

The files are installed in /usr/local/www/phpldapadmin.

Installation on Debian

The Debian package is simply called phpldapadmin. The installation scripts insist on configuring Apache, but since this configuration does not function with PHP-FPM, it can be removed immediately after the installation has completed.

```
debian# apt install phpldapadmin
debian# rm /etc/apache2/conf-enabled/phpldapadmin.conf
```

The PHP files are installed in /usr/share/phpldapadmin and the configuration files in /etc/phpldapadmin.

Installation on CentOS

The CentOS package is also simply called phpldapadmin.

```
centos# yum install phpldapadmin
```

The PHP files are installed in /usr/share/phpldapadmin and the configuration files in /etc/phpldapadmin.

Configuration Apache

The following lines should be added to the configuration for the virtual host *db.example.com* that listens on port 443; this means that these lines are inserted between the <VirtualHost *:443> and </VirtualHost> tags:

```
# Installation directories:
#   FreeBSD : /usr/local/www/phpldapadmin/htdocs
#   Debian  : /usr/share/phpldapadmin/htdocs
#   CentOS  : /usr/share/phpldapadmin/htdocs
```

```
Alias "/ldap" "/usr/local/www/phpldapadmin/htdocs"
<Directory "/usr/local/www/phpldapadmin">
  Options none
  AllowOverride Limit
  Require all granted
</Directory>

ProxyPassMatch "^/ldap/(.*\.php(/.*)?)$" \
"fcgi://127.0.0.1:9001/usr/local/www/phpldapadmin/htdocs/$1"
```

This makes phpLDAPadmin available at the URL *https://db.example.com/ldap.*

The `ProxyPassMatch` line must be inserted before the existing `ProxyPassMatch` line. These lines are tested in the order in which they are defined in the configuration file, and the existing line matches all URLs that end in `.php`. If the new line was inserted after the existing line, URLs that begin with `/ldap/` would be caught by the first line and thus never reach the newly added line.

The order for the other elements is not important.

If the web interface is only accessed from a single known IP address or a single set of known IP addresses (e.g., home and/or office), it is recommended to replace the line Require all granted with a line like

```
Require ip 192.0.2.125 203.0.113.12
```

This instructs Apache to reject requests from all IP addresses except those listed.

Configuration Nginx

The following lines should be added to the configuration for the virtual server *db.example.com* that listens on port 443; this means that these lines are inserted into the second server context:

```
location /ldap {
    # Installation directories:
    #   FreeBSD : /usr/local/www/phpldapadmin/htdocs
    #   Debian  : /usr/share/phpldapadmin/htdocs
    #   CentOS  : /usr/share/phpldapadmin/htdocs
```

275

```
    alias /usr/local/www/phpldapadmin/htdocs;
    location ~ \.php$ {
        fastcgi_pass 127.0.0.1:9001;
        fastcgi_index index.php;
        fastcgi_param SCRIPT_FILENAME $request_filename;
        include fastcgi_params;
    }
}
```

This makes the web interface available at the address *https://db.example.com/ldap*.

If the web interface is only accessed from a single known IP address or a single set of known IP addresses (e.g., home and/or office), it is recommended to add lines like the following:

```
allow 192.0.2.125;
allow 203.0.113.12;
deny all;
```

This instructs Nginx to reject requests from all IP addresses except for those listed.

Configuration PHP-FPM

The PHP-FPM pool configuration for *db.example.com* defines the php.ini option *open_basedir* to limit the number of directories that this pool has access to.

```
php_admin_value[open_basedir] = /srv/www/db.example.com:/usr/share
```

With this, PHP has the correct privileges to read phpLDAPadmin's installation directory. However, to grant PHP the right to read the configuration directory on Debian and CentOS, a directory must be added to this definition. For Debian, this would look like the following:

```
php_admin_value[open_basedir] =
/srv/www/db.example.com:/usr/share:/etc/phpldapadmin
```

This should be on a single line.

Furthermore, the configuration files belong to the www-data group (the web server). Since PHP-FPM is not executed with the web server's username, this must be corrected.

```
debian# find /etc/phpldapadmin \
        -group www-data \
        -exec chgrp www-db {} \;
```

(The combination of backslash and semicolon at the end of that command is important.)

Configuration phpLDAPadmin

The configuration files for phpLDAPadmin have been installed in /etc/phpldapadmin (/usr/local/www/phpldapadmin on FreeBSD). Currently, the only important file in this directory is config.php. A few settings must be modified in this file. These settings can be found in the section that begins about halfway the file with the following banner:

```
/*********************************************
* Define your LDAP servers in this section  *
*********************************************/
```

These are the settings that must be modified to allow a connection to the installed LDAP server:

- **$servers->setValue('server','name','ldap.example.com');**

  It is not mandatory to change this option; this value is only used as the displayed name of the server in the interface.

- **$servers->setValue('server','host','127.0.0.1');**

  In this line, the IP address 127.0.0.1 must be replaced with the path to the LDAP server's Unix socket; in that path, each slash must be replaced with %2f.

  On FreeBSD and CentOS (/var/run/openldap/ldapi), the new value becomes

  ldapi://%2fvar%2frun%2fopenldap%2fldapi

  and on Debian (/var/run/slapd/ldapi), it becomes

  ldapi://%2fvar%2frun%2fslapd%2fldapi

- **$servers->setValue('server','port',389);**

  Since the previous option defined the use of a Unix socket for phpLDAPadmin and Unix sockets do not use network sockets, this option can be disabled by placing two slashes at the beginning of the line.

- **$servers->setValue('server','base',array(...));**

  This option can be disabled by placing two slashes at the beginning of the line.

- **$servers->setValue('login','auth_type','session');**

  The session authentication type makes the most sense for the current setup.

- **$servers->setValue('login','bind_id','');**

  Leave the value for bind_id empty, like the comments in the file dictate when the auth_type has a value of session.

- **$servers->setValue('login','bind_pass','');**

  This value also stays empty, like the comments dictate.

- **$servers->setValue('server','tls',false);**

  This option stays disabled. A TLS certificate has been installed, but Unix sockets do not use TLS encryption. The certificate will be used to encrypt the connection between desktop clients, like Apache Directory Studio, and the server.

All other options in this file are optional and are left to the reader's creativity.

Connecting to phpLDAPadmin

It is now possible to log in to phpLDAPadmin at the address *https://db.example.com/ldap*. The *Login DN* used here is the olcRootDN that was defined in the LDIF file for the database. In the example file earlier in this chapter, that was

```
cn=Manager,dc=example,dc=com
```

The accompanying password in the example was helloldap.

The web interface regularly displays messages like "*Automatically removed objectClass from template*" and "*Automatically removed attribute from template*". This is normal behavior and can be ignored; to hide these messages, the *$config->custom->appearance['hide_template_warning']* variable in `config.php` can be given a value of `true`. More information about this can be found in the FAQ at the phpLDAPadmin website.

Apache Directory Studio

Apache Directory Studio is a desktop client for LDAP, developed in Java. The application is available for Windows, Linux, and Mac. Thus, Apache Directory Studio is not installed on the server, but on the PC or workstation.

Finding, downloading, and installing the application is self-explanatory, so that will not be discussed here. However, before the client can connect to the server, the Let's Encrypt intermediate certificate must be installed; this certificate makes Apache Directory Studio mark Let's Encrypt certificates as trusted.

Download the active certificate from `https://letsencrypt.org/certificates/` (first link). Save it without the `.txt` extension (`.pem` extension only).

Download, install, and start Apache Directory Studio. Then select **Window ➤ Preferences** in the menu and then in the configuration window that opens **Apache Directory Studio ➤ Connections ➤ Certificate Validation**. Click the **Add** button, and select the downloaded certificate.

A connection to the server can now be made by using hostname *ldap.example.com* and port 636 (ldaps). The *Bind DN* is the second *olcRootDN* that was defined in `slapd.ldif`—in the example earlier in this chapter that was `cn=Manager,dc=example,dc=com`—with the accompanying password.

The addition of users will be discussed in Chapter 12, "Email Basics".

Other Databases

Two other commonly used databases are DBM and SQLite. Both these databases do not function in a client-server model like the previously described databases, but instead create a single database file that can be integrated in an application and can be accessed using a software library.

The advantage of this is that no daemon needs to be running. A disadvantage may be that only a single process can write to these databases at the same time. These databases are most suitable for situations where write actions to the database are relatively rare, or where a single process writes to the database, while one or more processes read from it.

DBM

A DBM is a simple database that consists of a single table. DBM files are generated from text files containing two columns. The left column contains the keys that are used in searches, and the right column contains the values that are returned as search results.

An example of the use of this file format is the association of usernames and email aliases; this will be discussed in Chapter 12, "Email Basics". Software libraries for accessing these databases exist for many programming languages.

This file format is sometimes called Berkeley DB, after one of its implementations.

SQLite

An SQLite database is a relational database in a single file. As the name suggests, these databases can be accessed using SQL. A database can contain multiple tables.

The source code for SQLite was placed in the public domain by its developers, so it is entirely free from copyrights. In part due to this decision, software libraries for virtually every programming language exist for accessing these databases, and there are many applications for the management of these databases.

The system administrator who prefers to install a web interface for the management of SQLite databases could investigate phpLiteAdmin, a web interface for SQLite, comparable to the previously described phpMyAdmin for MariaDB/MySQL, phpPgAdmin for PostgreSQL, and phpLDAPadmin for LDAP.

Summary

In this chapter, two database management systems (MariaDB and PostgreSQL) and a directory service (OpenLDAP) were installed and configured. To facilitate the management of these services, web interfaces were installed for all three of them; these web interfaces are all hosted under the virtual host/server *db.example.com*, which was created at the beginning of this chapter. Finally, two single-file database systems (DBM and SQLite) were discussed.

LDAP and DBM will return in Chapter 12, "Email Basics", where they will be used for the storage of users and aliases, respectively.

Email Basics

Three protocols are involved in email communication: *SMTP* (*Simple Mail Transfer Protocol*) for sending messages and *POP* (*Post Office Protocol*) and *IMAP* (*Internet Message Access Protocol*) for receiving messages. The latter two protocols are often represented with their current version numbers: POP3 and IMAP4. If the communication is encrypted, using SSL/TLS, for example, the names used are SMTPS, POP3S, and IMAPS, where the added S means Secure.

The sender's mail client hands over the message to an SMTP server. This SMTP server sends the message to the receiver's SMTP server that stores the message. The recipient's mail client can then retrieve the mail and store it locally (POP) or display the message without moving it from the server to the client (IMAP). This is a strongly simplified representation of reality.

Thus, the main difference between POP and IMAP is that POP downloads messages from the server to the client before they can be read and IMAP leaves the messages on the server and only downloads a copy to present to the user. While IMAP generates more network traffic—unless the client is configured to store a copy locally, each message must be downloaded each time it is opened—IMAP's popularity increases. This is mainly due to the fact that more and more users access their email from a multitude of devices.

In some cases, a combination of POP and IMAP could be desirable: in this setup, an internal server would retrieve the messages from an external POP server and then serves them to internal users over IMAP. An advantage of such a setup is that the messages are securely stored behind an internal firewall and can be better and more easily protected from unauthorized access from outside of the local network. A consequence of this is, of course, that authorized access from outside the local network (field staff) also becomes more complicated; for these users, a *VPN* (*Virtual Private Network*) would have to be set up. VPNs are not discussed in this book.

This book presumes that this server's email users wish to access their mail from multiple devices (PC, smartphone, tablet, web mail) and have unlimited or extensive internet access. For this reason, only IMAP will be discussed for the retrieval of mail.

© Robert La Lau 2021
R. La Lau, *Practical Internet Server Configuration*, https://doi.org/10.1007/978-1-4842-6960-2_12

However, the selected IMAP server also supports POP, and the system administrator who wishes to make use of this should have no trouble enabling this.

These are some more common abbreviations in the world of email:

- **MUA**—Mail User Agent

  This is the user's email client. The MUA hands off messages to be sent to the MSA and presents messages received from the MDA to the user.

- **MSA**—Mail Submission Agent

  This program is part of the SMTP server and receives, after authentication and authorization, the mail from the user for delivery. The MSA receives messages from the MUA and hands them off to the MTA.

- **MTA**—Mail Transfer Agent

  This program is also part of the SMTP server and is responsible for the transfer of messages between SMTP servers. The MTA receives messages from the MSA or from another MTA and hands them off to another MTA or to the MDA.

- **MDA**—Mail Delivery Agent

  This program stores the messages to allow them to be presented to the user through POP or IMAP. The MDA is also called LDA (*Local Delivery Agent*) sometimes. The MDA receives messages from the MTA or from the MRA and gets them ready for the MUA or for the MRA.

- **MRA**—Mail Retrieval Agent

  This program retrieves messages from a remote server to hand them off locally for further processing; an example is the program that retrieves the messages from a remote POP server for the local IMAP server in the aforementioned combination of POP and IMAP. The MRA retrieves messages that were made available by a (remote) MDA and hands them off to a (local) MDA.

An email to a recipient on the same server travels the following path:

MUA → MSA → MTA → MDA → MUA

An email to a recipient on a different server:

MUA → MSA → MTA → MTA → MDA → MUA

An email to a recipient behind a company firewall:

MUA → MSA → MTA → MTA → MDA → MRA → MDA → MUA

Clearly, more variations than the aforementioned exist. It is also possible that a message travels over more MTAs. If one is interested in the way an email travels, one can view the `Received:` headers of received emails; every MTA adds such a header to the email.

For the processing of email, the following ports should be opened in the firewall:

- **25 (smtp), TCP**

  This is the port where the MTA listens. If other SMTP servers have mail for this server, it is handed off at this port.

- **53 (dns), UDP**

  Obviously, external SMTP servers must be allowed to make DNS lookups to find the MX server for the registered domains. But DNS will also be used for sender verification.

  As the DNS server has been configured in a previous chapter, port 53 should already be open.

- **587 (submission), TCP**

  The MSA listens on this port. The mail client connects to this port to send mails.

- **993 (imaps), TCP**

  The MUA (mail client) connects to this port to access mails through IMAP.

If POP3 is enabled, port 995 (pop3s, TCP) should also be opened.

DNS

A DNS record *mx.example.com* has already been created. The three domains *example.com*, *example.edu*, and *example.org* all have MX records pointing at *mx.example.com*, which means that this is the server that handles the mail for these domain names.

Essentially, this suffices. However, not only does it look better, it is also more recognizable for users if some additional DNS aliases are created.

```
imap  IN  CNAME  mx
smtp  IN  CNAME  mx
mail  IN  CNAME  mx
```

With these CNAME records in place, users will immediately understand what to enter in the email client settings for the IMAP server (*imap.example.com*) and the SMTP server (*smtp.example.com*). The *mail* alias will be used to host a web mail client at *https://mail.example.com/*.

An additional advantage of the use of these is that if the processing of email should ever get too demanding for this server, the IMAP server (or the SMTP server) could be moved to another server without requiring that users change their settings; the CNAME record is simply modified to point at another server.

TLS Certificate

Mail traffic will also be encrypted. A single certificate will be generated for IMAP, SMTP, and web mail.

The certificate will again be requested with the help of the specifically created directory. Since DNS records exist for *mx*, *imap*, *smtp*, and *mail*, but no virtual host has been created in the web server configuration yet, the web server will fall back to the default virtual host, *green.example.com*.

```
# certbot certonly --webroot \
    -w /srv/www/rfc5785 \
    -d mx.example.com \
    -d imap.example.com \
    -d smtp.example.com \
    -d mail.example.com
```

The certificate will be stored under the name `mx.example.com` (the first hostname listed on the command line).

The encryption of IMAP and SMTP traffic does not mean that the emails themselves are encrypted. TLS only guarantees the encryption of the traffic between the mail client and the server. To encrypt the messages themselves, a technique like OpenPGP could be used; this is not discussed in this book.

Internet Message Access Protocol (IMAP)

As indicated before, IMAP is the protocol that is used to access incoming emails. This protocol copies a message from the server to the client when it is opened by the user; many clients store local copies to avoid delays when messages are re-opened. However, the original mail stays on the server; when the message is moved to another folder, this is also done on the server; when the mail is marked as *Read* or *Important*, these marks are stored on the server. This way, the user always has the same view of their mailbox, regardless of the device used to access the mail.

Dovecot

Dovecot is the name of a stable and relatively easy-to-configure IMAP and POP3 server that adheres to all standards. Dovecot also provides the LDA, which means that the SMTP server hands off incoming mails for local users to Dovecot for local delivery.

In the configuration described here, Dovecot will also function as a *SASL* (*Simple Authentication and Security Layer*) server, which means that the SMTP server will make use of Dovecot for the authentication and authorization of users (who is allowed to send mails through this server and who is not). Dovecot, in turn, uses the LDAP server configured earlier as its user database.

Installation

During the installation, two users and groups are created, named *dovecot* and *dovenull*. These users are used internally by Dovecot.

FreeBSD

```
freebsd# pkg install dovecot
```

Example configuration files are installed into /usr/local/etc/dovecot/example-config. The files that will be used will be copied to /usr/local/etc/dovecot.

Debian

On Debian, Dovecot has been split up into a considerable number of sub-packages; it is important to select the correct ones.

```
debian# apt install dovecot-imapd dovecot-ldap
```

The configuration files are installed into /etc/dovecot.

CentOS

```
centos# yum install dovecot
```

The configuration is installed into /etc/dovecot.

Directory

The mail will be served from the directory /srv/mail. This directory is accessible to a single user, who acts on behalf of the owners of the mailboxes. Each mail user will have their own sub-directory in this directory, where not only the messages are stored but also the filter rules that will be discussed in a later chapter.

This directory is created at the same time its owner is created. This user is a system user, which in short means that the UID is lower than for regular users and that the user is not allowed to log in to the system; the contents of the skeleton directory will not be copied to this user's home directory.

```
freebsd# pw useradd vmail \
         -u 145 \
         -c "Owner /srv/mail" \
         -d /srv/mail \
         -m \
         -M 0770 \
         -s /usr/sbin/nologin
```

```
debian# adduser --system \
          --group \
          --gecos "Owner /srv/mail" \
          --home /srv/mail \
          vmail
centos# useradd --system \
          --comment "Owner /srv/mail" \
          --home-dir /srv/mail \
          --create-home \
          --user-group \
          --shell /sbin/nologin \
          vmail
```

Obviously, any other username may be chosen; the username *vmail* used in the
preceding code is the same name that is used in the Dovecot wiki, which may simplify a
future expansion of the configuration. For the FreeBSD user, any other UID may be used;
145 is an arbitrary choice. The idea is to find an unused UID under 1000, because the
UIDs for regular users start at 1000.

On Debian and CentOS, the permissions for the new directory must be set
separately.

```
linux# chmod 0770 /srv/mail
```

Configuration

The IMAP and SMTP users are stored in the LDAP directory service. This way, they do
not need a system password, which means the system is not at risk if a user password is
compromised. This type of users is called virtual users.

Dovecot is the only service to connect to the LDAP user database. The SMTP server
(Postfix) uses Dovecot's SASL to verify users.

Users

To not cause any confusion with the system users *diane* and *dimitri*, this chapter
introduces the users *alicia* and *arthur*. These users do not have a shell account and only
access their mail.

System users who also need to access the mail services must have LDAP accounts as well. These accounts may have the same name as the shell accounts, but this is not mandatory; the accounts are strictly separated.

The setup described in this book presumes that the addresses *alicia@example.com*, *alicia@example.org*, and *alicia@example.org* should all have user *alicia* as their final destination, and the same principle goes for user *arthur* and any other mail users.

Users can be added to the LDAP directory service with the help of LDIF files.

```
dn: uid=alicia,ou=users,dc=example,dc=com
objectClass: top
objectClass: account
objectClass: posixAccount
cn: alicia
gidNumber: 0
homeDirectory: /srv/mail/alicia
uid: alicia
uidNumber: 0
userPassword: {SSHA}gaXwDonGL5LGXXMaX54W2LgAs8gu6rWv
```

The `gidNumber`, `homeDirectory`, and `uidNumber` attributes are mandatory, but are not used in the current setup; their values are therefore not important. The `ou` (organizationalUnit) that is specified in the `dn` (Distinguished Name) is the element that was defined as the container for user records, in the section "Lightweight Directory Access Protocol (LDAP)" of Chapter 11, "Databases". The password hash is generated with the help of the `slappasswd` command, as it was done in the "Lightweight Directory Access Protocol (LDAP)" section in Chapter 11, "Databases".

The following command is used to load this LDIF file into the directory service:

```
# ldapadd -D "cn=Manager,dc=example,dc=com" \
    -f ./user-alicia.ldif -W
```

Some system administrators may prefer the use of phpLDAPadmin or Apache Directory Studio for user management.

If the web interfaces for the databases were installed as described in Chapter 11, "Databases", the phpLDAPadmin web interface can be accessed at *https://db.example.com/ldap*. The `olcRootDN` that was configured in the section "Lightweight Directory Access Protocol (LDAP)" (`cn=Manager,dc=example,dc=com`) and the associated password (`helloldap`) are used to gain access.

Completely unfold the tree structure in the left pane, and click the deepest **Create new entry here** link below **ou=users**. Select the **Default** option as the template. In the next screen, select the **account** and **posixAccount** objectClasses (hold the *Ctrl* key to select the second option), and click **Proceed**. Enter the following data:

Field	Purpose	Example
RDN	relative DN	userid (userid)
cn	username	alicia
gidNumber	arbitrary number (unused)	0
homeDirectory	arbitrary directory (unused)	/srv/mail/alicia
uidNumber	arbitrary number (unused)	0
userid	username	alicia
Password	user's password	5ecr3tPa5$
Hash type Password	SSHA	SSHA

Click **Create object**, verify the data, and click **Commit**. The new user now appears in the tree structure in the left pane; at first titled userid=alicia, but after clicking the **refresh** button, this changes to uid=alicia.

Apache Directory Studio functions in the same fashion. Connect to port 636 (ldaps) on server *ldap.example.com*. In the LDAP browser, entirely unfold the tree structure DIT (*Directory Information Tree*). Select **ou=users**, and select **LDAP ➤ New Entry** in the menu. Select **Create entry from scratch** and click **Next**. Select the **account**, **posixAccount**, and **top** objectClasses, and click **Add**; then click **Next**. Select **uid** in the first field for RDN, and enter the username in the second field. Click **Next**.

Enter the following data:

Field	Purpose	Example
cn	username	arthur
gidNumber	arbitrary number (unused)	0
homeDirectory	arbitrary directory (unused)	/srv/mail/arthur
uidNumber	arbitrary number (unused)	0

Then click the **New Attribute** button. Select the **userPassword** *Attribute type* and click **Finish**. Enter the password twice, select the **SSHA** *Hash Method*, and click **OK**. Click **Finish**.

Other tools exist for the management of directory services.

The different methods for record management can be used simultaneously, so each system administrator can use the tool they prefer.

Users can also use these tools to connect to the server and change their own password. However, these tools may be a bit overwhelming or confusing for nontechnical users. Several scripts can be found on the internet that allow users to change their password through a web interface without any other functionalities; it may be desirable to install one of these.

Dovecot

The Dovecot configuration consists of a considerable number of files. However, these files consist largely of comments.

Several settings allow variables to be used in their values. These variables are presented in the format *percent_sign-lowercase_letter*; an example is %u for username. Furthermore, these variables can be accompanied by so-called modifiers that automatically modify their value. These modifiers are represented by uppercase letters: L changes uppercase to lowercase (%Lu), U changes lowercase to uppercase (%Uu), and so on. The full list of variables and modifiers can be found on the Dovecot wiki.

On FreeBSD, a directory with example configuration files was installed.

```
freebsd# cd /usr/local/etc/dovecot
freebsd# cp -rp example-config/* .
```

The files in /usr/local/etc/dovecot can now freely be edited, while the originals are safely stored in the example-config sub-directory.

On Debian and CentOS, it is also sensible to have a copy of the original files.

```
linux# cd /etc/dovecot
linux# mkdir orig
linux# cp -rp * orig
linux# rmdir orig/orig
```

The cp command complains that the orig directory cannot be copied to itself; obviously, this is not a problem. An empty directory named orig/orig is created; this directory can be removed. The /etc/dovecot/orig directory now contains a copy of the original unmodified version of all configuration files.

The main configuration file is dovecot.conf. This file includes additional configuration files with the !include and !include_try directives; both directives include a file, but !include displays an error message if the requested file does not exist, and !include_try continues without an error message.

```
# nano dovecot.conf
```

The only setting that needs to be changed in this file is the definition of supported protocols. The *protocols* variable is used for this, the first variable in the file. Debian places this definition in separate files, but to keep some oversight, it is more practical to keep it in the configuration file. For now, only IMAP will be supported.

FreeBSD and CentOS:

```
# Protocols we want to be serving.
protocols = imap
```

Debian:

```
# Enable installed protocols
#!include_try /usr/share/dovecot/protocols.d/*.protocol
protocols = imap
```

These are the only other enabled lines in this file:

```
dict {
}
!include conf.d/*.conf
!include_try local.conf
```

These can remain as they are. The dict {} section can be used to refer external databases, but this section remains empty in the current setup. Then all files in the conf.d sub-directory of which the name ends in .conf are included. And lastly, Dovecot loads the file local.conf in the current directory, if it exists. The files in the conf.d sub-directory are loaded in alphanumerical order, which is why their names begin with a number: this forces the server to load the files in a certain order.

The following file determines the configuration for user authentication:

```
# nano conf.d/10-auth.conf
```

```
# Username format: lowercase.
auth_username_format = %Lu

# Expect non-encrypted passwords.
auth_mechanisms = plain

# Do not use the system's user database.
#!include auth-system.conf.ext

# Use the LDAP directory service for authentication.
!include auth-ldap.conf.ext
```

The value of auth_mechanisms seems unsafe, but a bit further in this chapter, Dovecot will be configured to require an SSL/TLS-encrypted connection. If the connection is encrypted, it is not necessary to additionally encrypt the password; the password can then be transmitted non-encrypted over the encrypted connection.

In the preceding file, the file auth-ldap.conf.ext is included. This file defines the database to use for user authentication (passdb) and the database that provides the other data—user id, group id, and directory—(userdb). The LDAP directory service will serve as the passdb; the user id and group id are the same for all users (the vmail user was created for this purpose), and the directory to use can be specified with a simple pattern.

```
# nano conf.d/auth-ldap.conf.ext
```

```
passdb {
    driver = ldap

    # This is the path for FreeBSD.
    # On Linux this is /etc/dovecot/dovecot-ldap.conf.ext.
    args = /usr/local/etc/dovecot/dovecot-ldap.conf.ext
}
userdb {
    driver = static

    # The home directory specified here is the directory
    # where mail and Sieve scripts are stored, and has
    # nothing to do with a possible system home directory.
```

```
    # Here too, it is important that the username is always
    # lowercase, regardless of what the user specified.
    args = uid=vmail gid=vmail home=/srv/mail/%Lu
}
```

Next, the LDAP parameters must be specified in the file dovecot-ldap.conf.ext. This file does not exist on CentOS, but an example can be found in /usr/share/doc/dovecot-<*version*>/example-config.

nano dovecot-ldap.conf.ext

```
# Multiple hosts may be specified, separated by spaces.
# Format: IP-address:port
hosts = 127.0.0.1:389

# Let the LDAP server handle the password verification.
auth_bind = yes
auth_bind_userdn = uid=%Lu,ou=users,dc=example,dc=com
```

The other lines in this file are not needed for this setup and may be deleted.

Dovecot is able to automatically find the directory where a user's mail is stored, but if it is defined explicitly, Dovecot can also automatically create this directory when a user logs in for the first time.

nano conf.d/10-mail.conf

```
# The mailbox location.
# The string 'maildir:' indicates the type of mailbox.
mail_location = maildir:/srv/mail/%Lu/Maildir

# These lines already exist in the file,
# and they can remain.
 namespace inbox {
    inbox = yes
}

# The minimum and maximum allowed user ids
# for access to /srv/mail.
# Enter the uid for user vmail twice.
 first_valid_uid = 117
 last_valid_uid = 117
```

```
# The minimum and maximum allowed group ids
# for access to /srv/mail.
# Enter the gid for group vmail twice.
 first_valid_gid = 123
 last_valid_gid = 123
```

The user id and group id for user vmail are displayed with the command

```
# id vmail
```

Additional directories that should be created automatically can be configured in the file 15-mailboxes.conf. A number of commonly used folders have already been defined in this file; to have them created automatically, the line auto = create or auto = subscribe must be added to each desired folder. The names for the already defined folders do not need to be translated; most mail clients do this automatically, based on the user's language settings. The defined virtual folders can be enabled, and other folders can be added, if desired.

```
# nano conf.d/15-mailboxes.conf
```

```
namespace inbox {

    # Drafts.
    mailbox Drafts {
        special_use = \Drafts
        auto = subscribe
    }

    # Spam.
    mailbox Junk {
        special_use = \Junk
        auto = subscribe
    }

    # Trash.
    mailbox Trash {
        special_use = \Trash
        auto = subscribe
    }
```

```
# Since there are two commonly used names for the folder
# for sent items, this folder will not be created
# automatically; this allows the mail client to decide
# which of those names will be used.
mailbox Sent {
    special_use = \Sent
}
mailbox "Sent Messages" {
    special_use = \Sent
}
}
```

And finally, the SSL/TLS parameters must be defined.

```
# nano conf.d/10-ssl.conf
```

```
# Use of SSL/TLS is required.
 ssl = required
```

```
# Certificate and key.
# Note the less-than sign; this means input redirection:
# the contents of the file are loaded, and not its name.
 ssl_cert = </etc/letsencrypt/live/mx.example.com/fullchain.pem
 ssl_key = </etc/letsencrypt/live/mx.example.com/privkey.pem
```

The Dovecot-LDA, which receives mail with a local destination from the SMTP server and delivers it to the mailbox in question, needs to be able to look up information in the userdb that was configured in the LDAP settings. The LDA is executed under the username vmail.

```
# nano conf.d/10-master.conf
```

```
service auth {
    unix_listener auth-userdb {7
        mode 0600
        user = vmail
    }
}
```

```
# nano conf.d/10-mail.conf
```

```
auth_socket_path = /var/run/dovecot/auth-userdb
```

The LDA will use this Unix socket to request the directory for mail delivery.

And Sieve (message filtering) must be enabled separately for the LDA.

```
# nano conf.d/15-lda.conf
```

```
protocol lda {
    mail_plugins = $mail_plugins sieve
}
```

This completes the configuration of IMAP and the LDA.

Email Client

With the preceding configuration in place, the mail client can now be configured with the following information to access user *alicia*'s mailbox:

- Server: **imap.example.com**

- Protocol: **IMAP**

- Port: **993**

- Encryption: **SSL/TLS**

- Authentication method: **normal password** (also called **plaintext**)

- Username: **alicia**

- Password: **5ecr3tPa5$**

Instead of port 993 with SSL/TLS encryption, it is also possible to use port 143 with STARTTLS encryption. This can be practical if a firewall only allows a few specific ports.

Test

Create the following text file, and save it as ~/testmail. Clearly, host- and usernames should be replaced. The date and time may be modified, but must be in so-called RFC822 date and time format. One empty line must be inserted between the headers and the body (or payload).

```
Return-Path: <alicia@green.example.com>
From: alicia@green.example.com
Date: Mon, 23 Nov 2020 17:48:18 +0200
To: alicia@green.example.com
 Subject: IMAP test

 It works!
```

Now execute the following command:

```
freebsd$ cat ~/testmail | \
           /usr/local/libexec/dovecot/dovecot-lda -d alicia

debian$ cat ~/testmail | /usr/lib/dovecot/dovecot-lda -d alicia

centos$ cat ~/testmail | /usr/libexec/dovecot/dovecot-lda -d alicia
```

If this message appears in user *alicia*'s mailbox in the mail client, IMAP and the LDA have been correctly configured.

Simple Mail Transfer Protocol (SMTP)

The protocol that is used to send mails is called SMTP. This protocol is both used for communication between mail client and SMTP server and for communication between SMTP servers.

Several open source SMTP servers exist. The server chosen for this book is Postfix, a server that is relatively simple to configure and that has a good reputation.

Postfix

Postfix development started over 20 years ago as an alternative for Sendmail, which has been the de facto standard SMTP server for a long time. Postfix's configuration is split into multiple text files and Berkeley DB or lmdb databases, but is despite that (or maybe even thanks to that) transparent and clear.

Installation

On FreeBSD and Debian, the Sendmail and Exim SMTP servers are installed, respectively; these must be disabled before Postfix can be enabled.

FreeBSD

Several packages exist that have *postfix* in their name. Some of those are Postfix editions, and others are Postfix add-ons. The Postfix version to be installed is simply called postfix. Some add-ons will be added later.

```
freebsd# pkg update
freebsd# pkg search postfix
freebsd# pkg install postfix
```

Postfix's configuration directory is /usr/local/etc/postfix.

The default SMTP server for FreeBSD is Sendmail. To completely replace Sendmail with Postfix, a few additional actions must be undertaken.

Sendmail must be stopped.

```
freebsd# service sendmail stop
freebsd# nano /etc/rc.conf
```

```
sendmail_enable="NONE"
```

Multiple Sendmail RC variables exist, but by assigning a value of NONE to *sendmail_enable* (instead of NO), all these variables are set to NO.

Then, a few scheduled Sendmail tasks must be disabled.

```
freebsd# nano /etc/periodic.conf
```

```
daily_clean_hoststat_enable="NO"
daily_status_mail_rejects_enable="NO"
daily_status_include_submit_mailq="NO"
daily_submit_queuerun="NO"
```

If this file does not exist, it must be created.

Now, indicate to the system that Postfix's sendmail command must be used instead of the original sendmail command.

```
freebsd# mkdir -p /usr/local/etc/mail
freebsd# install -m 0644 \
         /usr/local/share/postfix/mailer.conf.postfix \
         /usr/local/etc/mail/mailer.conf
```

The newly installed `mailer.conf` file shows that the command from the Postfix package is also called `sendmail`. This undoubtedly stems from the time that Sendmail was the standard SMTP package, and other scripts and applications hard-coded the name into their source code; the simplest way to replace Sendmail was then to have new projects use the same command names as the original. This is called a drop-in replacement; apart from the replacement itself, no additional modifications need to be made. The original `sendmail` command is installed in the `/usr/libexec/sendmail` directory.

The original `mailer.conf` file is installed in the `/etc/mail` Sendmail configuration directory. Deleting this directory is useless, because a system upgrade will create it again. It is a good idea, though, to create a file in this directory to indicate to system administrators that this directory is no longer in use.

```
freebsd# nano /etc/mail/UNUSED.DIRECTORY
```

```
See /usr/local/etc/mail and /usr/local/etc/postfix.

DATE - NAME
```

Debian

Debian also knows multiple packages with *postfix* in the name, but only the package simply called postfix contains the MTA. The other packages are add-ons; these will be discussed later.

```
debian# apt install postfix
```

First, `apt` indicates that Exim, the SMTP server per default under Debian, will be removed. Obviously, this is not a problem.

Next, `apt` asks to choose a configuration type. The option `Internet Site` should be selected here.

And lastly, `apt` asks to enter the hostname to be used. This should be the FQDN, the complete hostname, including the domain name. This hostname, prepended with an at sign, will be added to the sender, and possibly the recipient, of mails that are sent from the command line or by Cron. If this hostname is ever to be changed, the file `/etc/mailname` should be modified.

Postfix's configuration directory is `/etc/postfix`.

CentOS

Postfix is the MTA per default on CentOS, so it has probably been installed already. If it hasn't, the name of the package to install is simply postfix. The configuration directory is /etc/postfix.

As is often the case, CentOS is again way behind on its colleagues regarding the installed version; at the time of writing of this book, CentOS uses version 2.10.1, while FreeBSD uses version 3.4.9, and Debian's version is 3.1.14. However, this has no consequences for the configuration described here.

Configuration

Postfix listens on two ports: external mail servers hand off messages destined for this server on port 25 (smtp), and authenticated users hand off their messages destined for users on this server or elsewhere on the internet on port 587 (submission).

For user authentication, Postfix makes use of Dovecot-SASL (*Simple Authentication and Security Layer*), which in short means that Dovecot takes care of the authentication of users on behalf of Postfix, with use of the LDAP directory service that is also used for the authentication of IMAP users. This also means that every user who is allowed to receive mail through this server is also allowed to send mail through this server. To enable SASL in Dovecot, the lines in bold must be added to the Dovecot configuration file conf.d/10-master.conf:

```
service auth {
    unix_listener /var/spool/postfix/private/auth {
        mode = 0660
        user = postfix
        group = postfix
    }
}
```

This creates a Unix socket at the specified address when Dovecot is restarted; this Unix socket can then be used by Postfix to have Dovecot verify a name/password combination received from a user.

Lines in Postfix configuration files that begin with whitespace (space or tab) are considered to be a continuation of the previous line. As in many other configuration files, lines that begin with a hash sign are ignored. Parameters can be used as values for other parameters by prepending their name with a dollar sign, just like variables in some programming languages. The order of the parameters in the file is not important. However, when a parameter (before the = sign) accepts multiple arguments (after the = sign), the arguments are processed in the order in which they are defined.

Per default, the submission service is not enabled. This service can be enabled in the Postfix configuration file `master.cf`.

```
bsd# cd /usr/local/etc/postfix
```

```
linux# cd /etc/postfix
```

```
# nano master.cf
```

```
submission  inet  n  -  n  -  -  smtpd
  -o syslog_name=postfix/submission
  -o smtpd_tls_security_level=encrypt
  -o smtpd_tls_auth_only=yes
  -o smtpd_reject_unlisted_recipient=no
  -o smtpd_client_restrictions=permit_sasl_authenticated,reject
  -o milter_macro_daemon_name=ORIGINATING
```

The `master.cf` file already contains a configuration section for the submission service, but it is deactivated. Since the preceding settings are not quite the same as the original ones, it is advised to copy the preceding lines instead of modifying and enabling the existing lines.

Fundamentally, the submission service uses the same settings as the smtp service that will be configured later in this section; these settings will be stored in the `main.cf` configuration file. The settings specified previously (each `-o` argument represents an option) are exceptions and additions to those settings, specifically for the submission service.

Since all settings are documented extensively and clearly, it is not necessary to repeat this in this book. The meaning of each configuration option can be found in `postconf(5)`, and this man page can also be found as an HTML page at the Postfix website. In short, the most important settings specified previously activate the submission service, assure that this service requires TLS encryption, and make it available only to users who have a valid username and password in the Dovecot user database.

Another service is added to master.cf. This is the dovecot-lda that will take care of the delivery of messages to local (virtual) users.

```
# nano master.cf
```

```
dovecot  unix  -  n  n  -  -  pipe
  flags=DRhu user=vmail:vmail argv=/usr/lib/dovecot/dovecot-lda -f
${sender} -a ${original_recipient} -d ${user}
```

The second and third lines should be joined on a single line. The path to dovecot-lda specified here is valid for Debian; on FreeBSD, this is /usr/local/libexec/dovecot/dovecot-lda, and on CentOS, it is /usr/libexec/dovecot/dovecot-lda.

This service, a so-called virtual transport, hands off messages to the dovecot-lda with the message's sender, the original recipient, and the virtual user to whom the message must be delivered as arguments. The dovecot-lda is executed with username vmail and group name vmail, as configured before.

Next, the general settings can be made that form the settings for the SMTP traffic on port 25 and the basic settings for the traffic on port 587.

```
# mv main.conf main.conf.orig
# nano main.cf
```

```
# Some general matters.
smtpd_banner = $myhostname ESMTP $mail_name
biff = no
compatibility_level = 2
mynetworks_style = host

# Hostname. Change this!
myhostname = green.example.com

# Local aliases.
alias_database = hash:/etc/aliases
alias_maps = hash:/etc/aliases

# Domains for which mail is handled by this server.
virtual_mailbox_domains = example.com example.edu example.org

# Virtual aliases.
#    FreeBSD: /usr/local/etc/postfix/virtual
```

```
#    Debian : /etc/postfix/virtual
#    CentOS : /etc/postfix/virtual
virtual_alias_maps = hash:/etc/postfix/virtual

# Virtual transport.
# This is the 'dovecot' service that was created
# in master.cf (the LDA).
virtual_transport = dovecot
dovecot_destination_recipient_limit = 1

# SSL / TLS.
smtpd_tls_security_level = may
smtpd_tls_cert_file = /etc/letsencrypt/live/mx.example.com/fullchain.pem
smtpd_tls_key_file = /etc/letsencrypt/live/mx.example.com/privkey.pem
smtpd_tls_session_cache_database = btree:${data_directory}/smtpd_cache
smtp_tls_session_cache_database = btree:${data_directory}/smtp_cache

# SASL.
smtpd_sasl_auth_enable = yes
smtpd_sasl_type = dovecot
smtpd_sasl_path = private/auth
smtpd_sasl_security_options = noanonymous
smtpd_sasl_local_domain = $myhostname

# Restrictions.
smtpd_relay_restrictions =
  permit_mynetworks
  permit_sasl_authenticated
  reject_unauth_destination
smtpd_recipient_restrictions =
  permit_sasl_authenticated
  permit_mynetworks
  permit
```

The last two options determine which mails are accepted by Postfix and which are not. The default action for Postfix is to accept everything. The *smtpd_relay_restrictions* option determines the restrictions for the use of this server for sending mails to elsewhere on the internet, and *smtpd_recipient_restrictions* determines the restrictions for delivery of mails to the domains that were specified in the *virtual_mailbox_domains* option. Especially the latter may seem a bit strange, with three times `permit` in a row, but in Chapter 14, "Advanced Email", some other options will be inserted here.

The preceding configuration mentions several files. The first is `/etc/aliases`, in which local aliases are listed. The term `hash:` indicates that this file is a Berkeley DB. However, this database is based on a plain text file that lists several commonly used aliases. The format for this text file is very simple:

```
original_recipient:    new_recipient
```

If this file is opened in a text editor, it is clear that all local mail eventually ends up in user root's mailbox: a mail to *mailer-daemon@green.example.com* is forwarded to *postmaster@green.example.com* and then to *root@green.example.com*. It is recommended to forward root's mail to a "real" email address to assure that it is read regularly; the address that was made up for use in the DNS zone files could be used for this purpose: *sysadmin@example.com*. To add this alias, a single line must be added to `/etc/aliases`:

```
root: sysadmin@example.com
```

For clarity, it is advised to add this line somewhere at the top of the file. Note the colon in the first column.

When mail arrives, Postfix does not read this text file directly, but rather a database that was generated from it using the following command:

```
# newaliases
```

This command should always be executed when modifications were made to `/etc/aliases`; this created the database `/etc/aliases.db`. Even though the configuration specifies `/etc/aliases`, it is actually the file `/etc/aliases.db` that is used by Postfix.

The email addresses for which a user exists in the user database (*alicia@example.com*, *alicia@example.org*, *arthur@example.edu*, etc.) are recognized and delivered automatically; this is due to the value of the *mail_location* option in the Dovecot configuration. Other addresses must be created explicitly. This is what the second file that is mentioned in the Postfix configuration is used for. This is the file `virtual` in the Postfix configuration directory that is specified as the value for the *virtual_alias_maps* option. This file defines all aliases for the virtual users. This file also consists of two columns. However, there are a few differences with the file `/etc/aliases`:

- The values in the left column do not end in a colon.

- Both the addresses in the left column and the addresses in the right column contain a domain name.

- The left column defines a virtual alias or a catch-all address.

If the value in the right column does not contain a domain name, Postfix will try to deliver the mail to a system user. However, since the LDA was not configured for this purpose, this will generally not work.

A catch-all address is a definition for a single recipient for any address within a domain.

This is an example for the virtual file in the Postfix configuration directory:

```
finance@example.com       office@example.com
sales@example.com         office@example.com
office@example.com        arthur@example.com

procurement@example.edu   sales@example.com
sales@example.edu         @example.com
arthur@example.edu        arthur@example.com
@example.edu              alicia@example.com

@example.org              @example.com
```

This virtual user database results in the following:

- Mail to *finance@example.com* and *sales@example.com* is forwarded to *office@example.com*.

- Mail to *office@example.com*, including the mails forwarded earlier, is forwarded to *arthur@example.com*.

- Mail to *arthur@example.com* is not forwarded any further and is therefore delivered to the mailbox for the local (virtual) user *arthur*.

- Mail to other addresses in the *example.com* domain is rejected with the error message *Unknown user*.

- Mail to *procurement@example.**edu*** is forwarded to *sales@example.**com***, where it will be processed further according to the rule for that address.

- Mail to *sales@example.**edu*** is forwarded to *sales@example.**com***, where it will be processed further according to the rule for that address.

- Mail for any other address in the *example.**edu*** domain is forwarded to *alicia@example.**com***; this is called a catch-all address.

- Mail to *arthur@example.**edu*** is forwarded to *arthur@example.**com***; if a catch-all address is defined, as is done for the *example.edu* domain, it is important to also define the implicit addresses to prevent them from being caught by the catch-all address.

- Mail for *alicia@example.com* is not forwarded any further and is therefore delivered to the mailbox for the local (virtual) user *alicia*.

- Mail for any address in the *example.**org*** domain is forwarded to the same address in the *example.**com*** domain, where it will be processed further according to the rule that is defined for that address in that domain (mail to *warehouse@example.**org*** is therefore rejected, because the address *warehouse@example.**com*** has not been defined).

Obviously, the system administrator is completely free in the creation of the aliases, according to the existing requirements. However, three addresses have been used earlier in this book, so these aliases will need to be created in any case: *sysadmin@example.com* (DNS zone files and /etc/aliases), *tls-certificates@example.com* (TLS certificate request Let's Encrypt), and *fail2ban@example.com* (mail sent by fail2ban; see Chapter 4, "Network Basics and Firewall").

As with the local aliases file, a database must be generated from this text file; the following command will do so:

```
freebsd# postmap /usr/local/etc/postfix/virtual
```

```
linux# postmap /etc/postfix/virtual
```

This creates the file virtual.db that will be used by Postfix.

When the configuration has been modified, Postfix must be restarted; however, at this moment, the daemon has not been started yet on FreeBSD and CentOS.

```
freebsd# service postfix start
```

```
debian# systemctl restart postfix
```

```
centos# systemctl start postfix
```

When the files `aliases` and `virtual` have been modified, the respective commands `newaliases` and `postmap` must be executed; Postfix does not need to be restarted then.

Test

A basic SMTP server is now operational, and it is time to test the sending and receiving of email. These are the credentials for connecting to the SMTP server:

- Server: **smtp.example.com**

- Port: **587**

- Encryption: **STARTTLS**

- Authentication method: **normal password** (also called **plaintext**)

- Username: **alicia**

- Password: **5ecr3tPa5$**

Basic Mail Server Finished

A basic mail server has now been installed and configured. This mail server is fully functional and ready to be taken into production.

Chapter 14, "Advanced Email", will build upon this configuration and introduce techniques to filter incoming mails and to fight spam.

Summary

In this chapter, IMAP and SMTP servers were installed and configured for receiving and sending mail. Mail users and email aliases were also created.

The next chapter will discuss the more advanced configuration of the web server.

CHAPTER 13

Web Server Part 2: Advanced Apache/Nginx

The basic configuration for the web server has already been discussed in a previous chapter. PHP has also been installed already, together with the PHP FastCGI Process Manager. Furthermore, a few virtual hosts (Apache) or virtual servers (Nginx) have already been created: *green.example.com*, *db.example.com*, and *mail.example.com*. In the following paragraphs, some more advanced functionalities will be discussed, and a few instant, freely downloadable web applications will be presented.

www.example.com

To brush up on the knowledge acquired in previous chapters, the virtual host *www.example.com* will be created first. The following steps should be taken to achieve this:

1. **DNS alias**

   The name *www*(.*example.com*) is an alias for the hostname *green*(.*example.com*). A CNAME record is created for this purpose, the zone file's serial number is incremented, and the named configuration is reloaded.

2. **User**

   The PHP-FPM will be executed with the username www-www. This user has a group with the same name, and their home directory is /srv/www/www.example.com, but this directory is not created yet. The user does not have a login shell and is not a member of any additional groups.

© Robert La Lau 2021

R. La Lau, *Practical Internet Server Configuration*, https://doi.org/10.1007/978-1-4842-6960-2_13

3. **Directories**

   The main directory for this virtual host is /srv/www/www.example.com.
   This directory contains the sub-directories alias, bin, cgi-bin,
   conf, htdocs, and tmp. All these directories belong to user *webdev*
   and group *webdev* and are not accessible to other users. With
   the help of Access Control Lists, the web server and PHP-FPM
   are attributed read privileges; on top of that, PHP-FPM has write
   privileges for the tmp sub-directory.

4. **PHP-FPM**

   The PHP-FPM is configured to listen on port 9002. Since
   www.example.com is the main website and will therefore process
   more traffic than *db.example.com*, for example, the *pm* option has
   a value of dynamic; *pm.max_children* is set to 50, *pm.min_spare_
   servers* to 5, and *pm.max_spare_servers* to 30. The web server log
   files will need to be analyzed regularly to determine whether these
   values need to be adjusted. The PHP-FPM configuration is then
   reloaded.

5. **Virtual host or virtual server on port 80**

   The virtual host (Apache) or virtual server (Nginx) that listens on
   port 80 is called *www.example.com* and serves the website from
   the htdocs sub-directory. To simplify maintenance and analysis,
   the website has its own log files. Files with the .php extension are
   processed by the *fcgi proxy* that listens on port 9002. On Debian, a
   link to this configuration must be created in the correct directory
   to enable this website. The web server configuration is then
   reloaded.

6. **TLS certificate**

   The directory /srv/www/rfc5785 is used for requesting
   the certificate. The certificate is valid for the hostnames
   www.example.com and *example.com* (in that order).

7. **Virtual host or virtual server on port 443**

   The virtual host (Apache) or virtual server (Nginx) that was
   created before is moved to port 443, with SSL enabled, and a new
   virtual host or server is created on port 80, with as its only job the
   redirection of requests to port 443.

8. **HTML and PHP files**

   An HTML file named index.html with arbitrary contents is
   created in the htdocs sub-directory, and so is a PHP file with as its
   only contents the following PHP code:

   ```
   <?php phpinfo(); ?>
   ```

9. **Test**

   A request for *www.example.com* should now be redirected to the
   address *https://www.example.com/*, where the contents of the
   index.html file is displayed. A request for the file info.php should
   display an HTML page listing PHP settings and modules.

One parameter is added to the web server configuration that was not discussed before:
an alternative name for the same site. Since many users only enter example.com if they
want to visit the site *www.example.com*, it is practical to add the name example.com to the
configuration for the virtual host/server; if this name is not linked to this virtual host/server,
these users would end up at the default virtual host/server, *green.example.com*.

To add this alternative name in Apache, a line must be added to the VirtualHost;
directly under the ServerName line would be a logical spot:

```
ServerAlias example.com
```

In Nginx, the name is appended to the existing server_name line:

```
server_name www.example.com example.com;
```

An alternative solution that some system administrators implement is the creation
of an additional virtual server or host for the "hostname" *example.com* that forwards all
requests to *https://www.example.com/*. This solution is just as valid as an alternative
name; the choice depends on personal preference. The net difference between the two
solutions is the name that is displayed in the visitor's browser's location bar.

CGI (Common Gateway Interface)

CGI is short for *Common Gateway Interface*, an interface that allows the web server to execute command-line programs and scripts and present the result to the user (not to be confused with *Computer-Generated Imagery*, or computer animation). The PHP-FPM (*PHP FastCGI Process Manager*) discussed earlier is a CGI variant that is optimized for PHP.

The scripts or programs that should be executable by the browser are placed in a directory called `cgi-bin` (*Common Gateway Interface Binaries*). Instead of directly presenting the files in this directory to the user, the web server executes the scripts or applications and presents their result (*STDOUT*) to the user.

The format of the output of the applications and scripts in question must follow the following requirements:

```
<HTTP headers>
<empty line>
<content>
```

This is an example of a very short and simple CGI script:

```
#!/bin/sh

echo "Content-Type: text/html"
echo
echo "<h1>It works!</h1>"
```

If this script is saved in the `cgi-bin` for *www.example.com* as `test.sh` and it is made executable for the web server, a request for *https://www.example.com/cgi-bin/test.sh* will display an HTML page with the line "*It works!*". The first line that is written by the script is not displayed by the browser, but is interpreted as an HTTP header that instructs the browser to interpret the content (*body* or *payload*) as HTML; a *Content-Type* of `text/plain` would have instructed the browser to interpret the page as plain text, and the browser would have displayed the HTML tags on the screen.

It is also possible to configure the web server to execute certain files or file types outside the `cgi-bin` as CGI scripts, but for reasons of oversight and control, this is not recommended.

It is recommended to keep the `cgi-bin` outside the document root of the website. This is why the directories for the existing virtual hosts all contain a sub-directory named `cgi-bin`.

When executed, CGI scripts have several environment variables at their disposal. The list of available variables can, for example, be displayed with this simple CGI script:

```
#!/bin/sh

echo "Content-Type: text/plain"
echo
env
```

How these variables are used in the scripts depends on the programming language in question. In a Bash script this could be simply ${SCRIPT_NAME}, in a Perl script $ENV{SCRIPT_NAME}, in a Python script os.environ['SCRIPT_NAME'], and so on. More information about this can be found on the website for the selected programming language.

Apache

To set a certain directory as a cgi-bin, the following lines must be added to the definition of a VirtualHost:

```
ScriptAlias "/cgi-bin/" "/srv/www/green.example.com/cgi-bin/"
<Directory "/srv/www/green.example.com/cgi-bin">
  Require all granted
</Directory>
```

Obviously, the web server must be given the privileges to access the files in the directory, including the execute privilege on the scripts, using traditional permissions or ACL.

Nginx

Nginx cannot execute scripts itself. Just like the PHP-FPM is used to execute PHP code, an *application server* must also be installed and configured for the execution of programming languages like Perl and Python.

A description of this installation and configuration is beyond the goal of this book. The system administrator who wants to make use of this should search for information about *FastCGI* and/or *uWSGI*.

An alternative could be to use Apache as an application server. In such a setup, Nginx would listen on ports 80 and 443 for visitor requests and would forward requests for Perl and Python scripts to Apache that could, for example, listen on port 9050. Apache would then execute the scripts and send the results back to Nginx that would present it to the visitor. However, with such a setup, one could wonder why Nginx was chosen in the first place.

Alias

Sometimes, a single website is spread out over several locations on the server. An example of this would be a server that hosts multiple similar websites and stores the images for all these websites in a central directory. Another example would be an in-house developed website *www.example.com* that hosts a wiki at *www.example.com/wiki* that was not developed in-house. In this case, it would be advisable to completely separate the code for the website and the code for the wiki, on the one hand, to allow the wiki to be updated or upgraded without any risk to the website and, on the other hand, to prevent in-house developers from tinkering with the code for the wiki.

Apache and Nginx both have simple mechanisms to present these separate directories as an integral part of the website. The directive is called `Alias` in both web servers.

Apache

The Apache directive is used in the context of a virtual host:

```
<VirtualHost *:443>
    ServerName www.example.com

    # The Alias refers to an absolute path
    # somewhere in the file system.
    Alias "/images" "/srv/www/all_images"

    # Apart from the privileges defined here, Apache should
    # obviously also have access to the directory on the
    # file system level.
    <Directory "/srv/www/all_images">
        Require all granted
    </Directory>
</VirtualHost>
```

With this configuration in place, the URL *https://www.example.com/images/logo.png* refers to the on-disk location /srv/www/all_images/logo.png.

Multiple virtual hosts can make use of the files in this directory. These virtual hosts can all use their own name for the directory in question.

```
Alias "/afbeeldingen" "/srv/www/all_images"

Alias "/Bilder" "/srv/www/all_images"
```

The preceding aliases could, for example, be used for the URLs *https://nl.example.com/afbeeldingen/logo.png* and *https://de.example.com/Bilder/logo.png*.

An `Alias` can also refer to a directory inside the document root, but also then, the target should still be an absolute path.

```
Alias "/images" "/srv/www/www.example.com/htdocs/img"
```

In this case too, multiple `Alias` directives can refer to the same directory. For oversight and to prevent directories and files from being deleted when they are still in use by other sites, it is not a good idea to have an `Alias` refer to a directory in the document root for another website; it would then be better to separate the directory from the sites and create an alias for both sites.

If the alias uses PHP, a line must be added for the execution of the PHP-FPM. This directive must be added before the existing, more generic PHP-FPM directive, to avoid the new URL being caught by the wrong directive.

```
Alias "/wiki" "/srv/www/www.example.com/alias/dokuwiki"
<Directory "/srv/www/www.example.com/alias/dokuwiki">
    Require all granted
</Directory>

ProxyPassMatch "^/wiki/(.*\.php(/.*)?)$" \
"fcgi://127.0.0.1:9000/srv/www/www.example.com/alias/dokuwiki/$1"

ProxyPassMatch "^/(.*\.php(/.*)?)$" \
"fcgi://127.0.0.1:9000/srv/www/www.example.com/htdocs/$1"
```

Obviously, PHP-FPM should then have read privileges in the directory in question. There is no limit to the number of aliases a virtual host can contain.

Nginx

In Nginx, the directive is used inside a `location` context:

```
server {
    listen *:443 ssl;
    server_name www.example.com;

    location /images {
        # The alias refers to an absolute path somewhere
        # in the file system.
        # Obviously, Nginx should be able to access
        # this directory.
        alias /srv/www/all_images;
    }
}
```

With this configuration in place, the URL *https://www.example.com/images/logo.png* refers to the on-disk location /srv/www/all_images/logo.png.

Multiple virtual hosts can make use of the files in this directory. These virtual hosts can all use their own name for the directory in question.

```
location /afbeeldingen {
    alias /srv/www/all_images;
}

location /Bilder {
    alias /srv/www/all_images;
}
```

The preceding aliases could, for example, be used for the URLs *https://nl.example.com/afbeeldingen/logo.png* and *https://de.example.com/Bilder/logo.png*.

An `Alias` can also refer to a directory inside the document root, but also then, the target should still be an absolute path.

```
location /images {
        alias /srv/www/www.example.com/htdocs/img;
}
```

In this case too, multiple `Alias` directives can refer to the same directory. For oversight and to prevent directories and files from being deleted when they are still in use by other sites, it is not a good idea to have an `Alias` refer to a directory in the document root for another website; it would then be better to separate the directory from the sites and create an alias for both sites.

If the alias uses PHP, the PHP-FPM must be called.

```
server {
    listen *:443 ssl;
    server_name www.example.com;

    location /blog {
        alias /srv/www/www.example.com/alias/dotclear;

        location ~ \.php$ {
            fastcgi_pass    127.0.0.1:9000;
            fastcgi_index   index.php;
            fastcgi_param   SCRIPT_FILENAME $request_filename;
            include         fastcgi_params;
        }
    }
}
```

Obviously, PHP-FPM should then have read privileges in the directory in question. There is no limit to the number of aliases a virtual server can contain.

Access Control

Apache and Nginx both include functionality to manage access to websites (or parts thereof).

If a website's content is important enough to limit access to it, TLS encryption is not optional. This is even more important because, with the authentication method discussed here, passwords are sent to the server as plain text.

Apache

The most important Apache instruction for access control is `Require`; this directive defines the requirements that a user must fulfill to be granted or denied access. The main configuration for Apache contains the following lines:

```
<Directory />
  Require all denied
</Directory>
```

These lines assure that Apache does not have access to the root of the file system (/) and neither to the rest of the file system, because each directory inherits the settings from its parent directory; to grant access to a directory, the default denial of access must be overwritten explicitly.

As an example of this overwriting, the following line has already been used in the previously created virtual hosts:

```
Require all granted
```

The preceding line grants unconditional access to the directory in question (and its sub-directories).

The following line has also been touched upon briefly:

```
Require ip 192.0.2.125 203.0.113.12
```

That line limits access to visitors from the listed IP addresses. Variants of that last line are

```
Require not ip 192.0.2.125 203.0.113.12
```

```
Require ip 192.0.2
```

The former of those lines denies access to visitors from the listed IP addresses. The latter grants access to visitors from the class C subnet 192.0.2.0/24.

It is also possible to grant access based on a username/password combination with the help of the *mod_auth_basic* module. This module should be combined with a module like *mod_authn_file*, which allows the use of a text file as a password database. Both modules are loaded by default.

To make use of authentication based on username and password, a password file must be created first. The htpasswd command is used to manipulate this file.

```
# cd /srv/www/www.example.com
# mkdir ./htdocs/subdir
# echo "<h1>It works!</h1>" > ./htdocs/subdir/index.html
# touch ./conf/passwd.subdir
# htpasswd ./conf/passwd.subdir diane
```

```
New password:
Re-type new password:
Adding password for user diane
#
```

The name for the password file can be freely chosen, and the user does not need to have a user account on the system.

Then, the following lines are added to the virtual host definition for *www.example.com* (between the lines <VirtualHost *:443> and </VirtualHost>):

```
<Directory "/srv/www/www.example.com/htdocs/subdir">
  AuthType Basic
  AuthName "Confidential documents"
  AuthBasicProvider file
  AuthUserFile "/srv/www/www.example.com/conf/passwd.subdir"
  Require valid-user
</Directory>
```

Thanks to the line Require valid-user, this directory is accessible to all users who enter a valid username/password combination from the password file. To limit access even further, this line could be replaced with a line like the following:

```
Require user diane dimitri
```

With this line, access is only granted to users who enter the correct password for one of the usernames *diane* or *dimitri*, regardless of any other names in the password file.

If access to an entire virtual host is limited, it is important to explicitly grant unconditional access to the /.well-known directory to assure that certbot and other services which depend on this directory can do their work; see Chapter 10, "Traffic Encryption: SSL/TLS", for more information about certbot and the /.well-known directory.

The paragraph on *CalDAV* and *CardDAV* later in this chapter gives an example of the authentication of users against an LDAP directory service.

With the help of the mod_authz_groupfile module, Apache also supports user groups. Apache can also verify users against an SQL or DBM database. More information about authentication and authorization can be found at the Apache website.

Nginx

To grant or deny access based on the visitor's IP address, Nginx uses the `allow` and `deny` directives. These directives can appear multiple times and can be combined. They are checked in the order in which they are defined, and the first match determines what happens with the request.

```
location /subdir {
    deny 203.0.113.15;
    deny 203.0.113.64;
    allow 203.0.113.0/24;
    allow 198.51.100.23;
    allow 192.0.2.213;
    deny all;
}
```

The preceding configuration limits access to the URL */subdir*:

1. Visitors with IP addresses `203.0.113.15` and `203.0.113.64` are denied access.

2. Visitors with other IP addresses in the `203.0.113.0/24` subnet are granted access.

3. Visitors with IP addresses `198.51.100.23` and `192.0.2.113` are also granted access.

4. All other visitors are denied access.

It is also possible to grant access based on a username/password combination. For the manipulation of the password file, the `htpasswd` command is used, which is developed for the Apache web server. On FreeBSD, this requires the installation of the entire Apache web server; on Debian, the *apache2-utils* package suffices, and on Centos, the *httpd-utils* package.

```
# cd /srv/www/www.example.com
# mkdir ./htdocs/subdir
# echo "<h1>It works!</h1>" > ./htdocs/subdir/index.html
# touch ./conf/passwd.subdir
# htpasswd ./conf/passwd.subdir diane
```

```
New password:
Re-type new password:
Adding password for user diane
#
```

The name for the password file can be freely chosen, and the user does not need to have a user account on the system.

Then, the following lines are added to the virtual server definition for *www.example.com*:

```
location /subdir {
  auth_basic "Confidential documents";
  auth_basic_user_file
/srv/www/www.example.com/conf/passwd.subdir;
}
```

If access to an entire virtual host is limited, it is important to explicitly grant unconditional access to the /.well-known directory to assure that certbot and other services which depend on this directory can do their work; see Chapter 10, "Traffic Encryption: SSL/TLS", for more information about certbot and the /.well-known directory.

WebDAV

WebDAV (Web-based Distributed Authoring and Versioning) is an extension to HTTP that allows for the online creation, modification, storage, relocation, and deletion of files. Many *cloud-based* storage services use WebDAV, and most modern operating systems, including smartphones and tablets, support it. Most file managers (Windows Explorer, Finder, Nautilus, Dolphin, PCManFM, etc.) know how to access WebDAV storage, and office applications like LibreOffice, OpenOffice, and Microsoft Office have built-in functionality to open, edit, and save documents through WebDAV.

This makes WebDAV an ideal medium for online storage and sharing of files and indispensable for a modern internet server. But of course the usage of WebDAV is not limited to the sharing of files: with a small modification to the configuration discussed in the following, personal WebDAV directories can be created, which can be used, for example, for backing up files from a smartphone.

Several WebDAV server implementations exist, developed in several programming languages. The implementations discussed here are modules for the web servers that have been installed already.

While this would actually make an ordinary virtual host or server of the WebDAV server, the choice was made to separate the (read-write) WebDAV server from the (read-only) websites on the file system level. Clearly, this is not mandatory: the Filesystem Hierarchy Standard explicitly states that the system administrator is completely free in the arrangement and organization of the directory structure under /srv.

To assure that only the web server can write to these directories, the web server is the owner of this directory tree, and no additional access privileges are assigned using ACL.

```
# mkdir -p /srv/dav/dav.example.com/{conf,htdocs,tmp}
# chmod -R 0751 /srv/dav
# chmod 2770 /srv/dav/dav.example.com/*

freebsd# chown www:www /srv/dav/dav.example.com/*

debian# chown www-data:www-data /srv/dav/dav.example.com/*

centos+apache# chown apache:apache /srv/dav/dav.example.com/*

centos+nginx# chown nginx:nginx /srv/dav/dav.example.com/*
```

A DNS CNAME record is created for *dav.example.com* that points to green.example.com.

The following command is used to request the TLS certificate for this virtual host:

```
# certbot certonly --webroot -w /srv/www/rfc5785 -d dav.example.com
```

A virtual host or virtual server is then created in the web server configuration; this virtual host/server listens on port 443 and has /srv/dav/dav.example.com/htdocs as its document root. As this virtual host/server should serve the files just as they are stored on the server, instead of turning them into a website, PHP files are not sent to a PHP-FPM pool.

Since WebDAV is a read-write protocol, access control is of the utmost importance. As WebDAV is very suited for mobile clients, regulating access based on username/password combinations makes more sense than limiting access based on IP address. The setup discussed here makes use of a password file. The next section, "CalDAV and CardDAV", contains an example of the use of the LDAP directory service that is also used for the mail accounts; however, this option is only available for Apache.

```
# touch /srv/dav/dav.example.com/conf/passwd
# htpasswd /srv/dav/dav.example.com/conf/passwd diane
# htpasswd /srv/dav/dav.example.com/conf/passwd dimitri
```

Apache

The DAV modules must be installed and activated. On FreeBSD as well as on Debian and CentOS, the modules have been installed with the Apache package; however, on FreeBSD and Debian, they are not loaded automatically.

```
freebsd# ls /usr/local/libexec/apache24/
freebsd# grep -rs dav /usr/local/etc/apache24/httpd.conf
freebsd# nano /usr/local/etc/apache24/httpd.conf
```

```
LoadModule dav_module libexec/apache24/mod_dav.so
LoadModule dav_fs_module libexec/apache24/mod_dav_fs.so
LoadModule dav_lock_module libexec/apache24/mod_dav_lock.so
Include etc/apache24/extra/httpd-dav.conf
```

```
debian# ls /usr/lib/apache2/modules/
debian# cd /etc/apache2/mods-enabled
debian# ls dav* || ln -s ../mods-available/dav* .
```

```
centos# ls /usr/lib64/httpd/modules/
centos# grep -rs dav /etc/httpd/
```

In the file /usr/local/etc/apache24/extra/httpd-dav.conf on FreeBSD, all lines should be disabled (hash sign at the beginning of the line), except those starting with the word BrowserMatch.

In the file /etc/apache2/mods-available/setenv.conf on Debian, the following line must be modified:

```
BrowserMatch "^WebDAVFS/1.[0134]" redirect-carefully
```

And on CentOS, these lines must be added to the file /etc/httpd/conf.modules.d/00-dav.conf:

```
BrowserMatch "Microsoft Data Access Internet Publishing Provider"
redirect-carefully
BrowserMatch "MS FrontPage" redirect-carefully
BrowserMatch "^WebDrive" redirect-carefully
BrowserMatch "^WebDAVFS/1.[01234]" redirect-carefully
BrowserMatch "^gnome-vfs/1.0" redirect-carefully
```

```
BrowserMatch "^XML Spy" redirect-carefully
BrowserMatch "^Dreamweaver-WebDAV-SCM1" redirect-carefully
BrowserMatch " Konqueror/4" redirect-carefully
```

All these `BrowserMatch` corrections are workarounds for known flaws in certain
WebDAV clients.

A minimal configuration for the virtual host looks as follows:

```
<VirtualHost *:80>
    ServerName dav.example.com
    Redirect permanent "/" "https://dav.example.com/"
</VirtualHost>

<VirtualHost *:443>
    ServerName dav.example.com
    DocumentRoot /srv/dav/dav.example.com/htdocs

    # SSL/TLS.
    # Correct this path on FreeBSD.
    SSLEngine On
    SSLCertificateFile \
      "/etc/letsencrypt/live/dav.example.com/fullchain.pem"
    SSLCertificateKeyFile \
      "/etc/letsencrypt/live/dav.example.com/privkey.pem"

    # This file keeps track of which files are currently
    # open, and therefore cannot be opened by other users.
    # If the file does not exist, it will be created
    # automatically.
    DavLockDB /srv/dav/dav.example.com/tmp/DavLock

    <Directory "/srv/dav/dav.example.com/htdocs">
        # Enable WebDAV.
        Dav On

        # Security.
        AuthType Basic
        AuthName "Shared files"
        AuthBasicProvider file
```

```
        AuthUserFile "/srv/dav/dav.example.com/conf/passwd"
        Require valid-user
    </Directory>
</VirtualHost>
```

Depending on the client system, the WebDAV storage can now be accessed at one or both of the URLs *davs://diane@dav.example.com/* and *https://diane@dav.example.com/*; in this case, *diane* is the username. This WebDAV storage is shared by all users who have a name/password combination in the password file.

To give each user their own WebDAV storage, a separate virtual host could be created for each user. However, it probably makes more sense to create sub-directories inside the virtual host that was just created and add a line like the following to the configuration for each of those directories:

```
Require user diane
```

This simplifies the addition, modification, and deletion of users and facilitates the creation of backups.

Nginx

If the Nginx package that includes all modules was installed, as was discussed in a previous chapter, no additional installation is necessary. If a more limited installation was chosen, the *ngx_http_dav_module* must be installed.

With the necessary software installed, the following configuration turns the selected directory into a WebDAV storage:

```
server {
  listen *:80;
  server_name dav.example.com;
  return 301 https://dav.example.com/;
}

server {
  listen *:443 ssl;
  server_name dav.example.com;
  location / {
    root /srv/dav/dav.example.com/htdocs;
```

```
    # SSL/TLS.
    ssl_session_cache      shared:SSL:5m;
    ssl_session_timeout    10m;
    keepalive_timeout      75s;
    ssl_certificate \
      /etc/letsencrypt/live/dav.example.com/fullchain.pem;
    ssl_certificate_key \
      /etc/letsencrypt/live/dav.example.com/privkey.pem;

    # Directory for temporary files.
    client_body_temp_path /srv/dav/dav.example.com/tmp;

    # Allowed DAV methods.
    # Available: PUT, DELETE, MKCOL, COPY, MOVE
    dav_methods PUT DELETE MKCOL COPY MOVE;

    # Create non-existing directories.
    create_full_put_path on;

    # Permissions for stored files.
    dav_access user:rw group:rw all:rw;

    # Security.
    auth_basic "Shared files";
    auth_basic_user_file /srv/dav/dav.example.com/conf/passwd;
  }
}
```

Depending on the client system, the WebDAV storage can now be accessed at one or both of the URLs *davs://diane@dav.example.com/* and *https://diane@dav.example.com/*; in this case, *diane* is the username. This WebDAV storage is shared by all users who have a name/password combination in the password file.

To give each user their own WebDAV storage, a virtual server could be created for each user, or sub-directories could be created for each user in the existing virtual server, with a separate password file for each sub-directory.

CalDAV and CardDAV

CalDAV and *CardDAV* are extensions to the WebDAV protocol for serving calendars and address books, respectively. Contrary to WebDAV, no recent CalDAV and CardDAV web server modules are available.

However, a considerable number of CalDAV and CardDAV servers exist, both open source and closed source, developed in several programming languages. Most of these servers serve both CalDAV and CardDAV, but some servers exist that only serve a single protocol.

For this book, *Radicale* was selected, a free and open source CalDAV/CardDAV server with a decent reputation, developed in Python. An additional advantage of Radicale for this book is that this server functions as a daemon and by default only binds to *localhost* (which means that it is only available for the local machine and not for the rest of the network). This allows Radicale to be used to document how the web server can serve as a *reverse proxy* that makes a local service available and secures it on the internet. The advantage of the *reverse proxy* is that the calendars and address books are served on HTTPS port 443, and no additional ports need to be opened in the firewall.

Radicale's web interface is only used to create and delete calendars and address books, if the selected client does not support this functionality. The web interface generates a URL that allows the clients to access and manage the calendars and address books.

Radicale is available in the software repositories for the discussed systems, but unfortunately, Debian and CentOS only provide the old version 1.1.x; FreeBSD allows to select between versions 1 and 2. On Debian and CentOS, Radicale will therefore be installed using `pip`; see Chapter 3, "Software Management", for more information.

```
bsd# pkg install py37-radicale2
```

```
linux# pip3 install radicale
```

On FreeBSD, the configuration is installed in `/usr/local/etc/radicale2`. On the Linux systems, `pip` does not automatically create a configuration directory; by default, the `radicale` daemon tries to load its configuration from `/etc/radicale/config`:

```
linux# mkdir /etc/radicale
linux# touch /etc/radicale/config
```

No dedicated user for the `radicale` daemon is created either on the Linux systems.

```
linux# useradd --system \
        --user-group \
        --comment "Radicale daemon" \
        --shell /usr/sbin/nologin \
        --home-dir /srv/radicale \
        radicale
```

In the `config` configuration file, only a few options need to be defined.

```
[server]
# Only accept connections over the loopback device,
# on port 5232.
# Do not encrypt the connection.
hosts = 127.0.0.1:5232
ssl = False

[auth]
# Let the web server take care of authentication
# and authorization.
type = http_x_remote_user

[rights]
# All users can only access their own calendars
# and address books.
type = owner_only

[storage]
# The directory where the data is stored.
filesystem_folder = /srv/radicale/collections
```

Obviously, also other options may be defined. The documentation can be found on the Radicale website. When modifying the configuration, it is important to keep in mind that the web server will take care of authentication and authorization, so there is no need to configure this in Radicale. The web server is also responsible for SSL/TLS encryption. If the server could be considered a hostile environment (external users with shell access), it is advisable to configure Radicale's authentication and authorization, as well as the encryption of the traffic between Radicale and the web server that serves as its *reverse proxy*.

The directory where the calendars and address books are stored must be created and should only be accessible to user *radicale.*

```
# mkdir -p /srv/radicale/collections
# chown -R radicale:radicale /srv/radicale
# chmod -R 2770 /srv/radicale
```

On FreeBSD, Radicale was installed together with a startup script, but since Radicale was installed using pip on Linux, there are no such scripts for those systems. Debian and CentOS both use *systemd* as their *init system.*

```
linux# nano /etc/systemd/system/radicale.service
```

```
[Unit]
Description=CalDAV and CardDAV server
After=network.target
Requires=network.target

[Service]
ExecStart=/usr/bin/env python3 -m radicale
Restart=on-failure
User=radicale
UMask=0027
PrivateTmp=true
ProtectSystem=strict
ProtectHome=true
PrivateDevices=true
ProtectKernelTunables=true
ProtectKernelModules=true
ProtectControlGroups=true
NoNewPrivileges=true
ReadWritePaths=/srv/radicale/collections

[Install]
WantedBy=multi-user.target
```

And with that in place, the daemon can be started.

```
bsd# service radicale enable
bsd# service radicale start
linux# systemctl enable radicale
linux# systemctl start radicale
```

The CalDAV/CardDAV server is now running and listens on port 5232 on the loopback device (*127.0.0.1*). The selected web server, Apache or Nginx, will now serve as a *reverse proxy* to enable communication with the internet.

Firstly, a DNS alias must be created for the new virtual host. A software package that is used to manage personal information like calendars, agenda, and so on is sometimes referred to as *PIM* (*Personal Information Manager*) software, so *pim.example.com* could make sense as a hostname, but again, the system administrator is free to choose any name. The new alias points at *green.example.com*. (Do not forget to increment the serial number.)

The TLS certificate is installed using the following command:

```
# certbot certonly --webroot -w /srv/www/rfc5785 -d pim.example.com
```

The web server settings for Radicale are somewhat comparable to those for PHP-FPM, the FastCGI proxy that is used for the interpretation of CGI scripts.

Radicale and Apache

Apache supports the authentication of users against an LDAP directory service. This is the setup that will be discussed here: users will be verified against the directory service that is also used for the mail accounts; this way, mail users also have automatic access to synchronized calendars and address books. The configuration of the directory service is discussed in Chapter 11, "Databases". The previous section, "WebDAV", explains how users could be verified against a password file.

The Apache *proxy_http* module must be loaded to facilitate the communication between Radicale and the user. On CentOS, this module is loaded per default, but on FreeBSD and Debian, it isn't. Furthermore, authentication against an LDAP directory service requires the *ldap* and *authnz_ldap* modules. These modules are not installed by default on FreeBSD and CentOS; on FreeBSD, this requires the replacement of Apache, which was installed as a package, with an installation from the Ports Collection (mind you: this will take some time).

```
freebsd# cd /usr/ports/devel/apr1
freebsd# make deinstall && make reinstall clean
freebsd# cd /usr/ports/www/apache24
```

```
freebsd# make config
  Check: AUTHNZ_LDAP and LDAP
freebsd# make config-recursive
  Accept all default options
freebsd# make deinstall && make reinstall clean
freebsd# nano /usr/local/etc/apache24/httpd.conf
```

```
LoadModule proxy_http_module libexec/apache24/mod_proxy_http.so
LoadModule ldap_module libexec/apache24/mod_ldap.so
LoadModule authnz_ldap_module libexec/apache24/mod_authnz_ldap.so
```

```
debian# cd /etc/apache2/mods-enabled
debian# ln -s ../mods-available/proxy_http.load .
debian# ln -s ../mods-available/*ldap.load .
```

```
centos# yum install mod_ldap
```

The following lines optimize *Basic Authentication* for LDAP; they should be added to the end of httpd.conf (apache.conf on Debian).

```
LDAPSharedCacheSize 500000
LDAPCacheEntries 1024
LDAPCacheTTL 600
LDAPOpCacheEntries 1024
LDAPOpCacheTTL 600
```

And this is the configuration for the new virtual host:

```
<VirtualHost *:80>
  ServerName pim.example.com
  Redirect permanent "/" "https://pim.example.com/"
</VirtualHost>

<VirtualHost *:443>
  ServerName pim.example.com

  SSLEngine On
  SSLCertificateFile \
    "/etc/letsencrypt/live/pim.example.com/fullchain.pem"
```

```
    SSLCertificateKeyFile \
      "/etc/letsencrypt/live/pim.example.com/privkey.pem"
    # The /.well-known/ URL should not be handled by Radicale.
    <LocationMatch "^/.well-known/">
      ProxyPassMatch !
    </LocationMatch>

    # All other URLs should be handled by Radicale,
    # and must be secured with a password.
    <Location "/">
      AuthType Basic
      AuthBasicProvider ldap
      AuthName "PIM data - Password required"
      AuthLDAPURL \
  "ldap://localhost:389/ou=users,dc=example,dc=com?uid?one"
      Require valid-user

      # Pass requests to Radicale.
      ProxyPass "http://localhost:5232/" retry=0
      ProxyPassReverse "http://localhost:5232/"

      RequestHeader set X-Remote-User expr=%{REMOTE_USER}
    </Location>
</VirtualHost>
```

The last directive (RequestHeader set X-Remote-User [...]) assures that the username for the authenticated user is passed to Radicale.

Radicale and Nginx

Unfortunately, support for authentication via LDAP on Nginx is not (yet) as advanced as on Apache. Users will therefore be authenticated against a password file. The same users are created as were created for the mail server.

```
# touch /srv/radicale/passwd
# htpasswd /srv/radicale/passwd alicia
# htpasswd /srv/radicale/passwd arthur
```

And then, this is the configuration for the new virtual server:

```
server {
  listen *:80;
  server_name pim.example.com;
  return 301 https://pim.example.com/;
}

server {
  listen *:443 ssl;
  server_name pim.example.com;

  # The /.well-known/ URL should not be handled by Radicale,
  # and should not be secured.
  location /.well-known/ {
    alias /srv/www/rfc5785/.well-known/;
    auth_basic off;
    allow all;
  }

  # All other URLs should be handled by Radicale,
  # and must be secured with a password.
  location / {
    # SSL/TLS.
    ssl_session_cache      shared:SSL:5m;
    ssl_session_timeout    10m;
    keepalive_timeout      75s;
    ssl_certificate \
      /etc/letsencrypt/live/pim.example.com/fullchain.pem;
    ssl_certificate_key \
      /etc/letsencrypt/live/pim.example.com/privkey.pem;

    # Security.
    auth_basic "PIM data - Password required"
    auth_basic_user_file /srv/radicale/passwd;

    # Pass requests to Radicale.
    proxy_pass http://localhost:5232/;
    proxy_set_header X-Forwarded-For $proxy_add_x_forwarded_for;
```

```
      proxy_pass_header Authorization;
      proxy_set_header X-Remote-User $remote_user;
   }
}
```

The last directive (`proxy_set_header X-Remote-User [...]`) assures that the username for the verified user is passed to Radicale.

Clients

CalDAV and CardDAV are standards that are supported by many clients. These are the most important ones:

- iOS and Android support both protocols.

- Mozilla Thunderbird supports CalDAV through the *Lightning* add-on and CardDAV through the *CardBook* add-on.

- Microsoft Outlook supports both protocols through the *CalDAV Synchronizer Plugin.*

- macOS supports CalDAV in the Calendar application and CardDAV in the Contacts application.

- Evolution supports both protocols.

Logs and Statistics

Who manages a website will want to know how many visitors that website receives, where those visitors come from, what the peak times are, how visitors navigate the site, and so on, but also where the bottlenecks are and which requests resulted in a *404 error* (*Page not found*). And even though all this information can be distilled from the web server's log files, in /var/log—and it is absolutely advisable to analyze these regularly, each week, for example, to find and solve problems—these log files are not very user-friendly for daily use, and it is more practical and agreeable to use a specialized package that collects and aggregates this information and can present it in different ways.

AWStats and *Webalizer* are applications that try to make the log files more transparent. These applications import the web server log files and generate static HTML pages from the data, displaying the data in a graphical way and grouping the information by type.

Those applications are mainly oriented toward web server administrators. Marketing and sales departments may have slightly different requirements. For example, they may want to follow customers over the website to see which route a customer takes before the purchase is closed or to see where in the process potential customers abandon their purchase.

Many websites make use of external parties for the collection of these statistics. These external parties usually add a small piece of code to each page in the website and use this to analyze website visits. However, for websites that respect their visitor's privacy, sharing of their users' internet behavior may be an undesirable solution, and for websites that guarantee confidentiality, the involvement of a third party may conflict with the *General Data Protection Regulation*.

Matomo is an open source package that offers the exact same functionality as well-known third-party solutions, but can be hosted in-house and does not share any information with third parties. If desired or required, Matomo can be configured to anonymize collected data by masking the last two or three bytes of IP addresses, for example, or by respecting the *DoNotTrack request header*. A single Matomo installation can collect statistics for multiple websites; the access to the statistics is configured per user per website.

AWStats and Webalizer are both available in the software repositories for FreeBSD, Debian, and CentOS. Matomo is also available in the FreeBSD repository, but will need to be downloaded for Debian and CentOS. However, Matomo is a web application that is relatively simple to install, and the documentation on the website is vast and clear; the name of the free, *self-hosted* version is *Matomo On-Premise*.

Instant Web Applications

The last part of this chapter discusses some web applications that may be of interest to an organization running a web server. This is only a very small selection from an infinite number of available applications and only serves to give an idea of the possibilities.

Installation and use of these applications is not discussed. The websites for these applications, for which the links can be found in the online addendum for this book, give more information about this.

Many of these applications are installed with a file named `.htaccess` in the document root. This file contains configuration options for Apache and allows the developer or operator of a website to modify certain web server settings without the intervention of a system administrator; the system administrator determines which settings can be made in this way by setting the `AllowOverride` instruction in the web server configuration. If at all possible, it is recommended to copy the instructions from the `.htaccess` file to the `VirtualHost` configuration and to set `AllowOverride` to none. This prevents the web server from having to search for the `.htaccess` file in each directory with every request, which makes the web server use less memory and processing power and respond faster. Attention: since the name of this file starts with a dot, it is a hidden file; use `ls -a` to find it.

Notwithstanding the fact that these applications are self-hosted, a number of them load scripts, fonts, and/or images from external websites. These external websites are not always known for respecting users' privacy, so the use of these external websites could conflict with the privacy policy the operator of the web application has put in place. The use of these external websites is usually not mentioned in the documentation for these applications, but most of these applications run internet forums where information can be requested.

Complete Website

A *content management system* (*CMS*) is a (software) system that is used to publish information to the internet. A CMS is usually a web application that stores the information (*content*) on the server, in a database and/or the file system, to present it as a website using templates for layout and design. Most CMSs can be extended with modules (functionality) and themes (website design).

For an experienced *content manager*, a CMS can be an ideal solution that saves a lot of time. For people for whom website maintenance is not their daily work, a CMS can be complex and overwhelming because of the abundance of possibilities these systems often offer. Therefore, when selecting a CMS, it is important to not only look at the possibilities of the CMS but also at the person responsible for the maintenance of the website.

Furthermore, a CMS can be overkill because of all the built-in functionality that is not used, but still must be loaded into the interpreter, causing the website to use more memory and processing power than necessary.

Prominent examples of open source CMSs are *WordPress*, *Joomla*, and *Drupal*, which are all developed in PHP.

Ecommerce

An online store or web shop is a website that was developed for the presentation and sale of products and/or services. The content of the website consists mainly of items that are classified into collections and/or categories. The functionality for such websites focuses on search functions, order forms, "shopping carts" or "shopping baskets," and payment modules.

When selecting ecommerce software, it is important to verify that the software includes payment modules for the countries where the main market is located; examples of such payment services are *Secure Vault Payments* in the United States, *Interac* in Canada, *iDEAL* in the Netherlands, and *Giropay* in Germany.

Prominent examples of open source ecommerce packages are *OpenCart*, *PrestaShop*, *Zen Cart*, and *OsCommerce*, which are all developed in PHP.

Customer Service

Customer service software often consists of a combination of *knowledge base* and *issue tracker*.

A *knowledge base* is an online system where frequently asked questions are answered and common problems are documented. Customers (or employees) can use such a system to try and find an answer to their questions themselves.

An *issue tracker*, also called *ticket system*, is a system that allows customers (or employees) to pose questions and problems to a help desk or support department in a structured manner. The help desk or support department can then assign these problems (*tickets*) to staff members, and customer and staff can track the status of the problem online. The majority of issue trackers can be connected to one or more email addresses, allowing the communication with customers to take place via email while still being recorded in the system and thus being accessible, trackable, and analyzable for staff.

A customer support system can be a welcome or even necessary tool in the organization of the communication with customers or employees. In the startup phase, however, a considerable time span for planning and configuration must be taken into account; this phase includes the creation of ticket categories, the configuration of access rights for users, the email addresses to be linked, and so on. The knowledge base will also need to be updated frequently to prevent it from showing obsolete information and from missing new information.

Prominent examples of open source customer service packages are *Request Tracker*, developed in Perl, and *osTicket*, developed in PHP.

Wiki

A wiki is a website that can be modified by users, be it or not after username and password verification. Even though such a system is absolutely not suitable for every website, it is an ideal system for a website where a dedicated community of users shares information and looks to perfect this information over time.

The most prominent example of open source wiki software is obviously *MediaWiki*, the software *Wikipedia* runs on; *MediaWiki* is developed in PHP. Other examples are *TWiki*, developed in Perl; *XWiki*, developed in Java; and *DokuWiki*, developed in PHP, with text files as data storage instead of a database.

Personal Cloud Service

ownCloud and Nextcloud (which emerged from ownCloud) are both packages that offer some of the functionality that was described in this book (WebDAV, CalDAV, CardDAV); both packages can be extended with modules that add functionality.

These packages should absolutely be mentioned in a book about internet server management, but there are several reasons why that has not happened until now. First of all, a new system administrator learns more from configuring a web server to provide WebDAV than from installing a software package. Furthermore, it is overkill to install a large and complex package like ownCloud or Nextcloud if it is only used for WebDAV. These packages require quite some memory and processing power, and as stated before, every installed package potentially introduces additional risks.

Having said that, ownCloud and Nextcloud both deserve to be mentioned in this book.

Summary

This chapter discussed the more advanced functionalities web servers offer, like aliases, CGI scripts, and access control. The web server was also configured to deliver WebDAV services for the synchronization and backup of files, and a CalDAV/CardDAV server was installed for the centralization of calendars and address books. Lastly, some examples were given of commonly used open source instant web applications.

The next chapter dives deeper into the configuration of the mail server.

CHAPTER 14

Advanced Email

The SMTP and IMAP servers have been installed and configured, so mail can be sent and received. However, a modern mail setup is not complete without the possibility to filter mails and without anti-spam measures.

Sieve

Sieve is a scripting language for filtering incoming emails. This filtering is done on the server; when using IMAP, filtering on the client is rather useless, since the original messages remain on the server.

Sieve is an extension of the LDA that allows, for example, to move mails to certain folders based on the sender, recipient, subject, or other properties. Besides moved, mails can also be copied, deleted, rejected, marked, or forwarded; headers can be added, deleted, or modified; external applications can be executed; notifications can be sent through *XMPP* (*Jabber*); and so on.

Several clients exist for the *ManageSieve* protocol, the protocol that is used to edit Sieve filters. The system administrator can also add system-wide scripts that cannot be modified by users; this is used to add spam and virus filter headers.

This is an example of a small, simple Sieve script:

```
require ["mailbox", "fileinto", "reject"];
if header :matches "Subject" "*viagra*" {
    discard;
    stop;
}
elsif address :is :localpart "from" "marketing" {
    reject "Not interested in promotional content.";
    stop;
}
```

© Robert La Lau 2021
R. La Lau, *Practical Internet Server Configuration*, https://doi.org/10.1007/978-1-4842-6960-2_14

```
elsif address :is ["to", "cc"] "sales@example.com" {
    fileinto "Sales";
    stop;
}
else {
        keep;
}
```

Furthermore, the IMAP specification has been extended, allowing Sieve to be used to respond to user actions. A use case for this functionality could be the modification of spam filter rules when the user moves an email message to a designated folder (e.g., *Spam*). This extension is called *imapsieve*.

Dovecot supports most of the Sieve functionality, including *imapsieve*, through the *Pigeonhole* plugin.

To enable the manipulation of the filter rules, inbound traffic on TCP port 4190 (*managesieve*) must be allowed.

Installation

The Pigeonhole plugin is available from the software repositories of all discussed systems.

FreeBSD

```
freebsd# pkg install dovecot-pigeonhole
```

Example configuration files are installed into /usr/local/share/doc/dovecot/example-config. These files should be copied to the Dovecot configuration directory.

```
freebsd# cp /usr/local/share/doc/dovecot/example-config/conf.d/* \
        /usr/local/etc/dovecot/conf.d
```

Debian

On Debian, the Pigeonhole plugin has been split into two packages, one for the filtering and one for the manipulation of the filters.

```
debian# apt install dovecot-managesieved dovecot-sieve
```

The configuration files are installed into /etc/dovecot.

CentOS

```
centos# yum install dovecot-pigeonhole
```

The configuration is installed into /etc/dovecot.

Configuration

The Pigeonhole configuration files are installed into the conf.d sub-directory of the Dovecot configuration directory.

```
freebsd# cd /usr/local/etc/dovecot/conf.d
debian# cd /etc/dovecot/conf.d
centos# cd /etc/dovecot/conf.d
```

To enable Sieve filtering, the *sieve* plugin must be added to the (currently empty) list of mail plugins that must be loaded. This is done in the file 15-lda.conf:

```
protocol lda {
  mail_plugins = sieve
}
```

The *ManageSieve* protocol is enabled in the file 20-managesieve.conf:

```
protocols = $protocols sieve
```

The $protocols variable represents the old value of this variable, so sieve is added to existing list of supported protocols (instead of replacing it).

This is all the configuration that is necessary to enable regular email filtering. Some more configuration will be done later in this chapter when spam filtering is configured.

After these modifications, Dovecot must be restarted.

Manipulation of the Filters

Several applications exist for the management of Sieve filter rules, as well as plugins for mail clients and web mail packages. These applications connect to port 4190 at the server with the same username/password combination that is used for IMAP.

A user can have multiple Sieve scripts. One of those scripts is marked as *active*, and that is the main script; the LDA loads this script when mail arrives, and from this script, other scripts can be loaded.

Fine-tuning the Postfix Configuration

The cheapest way to fight spam is to have Postfix reject the most obvious cases "at the door". Several settings are available to achieve this.

Verification of HELO/EHLO Command

When a mail server wishes to deliver a message to another mail server, it starts the communication with the HELO or EHLO command, followed by its hostname. Since spam software does not always (completely) adhere to this requirement, part of the received spam can already be stopped by telling Postfix to not accept mails without this HELO command and that the HELO hostname must meet certain requirements. This is done by adding the following lines to the main.cf file:

```
smtpd_helo_required = yes
smtpd_helo_restrictions =
    permit_mynetworks
    reject_invalid_helo_hostname
    reject_non_fqdn_helo_hostname
    reject_unauth_pipelining
    regexp:/etc/postfix/helo.regexp
    permit
```

This makes Postfix reject any communication that is not started with the HELO command (smtpd_helo_required), any communication where the hostname in the HELO command does not meet the requirements of a regular hostname (reject_invalid_helo_hostname and reject_non_fqdn_helo_hostname), any communication where the sender tries to send other SMTP commands before the HELO command has been accepted (reject_unauth_pipelining), and any communication for which the helo.regexp file indicates that the hostname in the HELO command is not acceptable.

The `helo.regexp` file has the following contents:

```
/^green\.example\.com$/        550 Rejected
/^mx\.example\.com$/           550 Rejected
/^mail\.example\.com$/         550 Rejected
/^smtp\.example\.com$/         550 Rejected
/^imap\.example\.com$/         550 Rejected
/^ns\.example\.com$/           550 Rejected
/^www\.example\.com$/          550 Rejected
/^198\.51\.100\.156$/          550 Rejected
/^\[198\.51\.100\.156\]$/      550 Rejected
```

These rules prevent the sending server from impersonating this server.

Obviously, on FreeBSD, this file is located in the `/usr/local/etc/postfix` directory instead of the `/etc/postfix` directory.

Postfix needs to reload its configuration after these modifications have been made. If only the `helo.regexp` file was modified, Postfix does not need to be reloaded.

Verification of Addresses

Another simple measure is the verification of the addresses in the MAIL FROM and RCPT TO commands; these addresses must be in the correct format, they must contain *Fully Qualified Domain Names*, the destination domain must be handled by this server, and the sender domain must exist. The functionality to verify all this is included in Postfix.

Add the bold lines to `main.cf`:

```
strict_rfc821_envelopes = yes
smtpd_recipient_restrictions =
    permit_sasl_authenticated
    reject_non_fqdn_sender
    reject_non_fqdn_recipient
    reject_unauth_destination
    reject_unknown_sender_domain
    permit_mynetworks
    permit
```

After this modification, Postfix must again be reloaded.

Unused Addresses

If addresses exist that are no longer in use and currently only collect spam, these addresses can simply be blocked by putting them into a separate database in the Postfix configuration directory.

```
# nano recipients
```

```
sale2016@example.com        REJECT
enrollment2015@example.edu  REJECT
unused@example.org          REJECT
```

```
# postmap recipients
```

This creates the database `recipients.db` that can be queried in the same manner as the databases created in Chapter 12, "Email Basics". Add the bold line to `main.cf`:

```
smtpd_recipient_restrictions =
    permit_sasl_authenticated
    reject_non_fqdn_sender
    reject_non_fqdn_recipient
    reject_unauth_destination
    check_recipient_access hash:/etc/postfix/recipients
    reject_unknown_sender_domain
    permit_mynetworks
    permit
```

Clearly, on FreeBSD, that path should be `/usr/local/etc/postfix/recipients`. Reload Postfix.

To add addresses to this list, the text file `recipients` is modified, and a new database is generated with the help of the `postmap` command. This does not require Postfix to be reloaded.

These addresses could also have been blocked in the `virtual.db` database created earlier, but if a separate database is created, this check can be done early on in the process, preventing these messages from having to pass through the spam filter; this saves memory and processing power.

Greylisting

If an SMTP server cannot deliver a certain mail to the next SMTP server, it stores the mail temporarily and tries again later. Spam software often does not follow this convention; on the one hand, this would be expensive (time is money), and on the other hand, it is very probable that the spam server is already listed in all sorts of *blocklists* by the time a new attempt for delivery is made.

Greylisting is a technique that makes use of this lack of standards support for the fight against spam by temporarily blocking mails from unknown users. Legitimate SMTP servers will present the mail again after some time (the SMTP specification says 30 minutes, but often it is sooner); spam robots will abandon. This is a cheap and effective way to stop spam "at the door": mails that are blocked before they enter the server do not need to be processed by the spam filter and the virus filter, so this technique saves quite some memory and CPU time.

When implementing greylisting, it should be taken into account that mails from unknown senders will arrive with a certain delay. If this is a problem, it may be better to omit greylisting. On the other hand, it is good to realize that greylisting could result in a decrease of received spam messages of up to 90–95%.

Postgrey is a *Greylisting Policy Server* for Postfix. The software runs as a daemon and waits for requests from Postfix. Since (in the current setup) Postgrey only serves the Postfix installation on this server, no ports need to be opened in the firewall.

Installation

Postgrey exists in the software repositories for all three systems. On Debian, the service is started automatically after installation.

```
freebsd# pkg install postgrey
freebsd# service postgrey enable
freebsd# service postgrey start

debian# apt install postgrey

centos# yum install postgrey
centos# systemctl enable postgrey
centos# systemctl start postgrey
```

On FreeBSD and CentOS, the configuration files are installed in the Postfix configuration directory; on Debian, a directory named /etc/postgrey is created.

Configuration

The Postgrey daemon listens on a TCP socket on FreeBSD and Debian. Add the bold line to /usr/local/etc/postfix/main.cf (FreeBSD) or /etc/postfix/main.cf (Debian):

```
smtpd_recipient_restrictions =
    permit_sasl_authenticated
    reject_non_fqdn_sender
    reject_non_fqdn_recipient
    reject_unauth_destination
    check_recipient_access hash:/etc/postfix/recipients
    reject_unknown_sender_domain
    permit_mynetworks
    check_policy_service inet:127.0.0.1:10023
    permit
```

On CentOS, Postgrey is configured to listen on a Unix socket; when Postgrey was started, this socket was installed in /var/spool/postfix/postgrey. On CentOS, the following bold line should be added to /etc/postfix/main.cf:

```
smtpd_recipient_restrictions =
    permit_sasl_authenticated
    reject_non_fqdn_sender
    reject_non_fqdn_recipient
    reject_unauth_destination
    check_recipient_access hash:/etc/postfix/recipients
    reject_unknown_sender_domain
    permit_mynetworks
    check_policy_service unix:postgrey/socket
    permit
```

When these modifications have been saved, Postfix must be reloaded.

Postgrey supports allow lists for addresses that may pass unverified. More information about this can be found in the installed configuration files and in postgrey(8).

DNS Blackhole List (DNSBL)

A *DNS Blackhole List* or *Real-time Blackhole List* (*RBL*) is a list that contains hosts that are known for sending spam or other unsolicited mail. These lists are generally implemented as DNS servers, which allows mail servers and clients to simply and quickly request information about senders of emails: the receiving mail server sends the IP address of the sender to the DNSBL as a DNS lookup; if the DNSBL knows the IP address, which means that it is a known spammer, the DNS replies with an IP address—usually in the range 127.0.0.0/8—and if the IP address is unknown, the DNSBL sends an NXDOMAIN reply (*Domain not found*). This is a somewhat simplified representation of the reality.

A considerable number of public DNSBLs exist, and many of them can be used free of charge. Wikipedia is a good starting point to learn more about DNSBL and to find addresses. A few well-known DNSBLs are Spamhaus and SORBS.

The functionality to verify senders against a DNSBL is included in Postfix. To enable this functionality, only the address of the DNSBL needs to be specified; multiple DNSBLs can be specified. This check requires the full network stack, which requires more memory and CPU than a local check; it is therefore important to run this check toward the end of the series of checks when many unwanted mails have been discarded already.

Add the bold lines to main.cf in the Postfix configuration directory:

```
smtpd_recipient_restrictions =
    permit_sasl_authenticated
    reject_non_fqdn_sender
    reject_non_fqdn_recipient
    reject_unauth_destination
    check_recipient_access hash:/etc/postfix/recipients
    reject_unknown_sender_domain
    permit_mynetworks
    check_policy_service inet:127.0.0.1:10023
    reject_rbl_client sbl.spamhaus.org
    reject_rbl_client xbl.spamhaus.org
    reject_rbl_client dnsbl.sorbs.net
    permit
```

When the file has been saved, Postfix must reload its configuration.

```
bsd# service postfix reload
linux# systemctl reload postfix
```

Sender Policy Framework (SPF)

SPF is not so much a technique to protect users on this server against incoming spam, as it is a technique to help others protect themselves from spam that has a sender address in a domain that is hosted on this server. And in the same fashion, users on this server can be protected against spam by making use of the SPF configuration on other mail servers.

Everybody can put any sender address on an email. Spammers abuse this by sending spam with forged sender addresses to make it harder to block spam. The SPF protocol describes a *DNS TXT record* that lists which SMTP servers may be used to send mail for a certain domain.

An example to clarify this:

If *green.example.com* is the only SMTP server for the domain *example.com*, a TXT record can be created that indicates that the only valid emails with sender address *@example.com* are always sent through the host with IP address *198.51.100.156*. An SMTP server that receives a mail with a sender address *@example.com* executes a DNS lookup for the TXT record in question, and if the IP address for the SMTP server of the sender of the mail does not match the IP address listed in the TXT record, the receiving SMTP server knows that the mail was not really sent by a user in the *example.com* domain.

The DNS TXT record in question looks as follows:

```
 IN  TXT  "v=spf1 mx ip4:203.0.113.21
ip6:2001:db8:85a3:8d3:1319:8a2e:370:7348 -all"
```

This is all on a single line in the zone file for the domain in question.
This record states the following:

- The server uses SPF version 1 (`v=spf1`).

- There are three hosts that may be used as SMTP servers for this domain:

  - The host that is listed in the MX record for this domain (`mx`).

  - The host with IPv4 address *203.0.113.21*.

  - The host with IPv6 address *2001:db8:85a3:8d3:1319:8a2e:370:7348*.

- SMTP servers that receive a mail with this domain as the sender address, which was not sent through one of the SMTP servers listed previously, should consider this mail as unsolicited and reject it (`-all`).

As many hosts can be listed as necessary. All possibly employed SMTP servers should be listed, including backup mail servers and servers run by external providers.

This TXT record can be added to the zone files for all hosted domains. When the zone files have been modified, the serial number must be incremented, and named must reload its configuration.

A complete zone file could look like the following:

```
$ORIGIN example.edu
$TTL    3h
@           IN  SOA     ns.example.com.
sysadmin.example.com. (
                        2   ; Serial
                        3h  ; Refresh
                        1h  ; Retry
                        1w  ; Expire
                        1h  ; TTL
                      );
            IN  NS      ns.example.com.
            IN  MX      mail.example.com.
            IN  TXT     "v=spf1 mx ip4:203.0.113.21
ip6:2001:db8:85a3:8d3:1319:8a2e:370:7348 -all"
example.edu. IN  A      198.51.100.156
www          IN  CNAME  example.edu.
```

The new record can be verified with the help of the following command:

```
# dig @127.0.0.1 example.edu TXT
```

pypolicyd-spf

The DNS configuration described previously allows other servers to request the SPF record for this server. To allow this server to verify other servers' SPF records, an *SPF policy daemon* must be installed.

Several policy daemons exist for the verification of SPF records. The implementation discussed in this book is *pypolicyd-spf*, a daemon for Postfix, developed in Python.

```
freebsd# pkg install py37-postfix-policyd-spf-python
```

```
debian# apt install postfix-policyd-spf-python
```

```
centos# yum install pypolicyd-spf
```

On FreeBSD the configuration is installed in
/usr/local/etc/postfix-policyd-spf-python, on Debian in
/etc/postfix-policyd-spf-python, and on CentOS in /etc/python-policyd-spf.
This configuration is minimal, though, and usually needs no modifications.

Create a user and add some lines to the Postfix configuration to start and call the
policy daemon. On Debian, the user has already been created during the installation.

```
freebsd# pw useradd policyd-spf \
          -u 126 \
          -c "SPF policy daemon for Postfix" \
          -d /nonexistent \
          -s /usr/sbin/nologin
freebsd# cd /usr/local/etc/postfix
```

```
debian# cd /etc/postfix
```

```
centos# useradd --system \
          --comment "SPF policy daemon for Postfix" \
          --home-dir /nonexistent \
          --no-create-home \
          --shell /sbin/nologin \
          policyd-spf
centos# cd /etc/postfix
```

```
# nano master.cf
```

```
# SPF Policy Daemon
#   FreeBSD: /usr/local/bin/policyd-spf
#   Debian : /usr/bin/policyd-spf
#   CentOS : /usr/libexec/postfix/policyd-spf
policyd-spf unix    -  n  n  -  0   spawn
  user=policyd-spf argv=/usr/bin/policyd-spf
```

```
# nano main.cf
```

```
smtpd_recipient_restrictions =
    permit_sasl_authenticated
```

```
            reject_non_fqdn_sender
            reject_non_fqdn_recipient
            reject_unauth_destination
            check_recipient_access hash:/etc/postfix/recipients
            reject_unknown_sender_domain
            permit_mynetworks
            check_policy_service inet:127.0.0.1:10023
            reject_rbl_client sbl.spamhaus.org
            reject_rbl_client xbl.spamhaus.org
            reject_rbl_client dnsbl.sorbs.net
            check_policy_service unix:private/policyd-spf
            permit

bsd# service postfix reload

linux# systemctl reload postfix
```

DomainKeys Identified Mail (DKIM)

DKIM is comparable to SPF in the sense that the recipient of a mail can verify the sender's domain by means of a DNS record. Furthermore, a digital signature is added to the message. This signature is calculated based on the contents of the email, allowing the recipient to verify that the mail was not altered between the moment it was sent and the moment it was received. The digital signature is added to the *headers* of the message, and the public key to verify the signature can be found in a *DNS TXT record*.

OpenDKIM is a package that allows Postfix to add the DKIM signature to outgoing messages and to verify the signature on incoming messages. On Debian, this package is split into two separate packages.

```
freebsd# pkg install opendkim

debian# apt install opendkim opendkim-tools

centos# yum install opendkim
```

On FreeBSD the configuration file is installed as /usr/local/etc/mail/opendkim.conf and on Debian and CentOS as /etc/opendkim.conf. On CentOS, the directory /etc/opendkim is created for the storage of the keys; on the other systems, such a directory does not yet exist.

```
freebsd# pw groupadd opendkim -g 127
freebsd# pw useradd opendkim \
            -u 127 \
            -g opendkim \
            -c "OpenDKIM" \
            -d /nonexistent \
            -s /usr/sbin/nologin
freebsd# mkdir -p /usr/local/etc/opendkim/keys
freebsd# cd /usr/local/etc/opendkim
freebsd# touch KeyTable SigningTable TrustedHosts
freebsd# chgrp opendkim .
freebsd# chown opendkim:opendkim *
freebsd# chmod o-rwx *

debian# mkdir -p /etc/opendkim/keys
debian# cd /etc/opendkim
debian# touch KeyTable SigningTable TrustedHosts
debian# chgrp opendkim .
debian# chown opendkim:opendkim *
debian# chmod o-rwx *

centos# cd /etc/opendkim
```

The opendkim-genkey command is used to generate the private and public keys that are used to sign outgoing messages.

```
# cd keys
# mkdir example.com example.edu example.org
# opendkim-genkey --directory=./example.com \
    --domain=example.com \
    --selector=dkim
# opendkim-genkey --directory=./example.edu \
    --domain=example.edu \
    --selector=dkim
# opendkim-genkey --directory=./example.org \
    --domain=example.org \
    --selector=dkim
```

This generated in all three sub-directories a file called dkim.private (the private key) and a file dkim.txt (the DNS record containing the public key). The private keys must belong to user *opendkim* to allow them to be loaded.

```
# chown opendkim:opendkim */dkim.private
```

The files KeyTable and SigningTable are used to link the keys to the domains.

```
# cd ..
# nano KeyTable
```

```
dkim._domainkey.example.com
  example.com:dkim:/etc/opendkim/keys/example.com/dkim.private

dkim._domainkey.example.edu
  example.edu:dkim:/etc/opendkim/keys/example.edu/dkim.private

dkim._domainkey.example.org
  example.org:dkim:/etc/opendkim/keys/example.org/dkim.private
```

Attention: that is three lines and not six.

```
# nano SigningTable
```

```
*@example.com  dkim._domainkey.example.com
*@example.edu  dkim._domainkey.example.edu
*@example.org  dkim._domainkey.example.org
```

And lastly, the configuration file must be modified. It is advisable to put aside the original file and to start with an empty file.

```
freebsd# cd /usr/local/etc/mail
```

```
linux# cd /etc
```

```
# mv opendkim.conf opendkim.conf.orig
# nano opendkim.conf
```

```
# Should the daemon restart automatically after a crash?
AutoRestart yes
AutoRestartRate 10/1h
```

```
# Logging.
Syslog yes
SyslogSuccess yes

# Operation.
UserID opendkim:opendkim
PidFile /var/run/opendkim/opendkim.pid
Socket inet:8891@localhost
Mode sv
Canonicalization relaxed/simple

# The files created earlier.
# Directory:
#    FreeBSD: /usr/local/etc/opendkim
#    Debian : /etc/opendkim
#    CentOS : /etc/opendkim
KeyTable file:/etc/opendkim/KeyTable
SigningTable refile:/etc/opendkim/SigningTable
```

The record for the zone file is generated with the help of the opendkim-genzone command; the output of this command should be pasted into the zone file for the domain in question.

```
bsd# opendkim-genzone -D \
        -d example.com \
        -x /usr/local/etc/mail/opendkim.conf
bsd# opendkim-genzone -D \
        -d example.edu \
        -x /usr/local/etc/mail/opendkim.conf
bsd# opendkim-genzone -D \
        -d example.org \
        -x /usr/local/etc/mail/opendkim.conf
linux#  opendkim-genzone -D \
        -d example.com \
        -x /etc/opendkim.conf
linux#  opendkim-genzone -D \
        -d example.edu \
        -x /etc/opendkim.conf
```

```
linux#  opendkim-genzone -D \
          -d example.org \
          -x /etc/opendkim.conf
```

The output of this command spans multiple lines, but thanks to the parentheses, this is not a problem for named; the contents can be pasted into the zone file without any modifications. When the serial number has been incremented, the zone file has been saved, and named has been reloaded, the result can be verified with the help of the following command:

```
# dig @1278.0.0.1 dkim._domainkey.example.com TXT
```

If this works, the service can be started (and restarted on Debian).

```
freebsd# nano /etc/rc.conf
```

```
milteropendkim_enable="YES"
milteropendkim_uid="opendkim"
milteropendkim_gid="opendkim"
milteropendkim_cfgfile="/usr/local/etc/mail/opendkim.conf"
```

```
freebsd# service milteropendkim start
```

```
debian# systemctl restart opendkim
```

```
centos# systemctl enable opendkim
centos# systemctl start opendkim
```

And to complete the installation and configuration of DKIM, Postfix must be instructed to make use of the daemon.

```
bsd# nano /usr/local/etc/postfix/main.cf
```

```
linux# nano /etc/postfix/main.cf
```

```
smtpd_milters = inet:localhost:8891
non_smtpd_milters = inet:localhost:8891
```

```
bsd# service postfix reload
```

```
linux# systemctl reload postfix
```

Spam Filter

The preceding configuration rejects a lot of spam already. The messages that remain must now be analyzed by the spam filter to filter out the last spam messages.

Strangely, not many open source spam filters exist. One of the few projects that are open source, are updated regularly, and do only spam filtering without any bells and whistles is Bogofilter. The few other projects that exist also include functionalities like greylisting and DNSBL; a disadvantage of these more than complete applications is that they require much more memory and processing power than the setup described here, which separates all these functionalities.

Bogofilter is a learning, so-called *Bayesian*, spam filter. This means that the spam filter learns from the user, who indicates which mails are spam and which are not. This also means that new users will receive relatively much spam in the beginning; the longer a user uses the spam filter, the more it will adjust to the user's personal situation, until the user is virtually or even entirely spam-free.

It is the LDA that sends the messages through the spam filter, right before they are delivered. It is also possible to call the spam filter from the MTA (Postfix), but this would make it impossible to create a personalized spam database for each user.

In this setup, Bogofilter adds a header to each mail, indicating the probability that this mail is a spam message. In a strongly simplified fashion, it can be said that Bogofilter calculates this probability by comparing the content of the mail with a database of "bad" (*spam*) words and a database of "good" (*ham*) words. The more spam terms the message contains compared to the number of ham terms, the more probable it is that this message is spam. Obviously, the reality is a bit more complicated than that.

The use of the term *spam* is inspired by a Monty Python sketch about Spam, a brand of canned meat. The use of the term *ham* for non-spam references the difference between canned meat and "real" meat.

After Bogofilter has added the header to the message, the mail is delivered to the user as usual. The user then decides what will happen to the mail with the help of Sieve filters; the user could, for example, decide to have all mails with a score above a certain threshold deleted automatically. This way, the user keeps complete control over the messages they receive.

The user can also teach the spam filter which messages are or are not spam by feeding them back to the spam filter with the label *spam* or *ham*; this is sometimes called *training the spam filter*. This will make the spam filter automatically adjust the weighting.

```
freebsd# pkg install bogofilter
```

```
debian# apt install bogofilter
```

```
centos# yum install bogofilter
```

This setup requires several shell scripts and several Sieve scripts. It is practical to store these scripts together, separated from other scripts.

```
# mkdir /srv/mail/dovecot-bin
# mkdir /srv/mail/dovecot-sieve
```

Obviously, this means that no mail users can be created with the usernames *dovecot-bin* and *dovecot-sieve*, but the odds for users with those names were probably not great anyway. (If the *Filesystem Hierarchy Standard* is followed to the letter, these directories should not be here, but rather somewhere under /usr/local.)

Sieve scripts cannot execute shell scripts in just any directory. The created directory must be specified in Dovecot's configuration.

```
# nano conf.d/90-sieve-extprograms.conf
```

```
plugin {
    sieve_pipe_bin_dir = /srv/mail/dovecot-bin
    sieve_filter_bin_dir = /srv/mail/dovecot-bin
    sieve_execute_bin_dir = /srv/mail/dovecot-bin
}
```

Bogofilter won't function without a word list, so an empty word list should be created automatically when a user logs in for the first time.

Dovecot supports the execution of scripts between the login and the beginning of the IMAP session. This is the perfect moment for the execution of such an action: the user has been identified, but the list of folders has not been sent yet. The bold lines should be added to the Dovecot configuration file conf.d/10-master.conf (dovecot should be reloaded when the file has been saved):

```
service imap {
  executable = imap imap-postlogin
}

service imap-postlogin {
  executable = script-login /srv/mail/dovecot-bin/bogo-dirs.sh
  user = vmail
```

```
unix_listener imap-postlogin {
}
}
```

This will execute the bogo-dirs.sh script when a user logs in. This script can have any name. It is important to realize that this script is executed after each login and not only the first; it should therefore not do too much, because that would introduce a delay with every login. An example of such a script could look like this (it should be executable):

```
#!/usr/bin/env bash

# Base directory.
dir="/srv/mail/${USER}"

# Create bogofilter directory.
mkdir -p "${dir}/bogofilter"

# Create bogotmp directory.
mkdir -p "${dir}/bogotmp"

# Create wordlist.db file.
[ ! -f "${dir}/bogofilter/wordlist.db" ] && {
    echo | bogoutil -l "${dir}/bogofilter/wordlist.db"
}

# Without this last command this script won't function.
exec "$@"
```

This script guarantees that also in the unlikely case where the Bogofilter database disappears, it will be automatically recreated when the user logs in (but obviously, the new database will be empty).

The next script is the script that sends each received mail to bogofilter for verification.

It is possible to send the mail directly to bogofilter's *STDIN*. The problem with this solution is that it forces bogofilter to keep the entire message in memory while it is being processed. A better solution is to create a small script that saves the message to a temporary file, so that bogofilter can process the message on disk.

```
# nano /srv/mail/dovecot-bin/bogofilter-mail.sh
```

```bash
#!/usr/bin/env bash

# Temporary directory.
MAILHOME="/srv/mail/${USER}"
TMPDIR="${MAILHOME}/bogotmp"

# Create temporary files.
mkdir -p "${TMPDIR}" || exit 1
in=`mktemp --tmpdir="${TMPDIR}" --suffix=.in`
out=${in/%in/out}

# Send STDIN to a file.
cat > "${in}"

# Check the file,
# and create a new file that includes the header.
# The Pigeonhole 'spamtest' extension accepts
# no more than 4 decimals.
bogofilter -d "${MAILHOME}/bogofilter" \
    --spamicity-formats="%0.4f, %0.4f, %0.4f" \
    -p -I "${in}" -O "${out}"

# Send the new file to STDOUT.
cat "${out}"

# Clean up.
rm "${in}" "${out}"
```

That script is executed by a tiny Sieve script.

```
# nano /srv/mail/dovecot-sieve/bogofilter-mail.sieve
```

```
require "vnd.dovecot.filter";
filter "bogofilter-mail.sh";
```

And that Sieve script is executed from the Dovecot configuration.

```
# nano conf.d/90-sieve.conf
```

```
plugin {
  sieve_before = /srv/mail/dovecot-sieve/bogofilter-mail.sieve
  sieve_plugins = sieve_extprograms
  sieve_extensions = +vnd.dovecot.filter +spamtest +spamtestplus
  sieve_spamtest_status_type = score
  sieve_spamtest_max_value = 1
  sieve_spamtest_status_header = X-Bogosity: [[:alpha:]]+,
    tests=bogofilter, spamicity=([[:digit:]\.]+), version=[[:digit:]\.]+
}
```

The most important lines in the preceding script are the first (`sieve_before`) and the last (`sieve_spamtest_status_header`). The first line indicates that the script must be executed before the user's personal Sieve scripts. The last line defines the format for the header that `bogofilter` adds to the mail to indicate the spam probability (also called *spamicity*). It is important that this line has the exact same format; otherwise, Dovecot will not be able to parse it later to determine the value; it is a single long line with a single space after each comma.

```
bsd# service dovecot reload
linux# systemctl reload dovecot
```

To allow the execution of the Sieve script, it must be compiled. This must be done after dovecot has been reloaded, because the *vnd.dovecot.filter* extension must be loaded to compile the script.

```
# sievec /srv/mail/dovecot-sieve/bogofilter-mail.sieve
```

This can now be tested by sending a mail to a user at the server. The received mail should have a header that begins with "X-Bogosity:".

The *spamicity* given to the messages by Bogofilter is a value between 0 and 1, where 0 means *very probably not spam* and 1 means *very probably spam*. The following Sieve script, which could be a user's script, processes the mails based on the score they received:

```
require ["comparator-i;ascii-numeric", "fileinto", "mailbox",
"relational", "spamtest"];

if spamtest :value "ge" :comparator "i;ascii-numeric" "10" {
    discard;
}
elsif spamtest :value "ge" :comparator "i;ascii-numeric" "5" {
    fileinto :create "ProbablySpam";
}
elsif spamtest :value "ge" :comparator "i;ascii-numeric" "2" {
    fileinto :create "MaybeSpam";
}
```

This is what that script does.

First, a number of extensions are loaded; everything from the word *require* up to and including the semicolon is on a single line. The *spamtest* extension translates the score that was given by Bogofilter to a value between 1 and 10. Then, this calculated value is compared to a value of choice: if the value is *greater than or equal to* (ge) 10, the message is discarded. If the value is greater than or equal to 5, the mail is delivered to the ProbablySpam folder; if this folder does not exist, it is created. And if the value is greater than or equal to 2, it is delivered to the MaybeSpam folder. A mail that falls through all the tests—in this case, that is all mails with a *spamicity* less than 2—is delivered to the default INBOX.

Reclassification of Emails

The filter works as it should now, but it is not very functional yet. To be able to evaluate incoming mails, Bogofilter needs a word list, and that word list is still empty.

The first time a user logs in, a folder named Junk is created (see the Dovecot configuration file conf.d/15-mailboxes.conf). This folder can be used to feed spam messages back to bogofilter to fill the word list. A number of Sieve scripts must be created for this purpose; these scripts will be executed in response to the transfers of messages between folders.

These are the folders that (may) currently exist in a user's mailbox:

- **Junk**

  The LDA never delivers mail here; messages are only added manually. It is possible that the email client translates the name of this folder.

- **ProbablySpam**

  In this folder, mail is delivered that received a high spamicity score from Bogofilter. If it is indeed spam, the user moves the message to the Junk folder, and otherwise, the user moves the message to another folder.

- **MaybeSpam**

  In this folder, mail is delivered that received a lower spamicity score from Bogofilter. If it is indeed spam, the user moves the message to the Junk folder, and otherwise, the user moves the message to another folder.

- **Other folders**

  Mail that is not delivered to the ProbablySpam or MaybeSpam folders is delivered to another folder, depending on the other Sieve filter rules. If a spam message falls through, the user moves it to the Junk folder.

With the help of *ImapSieve*, the execution of scripts can be attached to users' actions. These are the actions that need scripts attached:

- A message is moved to the Junk folder.

  → Train it as spam.

- A message is moved out of the Junk folder.

  → "Untrain" it as spam, and train it as ham.

- A message is moved from the ProbablySpam or MaybeSpam folder to a different folder (but not Junk).

  → Train it as ham.

- A message is moved to the trashcan.

    → Do not train it.

This is the script that will be training Bogofilter:

```
# nano /srv/mail/dovecot-bin/bogofilter-train.sh
```

```
#!/usr/bin/env bash

case $1 in
    [sS]*)
        # spam
        FLAG="-s"
        ;;
    [hH]*)
        # ham
        FLAG="-n"
        ;;
    [rR]*)
        # retrain
        FLAG="-Ns"
        ;;
    *)
        exit 1
        ;;
esac

# Fork (&), so that Bogofilter does not block the copy.
cat | bogofilter ${FLAG} &
```

```
# chmod 755 /srv/mail/dovecot-bin/bogofilter-train.sh
```

This script expects a mail message on its STDIN and a single command-line parameter; this command-line parameter can begin with an s for *spam*, with an h for *ham*, or with an r if it must be retrained because it was taken out of the Junk folder. Then, the mail is sent to bogofilter with the correct parameters.

And these are the Sieve scripts that call the preceding shell script:

```
# nano /srv/mail/dovecot-sieve/train-spam.sieve
```

```
# * -> Junk

require ["copy", "imapsieve", "vnd.dovecot.pipe"];

pipe :copy "bogofilter-train.sh" ["spam"];
```

```
# nano /srv/mail/dovecot-sieve/train-ham.sieve
```

```
# MaybeSpam | ProbablySpam -> ! Junk

require ["copy", "environment", "imapsieve", "variables", "vnd.dovecot.
pipe"];

if environment :matches "imap.mailbox" "*" {
    set "box" "${0}";
}
if not string :is "${box}" ["Junk", "Trash"] {
    pipe :copy "bogofilter-train.sh" ["ham"];
}
```

```
# nano /srv/mail/dovecot-sieve/untrain-spam-train-ham.sieve
```

```
# Junk -> *

require ["copy", "environment", "imapsieve", "variables", "vnd.dovecot.
pipe"];

if environment :matches "imap.mailbox" "*" {
    set "box" "${0}";
}
if not string :is "${box}" ["Junk", "Trash"] {
    pipe :copy "bogofilter-train.sh" ["retrain"];
}
```

For this to work, the extensions and plugins in bold must be added to
`conf.d/90-sieve.conf`:

```
plugin {
    sieve_extensions = +vnd.dovecot.filter +spamtest +spamtestplus
+vnd.dovecot.environment +vnd.dovecot.pipe
    sieve_plugins = sieve_extprograms sieve_imapsieve
}
```

These are only two lines; the first begins with sieve_extensions and the second
with sieve_plugins.

To keep things transparent, it is practical to create a new configuration file where the
Sieve scripts are attached to the user actions.

```
# nano conf.d/91-sieve-bogofilter.conf
```

```
protocol imap {
  mail_plugins = $mail_plugins imap_sieve
}

plugin {
  imapsieve_mailbox1_name = Junk
  imapsieve_mailbox1_causes = COPY
  imapsieve_mailbox1_before = file:/srv/mail/dovecot-sieve/train-spam.sieve

  imapsieve_mailbox2_name = *
  imapsieve_mailbox2_from = Junk
  imapsieve_mailbox2_causes = COPY
  imapsieve_mailbox2_before = file:/srv/mail/dovecot-sieve/
  untrain-spam-train-ham.sieve

  imapsieve_mailbox3_name = *
  imapsieve_mailbox3_from = MaybeSpam
  imapsieve_mailbox3_causes = COPY
  imapsieve_mailbox3_before = file:/srv/mail/dovecot-sieve/train-ham.sieve

  imapsieve_mailbox4_name = *
  imapsieve_mailbox4_from = ProbablySpam
  imapsieve_mailbox4_causes = COPY
  imapsieve_mailbox4_before = file:/srv/mail/dovecot-sieve/train-ham.sieve
}
```

```
freebsd# service dovecot reload
```

```
linux# systemctl reload dovecot
```

```
# sievec /srv/mail/dovecot-sieve/train-spam.sieve
# sievec /srv/mail/dovecot-sieve/train-ham.sieve
# sievec /srv/mail/dovecot-sieve/untrain-spam-train-ham.sieve
```

And these scripts must also be compiled before they can be used.

Sieve scripts do not always need be compiled manually. Normally, Dovecot does it automatically if this is needed, but user *vmail* does not have write privileges for this directory.

And this concludes the configuration of the spam filter.

Web Mail

If the mail server serves ambulant users, it may be practical to support web mail. Wi-Fi access points sometimes block the usual email ports, but port 443 (*https*) is always open.

Obviously, it is important that the web mail software supports IMAP and is nothing more than a web front end for the existing email setup. Furthermore, it would be practical if the software supports Sieve, so that users can use web mail to edit their Sieve rules and do not need to find and install additional software. And in the previous chapter, a server for *CalDAV* (online calendars) and *CardDAV* (online address books) has been installed; it would be practical if the web mail client could access these address books.

Roundcube and RainLoop are two web mail clients that meet all these requirements. Both are developed in PHP and are documented extensively and clearly; a system administrator who keeps the acquired knowledge from this book and the websites for those web mail clients at hand should not have any trouble installing and configuring these web mail clients. This is left as an exercise for the reader.

Summary

The main focus of this chapter is the fight against spam. The Postfix configuration was tweaked, and *greylisting*, *DNSBL*, *SPF*, and *DKIM* were introduced. Finally, a spam filter was installed and configured. Throughout the chapter, examples of Sieve filters were given.

The next chapter will discuss backup of data and configuration files, and monitoring.

CHAPTER 15

Backup and Monitoring

The previous chapters all discussed the installation and configuration of services, the setting up of things. For a server, however, it is equally important to ensure that those services continue to function and that if they don't, they can be made functional again as soon as possible.

Three tasks are important in this respect:

- **Keeping the software up to date**

  Software updates are published with a reason: they add new functionalities, but more importantly, they bring more stability, reliability, and security. It is recommended to update the installed software at least once a week.

  More information about updating the software can be found in Chapter 3, "Software Management".

- **The creation of backups**

  Regular backups ensure that the state of the server can always be brought back to a point in time where everything still functioned as it was meant to.

- **System monitoring**

  The analysis of log files and other information helps anticipate problems or address them in time. The server and external systems can also be configured to alert the system administrator in case of problems.

© Robert La Lau 2021
R. La Lau, *Practical Internet Server Configuration*, https://doi.org/10.1007/978-1-4842-6960-2_15

Backup

An instant solution for the creation and restoration of backups cannot be given in this book, because the perfect solution depends heavily on the organization's specific requirements and on the available systems. A backup of an entire virtual server created by the provider demands a completely different scenario from a backup of a few specific directories to a local Windows server; and between these two extremes, many other scenarios are possible.

Many providers offer backups for physical or virtual servers. Obviously, this means that the provider needs access to the data on the server. If this does not pose a problem with respect to the General Data Protection Regulation, for example, it may be advantageous to delegate the creation of backups to the provider; this saves on planning, configuration, and disk space.

For the planning of backups, a few questions must be answered.

What Needs to Be Backed Up?

If the server is virtual, a backup of the entire virtual machine may be the most practical solution; this is the fastest way to bring the server back up in case of problems.

If it is not a virtual machine, a backup of the entire server is more complicated. In that case, a list will need to be created containing the directories that contain the data that is necessary to recreate the current server as rapidly as possible.

For the server that is discussed in this book, the most important directories are

- /etc (system configuration).

- FreeBSD: /usr/local/etc (additional system configuration).

- /var (databases, crontabs, at jobs, log files, DNS zone files on CentOS).

- /home and /root (notes, downloads, personal configurations).

- /srv (websites, email, etc.).

- /usr/local/bin and /usr/local/sbin may contain custom scripts.

If a new system should ever be installed based on that data, the list of packages that were installed on the original system can be determined with the following command:

```
freebsd# sqlite3 /var/db/pkg/local.sqlite \
        "select origin from packages"
```

```
debian# awk '/^Package:/ {print $2}' /var/lib/dpkg/status
```

```
centos# sed -n 'n;n;p;n;n;n;n;' \
        /var/lib/yum/rpmdb-indexes/pkgtups-checksums
```

Obviously, those paths should be relative to the created backups.

The obtained list can then be fed to the package manager on a new system to reinstall all the packages. Since the naming of packages differs between operating systems, it is important that the new system runs the same operating system as the old system for this to work; Debian's package list cannot be fed to yum, for example.

It may be practical to create partial backups. For example, it is quite unpractical to have to decompress the backup for an entire system, just to restore a single website or database. If hosting is provided to customers, it is practical to create a backup for each customer, containing the websites, databases, and email for the customer in question; the customer could then download this backup to have a copy of all the data on location.

It can also be practical to, for example, create a full system backup once a week and a smaller daily backup for the data that changes regularly, like databases and email.

Where Are Backups Stored?

Even if the backup is created by the provider, it is practical to have access to it oneself: if only one or a few documents need to be restored from a backup, it is not very practical to have to wait for the provider to do so and to have to pay the provider for the time spent.

For some things, a regular local backup can come in handy. A script that automatically copies the websites and their databases a few times per day can save a lot of time when a developer makes an error, and the state of a website must be rewound a few hours.

However, a local backup is useless if the server's hard disk crashes. An external backup will therefore need to be made as well. Is it worth it to acquire a second server for this, or might a server be available already in the local network? To guarantee the confidentiality of the data, these remote backups should only be made over a secure connection (*rsync + ssh, scp, sshfs*, etc.).

It will also have to be decided whether the backup should be incremental (a new backup modifies the existing backup) or multiple independent backups should be stored. If incremental backups are preferred, it is practical to select a system that implements version control, allowing to select the moment to which the system needs to be restored; it may happen that the last backup is not the most suitable one, if this backup was made after a certain problem began.

A final question to answer is whether the server itself initiates the backup and sends it to a storage or whether, for example, a local server at the office initiates the backup and retrieves it from the server.

If the backups are stored with an external party, like a cloud service, it may be necessary to encrypt the backups to guarantee the confidentiality of the data.

When getting rid of media that contained backups (or any other data for that matter), it is important to keep in mind that simply deleting a file using a command like rm does not actually delete the data: it merely unlinks the filename from its *inode*, leaving the data intact until it is overwritten by the storage of other data. Packages like *shred* and *secure_delete* can help truly destroy the data. Since these processes can be rather time-consuming, it may be worth the while to invest in the outsourcing of the data destruction to a specialized company if many hard drives must be wiped.

When Are Backups Created?

Will a weekly backup suffice, or must a backup be created multiple times per day? Clearly, this heavily depends on the type of data: it is usually more important to regularly back up the database for a website than its files. And a backup for a company's administration is usually more important than a backup of the employees' home directories.

Another question to be answered with respect to the "when" is the time of day when the backups must be created. For a company that works from 9 to 5, it makes sense to make the backups at night. But for a consumer web shop or a social network, the evening and night may be the busiest times when their clients are not working themselves. And international companies will usually have to consider time zones when colleagues are working.

Conclusion

Backup management is a complex subject, which should include more departments than only the system administrators. These are the steps to be taken for the implementation of an effective and reliable backup system:

1. Inventory of requirements and wishes from all involved departments

2. Inventory of the available infrastructure

3. Elaboration of the ideal scenario, which may be, and often is, a combination of multiple partial scenarios

4. Technical implementation

Since the choice of the software to be used is not made until step 4 of this road map, no concrete documentation can be given in this book for the implementation of a system for the creation and restoration of backups. Hopefully, the hints listed still give a solid basis to start from.

Monitoring

Monitoring is a necessary investment in the fight against all sorts of mischief, like bugs and foul play. A combination of passive and active monitoring is the most efficient.

Mailing Lists

All Linux distributions and BSDs maintain mailing lists to which administrators, users, and other interested parties can subscribe. Some of these lists are meant as a forum for discussion, and others are closed lists that are only used for making announcements. The online addendum for this book contains links to the collections of mailing lists for FreeBSD, Debian, and CentOS.

A **FreeBSD** administrator should at least be subscribed to the list **freebsd-security-notifications@freebsd.org**.

A **Debian** administrator should at least be subscribed to the list **debian-security-announce@lists.debian.org**.

A **CentOS** administrator should at least be subscribed to the list
centos-announce@centos.org.

These lists are used to announce security problems and therefore receive mails that require system administrators to take action immediately. These lists do not receive a large volume of mail.

Other Unices maintain similar mailing lists.

Monitoring Locally

The simplest thing a system administrator can do to monitor the server is simply log in regularly and verify that all services are activated that must be activated, check the *load* of the server, see which users are logged in, and verify that no unknown services are active or services that should not be active. The commands that can be used for this have already been discussed in previous chapters: uptime, ps, top, service, systemctl, who, w, and so on.

But, while very important, these actions always only provide a snapshot. In the following, a few possibilities are discussed that will help the system administrator to expand their field of view.

Log Files

Beginning Unix administrators coming from other environments often neglect the log files. However, these files contain a huge amount of information about the functioning of the system.

The log files can usually be found in /var/log. Most log files are plain text files, which can be opened with commands like less and more.

A few binary files exist:

- wtmp and btmp

   The wtmp file records successful login attempts, and the btmp file records unsuccessful login attempts. The /var/log/btmp file can grow rapidly when a *brute-force attack* is in progress on the server. These files can be accessed with the help of the respective commands last and lastb. See last(1) for more info.

- `lastlog` and `faillog`

  The `lastlog` and `faillog` files also record, respectively, the
  successful and unsuccessful login attempts per user. These files can
  be accessed with the commands of the same names, `lastlog` and
  `faillog`. See `lastlog(8)` and `faillog(8)` for more information.

- `tallylog`

  The `tallylog` file records the failed login attempts per username.
  The *pam_tally2* module can use this information to block access
  for certain users; this module is disabled by default. More info in
  `pam_tally2(8)`.

The log files for *systemd* (the *init* system for Debian and CentOS) are also binary and
can be accessed using the `journalctl` command.

```
linux# journalctl

linux# journalctl --catalog --pager-end

linux# journalctl --unit dovecot
```

Scripts

As indicated earlier, *cron* mails all program and script output to the owner of the crontab.
This functionality can be used for the monitoring of the server. As an example, a cronjob
that is executed every four hours to mail an overview of free and used disk space:

```
MAILFROM=monitor-df@example.com
MAILTO=sysadmin@example.com
* */4 * * * /bin/df -h
```

The usefulness of this specific cronjob may be questionable, but the concept is clear.
Another example that is a bit more useful:

```
@reboot echo "The server just rebooted."
```

Obviously, this is not limited to the standard commands; custom scripts can be
created and executed as well. The following little script, for example, only outputs
something if a partition is more than 90% full. This script could be executed each hour by
`cron`, but a mail will only be sent if there is something to report.

```
#!/usr/bin/env bash

while read line; do
    percentage=$(echo ${line} | awk '{print $5}')
    [ ${percentage/\%/} -gt 90 ] && echo "${line}"
done < <(/bin/df -h | grep '^/dev/')
```

Instead of email, or in addition to, SMS messages could be sent. Several companies can be found online that offer an SMS gateway (for a fee).

Remote Monitoring

It is very practical to configure the server to monitor itself. But in case of network trouble, the server will not be able to report them, because it will not be able to send any mails. Therefore, there should also be monitoring in the other direction.

The simplest way to achieve this is to configure a local server to periodically make requests to the most important ports on the server (ssh, dns, http, https, imaps, smtps) and to raise an alert if a port cannot be reached or has an unacceptable long delay. Several free and paid services exist for making these requests.

Software packages exist for monitoring entire server parks (or a single server, of course). These packages go further than a periodical *ping* and an email if a disk is almost full. They often offer a dashboard that allows the monitoring of everything that can be monitored from the free space on the hard disks and the memory usage to the temperature of the CPUs and the amount of data that is sent and received through the network interfaces.

A few open source examples of such packages are *Zabbix*, *Pandora FMS*, and *Netdata*.

Summary

This chapter laid the foundation for the implementation of a backup system. Also, the reader was given pointers for the monitoring of the system. Furthermore, the system administrator is now subscribed to at least one mailing list concerning their operating system of choice.

The next chapter will complete this book by giving the reader some hints on subjects that will help bring the server (and the system administrator) to the next level.

CHAPTER 16

Taking It Further

This chapter provides a few more topics that will not be explored in depth, but which the inquisitive system administrator can get to work with on their own.

chroot and Virtualization

The purpose of *chroot* (*change root*) is to change the system root directory from the point of view of a certain process.

To illustrate this with an example, if a *chroot* is done for the `processx` daemon to the `/chroot/processx` directory, that directory will be the `/` directory from the point of view of that process; in principle, the daemon will not be able to escape from this directory. As a consequence, if there happens to be a bug in the `processx` daemon that allows users to break out of the program and gain shell access, these users will still not be able to escape from the directory in question.

This does mean, however, that all programs and libraries necessary for the execution of the process in question must be copied to this directory, because the process will not be able to access files outside this *chroot jail*. The process inside the *chroot jail* still shares things like memory, CPU, and network with the rest of the system. A *chroot* can only be done by *root*, and the process inside the *chroot jail* must not be executed with root privileges.

The *chroot call* is only one of the layers of a server's security, and it must be taken into account that ways exist to escape from a *chroot jail*.

A system that takes things further than a *chroot* is *operating-system-level virtualization*. With this form of virtualization, processes, or even entire systems, are executed in a virtualized environment that only shares the kernel with the host system (the system that harbors the virtualized environments). Apart from its own root directory like the *chroot jail*, the virtualized environment also has its own IP address and hostname, its own set of users, and even its own root user. Since the kernel is shared with the host system, the virtualized environments run on the same operating system.

© Robert La Lau 2021
R. La Lau, *Practical Internet Server Configuration*, https://doi.org/10.1007/978-1-4842-6960-2_16

Examples of operating-system-level virtualization are *FreeBSD jail* and *Linux Containers* (*LXC*).

Full virtualization takes things even further and completely separates the virtualized environment (the *guest system*) from the host system. In this setup, the guest system runs its own kernel, so the operating system may be different from that of the host system.

In all three of these setups—*chroot, operating-system-level virtualization,* and *full virtualization*—it is possible to access the guest system from the host system.

Kernel Configuration

The *kernel* is the central part of the operating system and acts as the gateway between the software and the hardware. The kernel decides which process has access to the processor or the memory at which moment. With the help of drivers, usually called *kernel modules* in the Unix world, the kernel also facilitates access to the other hardware, like keyboards, network cards, USB ports, and so on. These kernel modules can be deployed in two manners: they can be compiled into the kernel, or they can be compiled as separate software libraries and loaded when needed.

To support as many hardware components as possible, a great number of modules are compiled into the BSD and Linux kernels by default, and even more modules are included separately. This makes it inevitable that modules are included that are not used on the current server.

The system administrator can determine which hardware is supported in which manner by disabling certain modules or by removing them from the kernel. Obviously, this saves memory—the kernel is smaller if certain modules are not loaded—but it can also be an extra layer in the server's security. For example, a server usually does not need its USB ports. If USB support is then completely removed from the kernel, making it impossible for software to access the USB ports, this eliminates the risk of an attacker using the USB ports to load malicious software onto the server.

The configuration of the kernel can be a time-consuming process, especially the first time (the kernel configuration can be saved and reused for new kernel versions), but it is also an interesting and educational process.

Some Linux and BSD administrators state that one is not a real system administrator until one has configured and compiled a kernel. That might go a bit far, but it is a fact that configuring and compiling a kernel brings the system and the administrator closer together.

Most, if not all, Unices document kernel configuration. Links for FreeBSD, Debian, and CentOS can be found in the online addendum for this book.

Load Balancing

It may happen that at a certain moment the workload becomes too heavy for a single server. The first action in such a case would obviously be the deployment of more powerful hardware, and a second action would be the separation of services: to begin, the mail processing and web traffic can be separated to different servers; then, regarding email, IMAP and SMTP can be processed on different servers, and regarding web traffic, separate servers could be deployed for, for example, web server and file storage, database, and PHP-FPM; the DNS could move to a separate server. But at some point, this ends: each service then runs on its own server, and each server is dedicated to a single service. That is the moment where one starts planning to have a single service provided by multiple servers.

One of the ways to achieve that is *load balancing*. This technology allows multiple servers to be deployed for the provision of the same service and to have a *load balancer* determine which requests are sent to which server.

The load balancer can make this decision in several manners. For example, a load balancer could be in constant contact with the cluster behind it to always have information about the load on the different servers and send requests to the server with the lowest current load. But the load can also be distributed geographically, sending all requests from a clearly defined region to a dedicated server or cluster; depending on the service and the area that is served, this could result in dedicated servers for each continent or for each country.

Clearly, it is important that the servers behind the load balancer are in constant contact and synchronize their data, to ensure that users are always presented with the same information, regardless of the server they are assigned to. However, load balancers are usually configured to send follow-up requests to the same server as the initial request, to make sure that session data remains consistent; this is also known as *session affinity* or *sticky sessions*.

Load balancers also facilitate repairs and replacements: new servers can simply be added to the cluster and take over the job of a server that needs repair or replacement; the old server can then be removed from the cluster.

A load balancer can be an apparatus that was developed especially for this purpose, but it can also be an "ordinary" server with a modified DNS configuration and/or a script or program that makes the decisions.

RAID

RAID (*Redundant Array of Independent Disks*) is a system that joins multiple hard disks into a single storage unit. This is used to expand storage space, to increase the reliability of the storage, to enhance the data writing speed, or a combination of those.

The different manners in which disks can be joined are called *levels*. Seven default RAID levels exist:

- **RAID 0**

  This level is also called *striping* and joins two or more disks into a single large storage unit. Data is distributed equally over the disks in the *array*, which allows for writing to multiple disks at the same time, which enhances the writing speed.

  All disks in the array only use the amount of disk space that is available on the smallest disk; therefore, a *RAID 0 array* consisting of a 300GB disk and a 500GB disk will have a total storage space of 2 x 300GB = 600GB.

  If one of the disks in the array is damaged, all data in the array is lost.

- **RAID 1**

  This level is also called *mirroring* and can consist of two or more disks. The data is written to all disks at the same time, ensuring that all disks contain the same data. This means that the storage space does not expand by combining the disks.

  All disks in the array only use the amount of disk space that is available on the smallest disk; therefore, a *RAID 1 array* consisting of a 300GB disk and a 500GB disk will have a total storage space of 300GB.

If one of the disks in the array is damaged, the other disks can relieve the damaged disk, because all disks contain all data; the damaged disk can then be replaced, and a new *mirror* can be created on the new disk.

- **RAID 2**

  RAID level 2 has built-in error correction. In practice, RAID 2 is hardly used.

- **RAID 3**

  RAID level 3 also has built-in error correction (but not the same as RAID 2). This level is also hardly used.

- **RAID 4**

  This level requires at least three disks: one disk is used for error correction (*parity bits*), and the data is distributed over the other disks, just like RAID 0 does. Thanks to the *parity bits*, the data from a damaged disk can be reconstructed.

- **RAID 5**

  RAID level 5 somewhat resembles RAID 4, but distributes the *parity bits* over all disks in the array, instead of storing them on a single dedicated disk. As a consequence, the writing speed is higher, because the *parity bits* for all disks in the array are no longer written to a single disk. This also eliminates the risk of losing redundancy because of damage to the single disk holding the *parity bits*. Another consequence is that RAID 5 does not tolerate more than a single damaged disk at the same time.

- **RAID 6**

  RAID level 6 is an evolution of RAID 5 and stores all *parity bits* twice on different disks in the array. This gives RAID 6 a larger redundancy than RAID 5; RAID 6 can recover from two damaged disks. The writing speed is a bit less than for RAID 5, because all *parity bits* are written twice.

A few vendor-specific variants exist apart from these seven default levels. Also, several combinations of the standard RAID levels, so-called *nested RAID levels*, have been created. One of these nested RAID levels is *RAID 10* (also called *RAID 1+0*), a combination of RAID 0 and RAID 1, or more precisely a RAID 0 array of RAID 1 mirrors; it is currently the most reliable RAID setup for speed and data safety.

Both hardware and software solutions exist for the implementation of a RAID system.

A RAID system does not invalidate the need for backups! If, by error or by malicious intent, files are deleted, this deletion is propagated over the RAID system just like any other deletion; the system does not see a difference. In such a case, the original data must still be retrieved from a backup.

Reduce the System Administrator's Work

The vast majority of the work in this book was manual labor: the command line will always be the basis for administrators of Unix-like systems. But of course projects exist that try to off-load some work from the system administrator, automate the work, or move the work a bit more toward the desktop.

Web Hosting Control Panel

As the name indicates, web hosting control panels are mainly developed for web hosting companies. However, they can be deployed in any situation where less technically skilled persons must be made responsible for a part of the management of internet services.

A web hosting control panel is a web interface that allows the delegation of certain, usually simple and common tasks to users or customers. Examples of such tasks are the management of the DNS server, the web server, email addresses, databases, and so on. The system administrator determines which tasks for which domains are delegated to which users.

Most web hosting control panels are commercial products. The most prominent example of an open source control panel is *Virtualmin*, which is based on *Webmin*, a web interface for system administration.

Configuration Management

A configuration manager allows the system administrator to roll out configurations over multiple servers at the same time while still allowing individual differences. Configuration managers can also be used to execute commands on multiple servers at the same time, to back up the configurations of the servers in a server park, to join configurations, and to monitor a server park.

A system administrator who wishes to control a large server park should look into *Ansible, Chef, Puppet,* and *SaltStack.*

Summary

This chapter listed some subjects the inquisitive system administrator may be interested in after having read this book. The presented subjects were *chroot* and virtualization, kernel configuration, load balancing, RAID systems, web hosting control panels, and configuration managers.

APPENDIX

Default Port Numbers

These are the default port numbers for the services described in this book:

Service	Port	Protocol
dns	53	tcp, udp
http	80	tcp
https	443	tcp
imaps	993	tcp
ldap	389	tcp
ldaps	636	tcp
managesieve	4190	tcp
mariadb	3306	tcp
mysql	3306	tcp
ntp	123	udp
pop3s	995	tcp
postgresql	5432	tcp
smtp	25	tcp
ssh	22	tcp
submission	587	tcp

© Robert La Lau 2021
R. La Lau, *Practical Internet Server Configuration*, https://doi.org/10.1007/978-1-4842-6960-2

Index

A

© Robert La Lau 2021
R. La Lau, *Practical Internet Server Configuration*, https://doi.org/10.1007/978-1-4842-6960-2

Printed in the United States
by Baker & Taylor Publisher Services